How to Live / What to Do

How to Live

What to Do

H.D.'s
Cultural Poetics

Adalaide Morris

University of Illinois Press
Urbana, Chicago, and Springfield

⊗ This book is printed on acid-free paper.

The Library of Congress cataloged the cloth edition as follows:
Morris, Adalaide Kirby, 1942–
How to live/what to do : H.D.'s cultural poetics /
Adalaide Morris.
p.   cm.
Includes bibliographical references and index.
ISBN 0-252-02796-5 (alk. paper)
1. H.D. (Hilda Doolittle), 1886–1961—Criticism and interpretation.
2. Women and literature—United States—History—20th century.
3. Conduct of life in literature. I. Title.
PS3507.O726Z78   2003
811'.52—dc21   2002007555

PAPERBACK ISBN 978-0-252-07591-9

For W.D.

For a writer, it is language that carries thought, perception, and meaning. And it does so through a largely metonymic process, through the discovery and invention of associations and connections. Though it may seem merely technical, the notion of linkage—of forging connections—has, in my mind, a concomitant political or social dimension. Communities of phrases spark the communities of ideas in which communities of persons live and work.

—Lyn Hejinian, *Language of Inquiry*

Contents

Acknowledgments

"Poems," Jack Spicer told his friend Robin Blaser, "should echo and reecho against each other. They should create resonances. They cannot live alone any more than we can" (*Collected Books* 61). This book, which reflects on sounds, transmissions, and resonances of many different sorts, emerges from an echo chamber of interchanges with colleagues, students, and friends whose thoughts have shaped and inflected my own. Written during particular years, reworked some time later, published later still, and revised and expanded for this book, each chapter is dense with debts I can only begin to acknowledge here. The merit in the book is dedicated to all those who have created its resonances; the flaws, of course, are my own.

My first debt is to a changing group of scholars whose intelligence, energy, and generosity made this book possible. When I began to read H.D. in 1982, very little of her work was in print; by 2002, most of her major writings have been published, discussed, debated, and, in some cases, published again in more substantial editions. Susan Stanford Friedman laid the foundations for this scholarship in a series of groundbreaking books and essays on H.D. Like all H.D. scholars, I have benefited continuously from her knowledge, her insights, and her liberality of spirit. Rachel Blau DuPlessis, Eileen Gregory, and Donna Krolik Hollenberg have each been crucial to the process of writing. I am deeply grateful for their companionship.

My colleagues at the University of Iowa provided impetus for this work from beginning to end. I would especially like to thank Ed Folsom, with whom I first taught *Trilogy,* and Huston Diehl and Mary Lou Emery, who read portions of the book as it developed. The thinking of N. Katherine Hayles, my colleague at Iowa when the book began, and Garrett Stewart, my colleague as it comes to its close, have also been integral to the development of my argument. The poets Jane Cooper, Lyn Hejinian, and Meredith Stricker—all of whom I came to know at Iowa—have enriched my apprehension of the complexity, diversity, and energy of poetic knowledge.

Of necessity at first and habit later, much of the work for this book was done in archival collections, again with indispensible help from others. I am especially indebted to the late Louis H. Silverstein, the archivist of the H.D. papers at the Beinecke Rare Book and Manuscript Library. I would also like to thank David Schoonover and Patricia C. Willis, the former and current curators of the Beinecke's Collection of American Literature, and Steve Jones and Kate Sharp, library service assistants. For help in the Henry W. and Alfred A. Berg Collection of English and American Literature at the New York Public Library, I thank Steve Crook, archivist, and Frank Mattson, acting curator. And, finally, my thanks to Charles E. Jones, research associate and bibliographer at the Oriental Institute of Chicago, and to Ellen Fowles Morris for help with matters Egyptological.

The students in my early seminars on H.D.—among them Jeff Gardiner, Shannon Hengen, Larry McCauley, Jim McKean, Dana Shugar, Meredith Stricker, Edith Walden, Sarah Witte, and Shari Zeck—were instrumental in the formation of my thinking about H.D. I would also like to thank the students in the poetry research group with whom I have read contemporary experimental poetry. For two extended stays at the University of Iowa Obermann Center for Advanced Studies, I thank Jay Semel, director, and Lorna Olson, the center's able secretary. Over the years, I have also benefited from the research assistance of Lisa Angelella, Kelli Beer, Maura Brady, Angela Brown, Jim Conner, Jessica DeSpain, Laura Dubek, Jeff Klinzman, Rick Lattanzio, Katherine Lewis, Sue Loellbach, Joyce Meier, and Angela Nepodal. José F. Candelaria, of the University of Iowa Department of Mathematics, produced the diagrams for figures 6, 10, and 11. Sarah Courteau helped with the final details.

This book began with the generous support of a fellowship from the American Association of University Women, continued some years later with the help of a University of Iowa Senior Faculty Fellowship, and was sustained along the way by crucial University of Iowa developmental leaves. I am grateful to the Beinecke Library for a Beinecke Research Fellowship, which allowed me to spend a month in New Haven immersed in the materials of the H.D. archive. The University of Iowa English department's Evelyn Harder Glick Fund helped to fund travel to these various archives.

I am grateful to Joan Catapano, the editor in chief of the University of Illinois Press, for her wisdom, patience, and impatience. For their readings of the full manuscript, I am indebted to two astute readers for the University of

Illinois Press, Professors Michael Davidson and Eileen Gregory. I am grateful for the care and clear eye of my copyeditor, Matt Mitchell.

Finally, at last and lastingly, this book is for—and because of—Wendy Deutelbaum and Ellen Fowles Morris.

*   *   *

Grateful acknowledgment is made for permission to reprint in revised form the following articles and book chapters:

"Sound Technologies and the Modernist Epic: H.D. on the Air," in *Sound States: Innovative Poetics and Acoustical Technologies,* ed. Adalaide Morris (Chapel Hill: University of North Carolina Press, 1997), 32–55. © 1998 by the University of North Carolina Press. Used by permission of the publisher.

"The Concept of Projection: H.D.'s Visionary Powers," *Contemporary Literature* 25.4 (Winter 1984): 411–36. © 1984 by the Board of Regents of the University of Wisconsin System. Reprinted by permission of the University of Wisconsin Press.

"A Relay of Power and of Peace," *Contemporary Literature* 27.4 (Winter 1986): 493–524. © 1986 by the Board of Regents of the University of Wisconsin System. Reprinted by permission of the University of Wisconsin Press.

"Science and the Mythopoeic Mind: The Case of H.D.," in *Chaos and Order: Complex Dynamics in Literature and Science,* ed. N. Katherine Hayles (Chicago: University of Chicago Press, 1991), 195–220. © 1991 by the University of Chicago. All rights reserved.

"Angles of Incidence/Angels of Dust: Operatic Tilt in the Poetics of H.D. and Nathaniel Mackey," in *H.D. and Poets After,* ed. Donna Krolik Hollenberg (Iowa City: University of Iowa Press, 2000), 235–54. © 2000 by the University of Iowa Press. Reprinted by permission of the University of Iowa Press.

Grateful acknowledgment is given to New Directions Publishing Corporation for permission to quote from the following copyrighted works of H.D.:

Collected Poems, 1912–1944, © 1982 by the Estate of Hilda Doolittle. Reprinted by permission of New Directions Publishing Corporation.

Helen in Egypt, © 1961 by Norman Holmes Pearson. Reprinted by permission of New Directions Publishing Corporation.

The Gift, © 1969, 1982 by the Estate of Hilda Doolittle. Reprinted by permission of New Directions Publishing Corporation.

Trilogy, © 1944 by Oxford University Press; © renewed 1972 by Norman Holmes Pearson. Reprinted by permission of New Directions Publishing Corporation.

Previously unpublished materials by H.D. © 2003 by The Schaffner Family Trust. Used by permission of New Directions Publishing Corporation.

Material by H.D. published in periodical form or out-of-print material is quoted by permission of New Directions Publishing Corporation, agents for Perdita Schaffner.

Excerpt from Norman Holmes Pearson's notes for a biography of H.D. is used by permission of Yale University through the Yale Committee on Literary Property.

I am grateful to Leslie Scalapino for permission to quote from "Dahlia's Iris: Secret Autobiography and Fiction," forthcoming from Fiction Collective Two.

How to Live / What to Do

Introduction:
H.D.'s Ongoingness

"'I know what the letters H.D. stand for,'" a physician announced to the poet Barbara Guest as she approached completion of her biography of H.D. "'They stand for Have Done'" (qtd. in "Intimacy" 62). As numerous poets and critics before me have found, however, it's not easy to have done with H.D. For Guest, this hesitation to conclude is a mark of the "passionate absorption" in the labors of "research, detection, introspection, intuition, identification" necessary to any prolonged thinking about another person's thought (62). But there is an additional factor that makes it hard to have done with H.D., a factor this book imagines as a pressure of ongoingness, a generativity that belongs both to the poetry of H.D. and more generally to the properties of poetic language.

In this introduction, I want to make a case for poetic language less as a medium for identification and introspection than as an agent of thought, perception, and meaning in the ongoing life of a culture. Because of the predominance of the lyric in postromantic Western poetry, it's difficult not to read poems as guidebooks to the psyche—I do it, and gleefully, many times in the pages to come—but biographical and/or psychological reading is not the burden of this book. My argument situates H.D.'s poems as a cultural link, a relay, a connection, tie, or bond among three interdependent realms: the printed page, recorded voice, and filmstrip of modernist aesthetic practice, the socioeconomic crises of the first half of the twentieth century, and the matrix of ideas through which thinkers in different fields have struggled to comprehend these crises. H.D.'s poems, the following chapters argue, draw from, participate in, and contribute to our understanding of the ways in which modernist artists and scientists address the conundrum Wallace Stevens calls "How to Live. What to Do."[1]

When poems are taken to be predominantly biographical or psychological, they make sense by virtue of meanings understood to reside in the person who writes or the person who reads. When poems are taken as historical documents, they make sense by virtue of their alignment with identifiable events in a particular time, a particular space. In both cases, the poem's utterance is taken to be referential: it is *about,* it *points to* something outside the poem. As I worked with the poetic language of H.D.'s *Sea Garden, Trilogy,* and *Helen in Egypt,* however, what seemed most remarkable was not that these poems generate a series of compelling and complicated subject positions—although they do—or that they draw our interest to events off the page—although, again and very importantly, they do. What fascinates me in these poems is not just *what* but *how* they think. As forms of cultural meditation and mediation, they instantiate, exercise, and advocate a kind of attention that is crucial to the ongoing life of a culture. In this sense, they think *about* thinking and they think *toward* action: they are, that is, philosophical and ethical. They do cultural work.

The opposing point of view—that poetry, however "cultured," is, in the end, peripheral to a culture's life—takes both colloquial and refined forms. The offhand phrase "that's just poetry"—a dismissal that means, more or less, "that's nice," "that's pretty," or, with an edge, "so?"—takes poetic language out of the loop into the bright, thin air of beauty associated with high art. Inherited from romanticism, this notion of aesthetic autonomy holds poetry apart from the market exchanges through which it circulates and the historical debates in which it participates. "[P]oetry makes nothing happen," as W. H. Auden puts it in his poem "In Memory of W. B. Yeats": "it survives / In the valley of its saying where executives / Would never want to tamper" (50). Like more popular dismissals, Auden's lines allude to the poet's art as an isolated, rarified skill, fascinating to its practitioners, perhaps, but of little more use to the men and women who administrate a country's laws and spend its money than the art of dancing in armor.

It is easy to caricature positions that argue for a use in poetry beyond psychological insight or aesthetic exaltation. Despite Yeats's artistry, Auden goes on, "Ireland has her madness and her weather still" (50). Despite Ezra Pound's delivery of a copy of *A Draft of XXX Cantos* to Mussolini in January 1933, to give a more extreme example, despite his effort to explain economic principles to Roosevelt's agriculture secretary Henry Wallace in April 1939, despite the politically inflected poetry he read over the radio in the early 1940s, worldwide depression continued to devolve into worldwide war.[2] From a cause-and-effect or instrumental point of view, an attempt to use poems to bolster fascist ideology or right-wing church-and-state authoritarianism differs little from an attempt to use poetic language to undermine governmental bureaucracy. The Marxist critic Terry Eagleton, therefore, fires with equal sarcasm in both directions: on the right, he finds T. S. Eliot's *The Waste Land* "a poem which intimates that fertility cults hold the clue to the salvation of the West" (41); on the left, he finds Julia Kristeva's *Revolution in Poetic Language*—the book in which she sets up guerrilla headquarters in "the valley of [poetry's] saying"—not only "dangerously formalistic" but downright silly. "[W]ill reading Mallarmé," Eagleton asks, "bring down the bourgeois state?" (190).

It is not necessary to reduce poetic language to an instrumental agent, however, to make the claim that it does useful cultural work. In *Repression and Recovery: Modern American Poetry and the Politics of Cultural Memory, 1910–1945*, Cary Nelson argues for a much more capacious poetic canon—the canon instantiated in his recent *Anthology of Modern American Poetry*—on the grounds that poems are sites of social as well as artistic practice. Working-class poems, African American experimental poetry, political poetry of the 1930s, poems written by Chinese immigrants on Angel Island, and contemporary performance poetry are all levered into a tradition severely constricted by previous anthologies of modern American poetry under the pressure of the following questions: "What have we entirely forgotten and why? How has the selectivity of our literary memory facilitated and inhibited (and been directed by) our development as a culture? How might both the present and the future be altered if we rediscover the literature we have lost?" (*Repression* 51).

Although Nelson makes his case predominantly on the grounds of content, his argument for the power and importance of American poetry makes it clear "that much more than the *subject matter* of poetry is at stake":

> Poetry, for a time, had the power to help people not only come to understand the material conditions of their existence but also to envision ways of changing them. Poetry offered people oppositional language they could quote and identify with—socially critical perspectives of anger and idealization they could accept as their own. In part because of its long historical links with song and with the speaking voice, and in part because we are especially aware of its formal properties, poetry offers us subject positions we can take up consciously and with a paradoxically self-conscious sense of personal identification. Compared to prose, and certainly in contrast to many forms of public rhetoric, poetry is perhaps less likely to write itself out on our tongues unawares. (124)

Nelson is speaking here of American poetry of the 1930s, but his words could also be used to describe readings of H.D. that began in the 1980s to discern an array of oppositional strategies in poems previously considered chaste and classical. Like Nelson's anthologizing of Japanese American concentration camp haiku next to such canonized lyrics of World War II as Randall Jarrell's "The Death of the Ball Turret Gunner," the insertion of H.D.'s revisionary mythmaking, lesbian erotics, and antipatriarchal poetics into the context of Eliot's *The*

Waste Land, Pound's *Cantos,* and William Carlos Williams's *Paterson* forces a reconceptualization of modernism's relation to gender, history, and politics.[3]

To borrow an insistence made in another context by the poet and critic Barrett Watten, historical and cultural material in poetry is not only a question of "the world in the work" but also a matter of "the work in the world" ("Politics" 58). Although they don't operate with the cause-and-effect tidiness parodied in Eagleton's swipes at Eliot and Kristeva, poems do play a part in the labor of altering the present and the future. What I hope the chapters that follow will add to arguments made by Nelson, Watten, and others is a sense of the ways in which H.D.'s poetic forms and vocabulary participate in this work. On the assumption that it is language that carries and contours thought, perception, and meaning, the three parts of this book take up, in sequence, the foundations of H.D.'s language in sound, its coalescence in the charged words of her poems, and its transmissions and transmutations in the work of more contemporary poets. The first part considers the dynamic materiality of poetic language through an extended analysis of sound in H.D.'s poems; the second looks at the conceptual charge detonated by three terms from H.D.'s poetic lexicon; the final part looks at interactions between H.D. and three more recent poets—Jack Spicer, Nathaniel Mackey, and Leslie Scalapino—who also use poetic formulations to think through catastrophic events of the twentieth century. Because these poets all use poetic language to tamper with the roots of cultural thinking, they belong, it seems to me, not so much to high modernism, the aesthetic quarters to which H.D. is usually assigned, or to postmodernism, the rubric under which Spicer, Mackey, and Scalapino are usually housed, but to the century-long tradition critics have called radical modernism.[4]

*   *   *

For many contemporary critics, readings launched from poetic form—so-called formalist or close readings—smack of a now quite old New Criticism. Although, as Gerald Graff has pointed out, New Criticism began in a series of essays that used analysis of poetic language to make passionate statements about "the dissociation of sensibility, technical rationality, the collapse of the Old South, or some other equally large theme," at a certain moment in its development, "the argument that the politics of literature should be seen as part of its form modulated subtly into the idea that literature had no politics, except as an irrelevant extrinsic concern" (150). For John Guillory, the moment at which New Criticism began to fetishize the lyric as a genre isolated, even insulated, against the world's mire and contingency, its executives and chaotic weather, was the publication of Cleanth Brooks's *The Well Wrought Urn* in

1947.[5] Brooks's title—borrowed, of course, from John Donne's "The Canonization"—has become an emblem of the New Critical view of the poem as a rarified object to be showcased under bright lights in the Musée des Beaux Arts. Understood as an aesthetic artifact abstracted from its historical, political, and ideological contexts, "the poem itself," as the New Critics liked to call it, was cultural ink uncontaminated by links with politics, history, and ideology.

To argue that poetic form has cultural bearing, it is necessary to begin by relinking a poem's formal properties with its discursive content. In 1950, when Charles Olson drafted his manifesto "Projective Verse," this was not an obvious connection. Amplifying Robert Creeley's dictum to make it heard over prevailing formalist doctrine, Olson shouted in cold block type, "FORM IS NEVER MORE THAN AN EXTENSION OF CONTENT" (240). The point performed here is that poems are material forms of thinking: they enact ideas, extend them, project them, throw them forward. As Michael Davidson puts it in *Ghostlier Demarcations: Modern Poetry and the Material Word,* poetic forms "derive from and generate critical frames" (133). This overlap makes it not only possible but imperative for a critic to move between formal procedures and socioeconomic contexts, "two materialities," Davidson concludes, "that cannot easily be separated" (226).

In his 1997 review of Davidson's book, Lytle Shaw situates it as part of "a significant (if still comparatively marginal) movement within poetry theory that explores the ways modern and contemporary poetry encodes, engages and enacts the social" (173). Shaw mentions Barrett Watten's *Total Syntax* (1984), Charles Bernstein's *Content's Dream* (1984) and *A Poetics* (1991), Ron Silliman's *The New Sentence* (1987), Cary Nelson's *Repression and Recovery* (1989), Alan Golding's *From Outlaw to Classic* (1995), Jed Rasula's *The American Poetry Wax Museum* (1996), and Bob Perelman's *The Marginalization of Poetry* (1996), a roster to which must now be added Lyn Hejinian's essays, collected under the title *The Language of Inquiry* (2000), and Rachel Blau DuPlessis's *Genders, Races, and Religious Cultures in Modern American Poetry, 1908–1934* (2001). This lineage reaches back to Theodor Adorno's warning that the lyric's "relation to social matters . . . must not lead us away from the works, it must lead us more deeply into them" ("Lyric Poetry" 56) and outward to Jerome McGann's exploration of the modern lyric as a typographical event in a bibliographic field that has much to do with commodity culture and the chaos of the marketplace. Marjorie Perloff's sustained work on innovative traditions in modern and contemporary poetry, finally, has been foundational to this movement to capture the dynamic reciprocity between poetic language and forms, cultural ideologies, and social circumstances.[6]

To name this tradition of reading poems requires at least two terms: one to reclaim poetry as a complex set of formal dynamics, the other to situate it in its social, historical, and ideological contexts. To ignore the first in favor of the second is to assume what DuPlessis aptly calls "an extractive attitude to texts," an attitude that reduces the poem to little more than "an odd delivery system for ideas and themes" (*Genders* 7); to ignore the second in favor of the first is to sheer off from crucial contemporary debates into one or another aesthetic cul-de-sac. Like Davidson's term "ideology of form" (133) and Watten's term "social formalism" ("Social Formalism"), DuPlessis's term of choice—"social philology"—emphasizes the founding assumption of this approach: the insistence that "social meanings and debates, textual irruptions of subjectivities, contradictory or self-consistent, must be examined not just *in* poetry but *as* poetry" (11).

The terminology of this practice diverges sharply from the New Critical lexicon that continues to dominate poetry handbooks. The terms favored by the New Critics tended to be two-part tropes like metaphor, allegory, parallelism, ambiguity, paradox, or irony. Tacitly binary and happily organic, these tropes move the poem toward a formal resolution in which the trope's two parts dissolve into one. Operating with this ideal in mind, New Critics used "close reading" to, in effect, close the poem by pulling its tenor and vehicle, its apparent sense and its other-sense, its parallel syntactical patterns and contradictory emotional patterns into a unity, wholeness, or identity understood to be the poem's purpose and mode of being. Such procedures, needless to say, drop out "mad Ireland and her weather," have little to say about economics, and appear to take no position at all in the political fray that surrounds them.[7]

The "reactivation of close reading" (DuPlessis, *Genders* 1) by postformalist critics mobilizes a more elastic and elusive set of terms to align a poem's formal dynamics with its trajectory as social and political communication within a historical field. Insisting that "stylistic innovations be recognized not only as alternative aesthetic conventions but also as alternative social formations," Bernstein emphasizes the need for critics to develop "a synoptic, multilevel, interactive response" to poetry (*A Poetics* 227). Instead of metaphor, allegory, or irony, therefore, critics like Bernstein, Davidson, DuPlessis, and Perloff emphasize tropes of indeterminacy and uncertainty.[8] The figures that catch the eye of these critics are targets that flicker and gyrate across contexts, enact transitoriness instead of permanence, and promote generativity rather than stability. Using, among other devices, metonymy, allusion, syntactical fracturing, and the spatial field of the page to emphasize gaps and incongruities, poets in this tradition foreground not form but deformities or, better, "multiformities," like the staggered line in the poems of William Carlos Williams, "the offbeat or eccentric accent" in the poetics of Nathaniel Mackey (*Discrepant* 244), and the stutter in the work of Susan Howe ("*Talisman* Interview" 181). In order to assess the ways in which the materiality of the page interacts with the materiality of social forms on a multitude of levels, Michael Davidson merges the words *palimpsest* and *text* to coin the term "palimtext" (67). "By this word," he writes, "I mean to emphasize the intertextual—and interdiscursive—quality of modern writing as well as its materiality. The palimtext is neither genre nor object but a writing-in-process," a writing that "retains vestiges of prior inscriptions out of which it emerges" (67–68).

Borrowing a term from the psychoanalysts Maria Torok and Nicolas Abraham and from the critic John Shoptaw, DuPlessis reads for "crypt words" or "crypt phrases" in a poem. In DuPlessis's generative interpretations, words like "whit" in Countee Cullen's "Incident" or phonemic sequences like "hoo hoo hoo" in poems by Vachel Lindsay, Wallace Stevens, and T. S. Eliot release their meanings like seedpods spilling seeds. Caught in the crosshairs of DuPlessis's "social philology"—"the point at which cross both lateral metonymic associations and a vertical semantic coring"—the word "whit" in Cullen's poem signifies particle or iota; sounds like "wight," meaning person or human creature; evokes ethical considerations of courage or valor; and, above all, at last, condemns the white child who although "no whit bigger" is empowered to use a term that interpellates both children into their positions in the racial system of the United States (*Genders* 18). Synchronizing the words of the black child with the ballad stanza of Western normative culture, Cullen rhymes the size of the white child—"no whit bigger"—with the upshot of the encounter: "called me, 'Nigger.'"[9] In this reading of the poem, Cullen's manipulation of the resonances of the word "whit" carries as much weight as any paradox or irony in a New Critical reading,[10] but the effect of heightened attentiveness to a crypt word is not to isolate or insulate the poem from the world's discrepancies and contingencies but rather to bring its historical, political, and ethical crosscurrents fully into view.

The key words of this study—most importantly, the terms *phonotext, manaword,* and *radical modernism*—converge to describe a kind of kinetic, insurgent, processual thinking for which H.D.'s poetry provides a productive example. My aim is to use these terms not to stabilize the meanings of H.D.'s poems, pinpoint their truths, or exclaim over their beauty but rather to catch thought in action as it cuts across reality-generating fields. For this reason, the chapters take up, in turn, discourses such as poetics, psychoanalysis, cinema studies, mapping, mysticism, anthropology, and science through which H.D. describes a material world that can never be fully, adequately, or finally represented. To think about thinking in a landscape of crisis is not, as Stevens knew, an exercise in the Academy of Fine Ideas but a practice with an ethical horizon and social, political, and spiritual effects.[11]

Part 1 of this book—"Sounds"—focuses on the acoustical churn of phonemes, syllables, words, and phrases as they pull into play and keep in circulation multiple and simultaneous articulations of information from several different cultural fields at once. To foreground sound in poetic language is to engage a proliferation of meaning that cannot be halted, an ongoingness of signification that exceeds binary oppositions and resists closure. As the ensuing readings of H.D.'s poems will show, however, this openness is not a rejection of communication in favor of an endless—and perhaps pointless—playfulness and pluralism, much less a rejection of cultural reference, but rather a generation of conceptual links through which poets and readers access, activate, refresh, and sustain the cultural materials through which crises are understood and addressed.

During H.D.'s lifetime, the rapid proliferation of telephones, radios, microphones, loudspeakers, and talking films changed not only the ways in which sound circulated through the culture—its reach and timbre, its range and pervasiveness—but also the information sound carried and the manner in which the mind seized and processed that information. The change apprehended by scholars like Eric A. Havelock, Walter J. Ong, S.J., and Marshall McLuhan led them to postulate the emergence of a postliterate "secondary orality," a newly energized alertness to sound that in its turn energized and reconfigured modernist literary production and reception. This resurgent aurality in the work of H.D. and her modernist contemporaries, part 1 will argue, gives us new ways to think toward and through the links between poetics and culture.

Part 2 of this book—"Mana-Words"—borrows a term from Roland Barthes for words that function in a writer's vocabulary as nodes and relays of thought. These words, Barthes explains, are rarely the capitalized nouns of philosophy, history, and religion—*Beauty*, for example, or *Truth*—but more elusive and elastic words, words that are "neither eccentric nor central" yet nonetheless impart "the illusion that by this word one might answer for everything" (*Roland Barthes* 129). The distinguishing characteristic of the mana-word, Barthes explains, is its capacity to move across registers of thinking, "always atopic (escaping any topic), at once remainder and supplement, a signifier taking up the place of every signified" (129). Barthes's example of word-as-mana is the word *body* (130). Three examples from H.D.'s poetry, each of which anchors a chapter in part 2, are the mana-words *projection, gift,* and *science.*

Although it emerges in a different context, Hugh Kenner's description of the Chinese ideogram in Pound's thought provides a useful entry to the mana-word in H.D.'s thinking. As Pound learned from Ernest Fenollosa, the ideogram is "alive and plastic, because [in its formulations] *thing* and *action* are not formally separated" (Fenollosa 17). In Fenollosa's theory, Kenner elaborates, the Chinese character "sketches a process, seizes some continuous happening—the movement of attention through an eye, the flow from roots to branches within a tree—and fixes it, like Buckminster Fuller's knot, with three or four minimal vigorous spatial gestures" (*Pound Era* 160). Kenner's reference is to Fuller's figure of a slip knot sliding along a rope spliced in sequence of hemp, cotton, and nylon: this knot is, for Fuller, a patterned energy made visible by but not dependent on the particular substances—hemp, cotton, nylon—that momentarily instantiate it. "Like molecules of water in fountain or vortex," Kenner elaborates, "particulars of the pattern mutate; the pattern is stable, an enduring integrity, shaped by the movement, shaping it" (*Pound Era* 147).

H.D.'s mana-words point to and put into play patterns of energy that move across contexts without significantly altering their form. For H.D., these processes are the engines of ongoingness: they link cultural fields, bind together social groups, tribes, or nations, and replicate across scales in material and social phenomena. *Projection,* then, is a throwing forward of energy in the practice of poetics, psychoanalysis, cinema, mapping, and alchemy; the *gift,* a transfer of goods that creates and maintains connections among groups, a relay, as H.D. thought of it, of power and peace; and *science,* an unfolding sequence of principles by which we come to comprehend relations between processes, events, and beings in the world.

The difference between Pound's ideograms and H.D.'s mana-words is subtle but important, for it allows us to see a spread or separation between two differently inflected "modernisms." As many critics have pointed out, Pound enlisted Fenollosa's notion of the Chinese written character to serve the totalizing vision that is frequently used to define "high modernism." When the notion of a replication of patterns across contexts becomes exact or rigid—as it does, for example, when Pound makes the ideal of a good ruler or an orderly society into a transcendental norm equally applicable to rural and urban, feudal and capitalist, European and non-European cultures—the ideogram enters the service of a politics of hierarchy and mastery. In this economy of enforced sameness, the ideogram turns into the measuring stick that Bernstein calls "the Pound standard [of] the absolute worth of the cultural production of all the societies of earth" ("Pounding Fascism" 121).

As Bernstein goes on to argue, however, even Pound himself diverges from the Pound standard: "the success of *The Cantos* is that its coherence is of a kind totally different than Pound desired or could—in his more rigid moments—

accept. For the coherence of the 'hyperspace' of Pound's modernist collage is not a predetermined Truth of a pancultural elitism but a product of a compositionally decentered multiculturalism" (122–23). If the Pound standard enforces a coercive equation of like to like, a relationship of similarity, the paratactic forms of *The Cantos*—collage, documentary fragments, polyphonic cross-language punning—defeat such an equation, for in these forms there is always something left over, a remainder from which difference or change emerges. This overrun of significance, a key characteristic of poetic language, is also the identifying trait of the mana-word and the seed of H.D.'s radical modernism.

Part 3—Radical Modernisms—develops some of the implications of H.D.'s position between a series of different modernisms. My interest here is not in proposing another large theoretical framework for modernism but rather in using a third term to interrupt the binary opposition between "modernism" and "postmodernism" that not only reduces the poets it would describe but makes it all but impossible to see the generative links between them. Like Bernstein's essay on Pound, the chapters in part 3 acknowledge contradictory elements in H.D.'s poetics and seek to identify those that have proved useful to poets in subsequent generations. In looking at the writings of Nathaniel Mackey, Jack Spicer, and Leslie Scalapino and attending to their interpretations of H.D.'s sounds, mana-words, and mythological constructs, once again my emphasis is on the intersection of aesthetics and ethics in a context of historical and political crisis. My goal is to come to terms with poetic language that suggests alternate methods of thinking, alternate relationships among components of thought, and alternate approaches to the question of how to live, what to do.

*   *   *

Although this book follows several strands in the weave of H.D.'s historical moment, her life, and her work, it does not offer another reading of the career of a major modernist. When I take up H.D.'s unpublished and/or slighter works, her letters and journals, and the writings of thinkers whose work she read, I use them for the most part not to trace her development but to pursue her thinking through several complex and compelling texts—most importantly, the lyrics of *Sea Garden*, the long poems *Trilogy* and *Helen in Egypt*, her fictionalized memoir *The Gift*, and her novel *HERmione*. As will be clear in the chapters that follow, I am moved by her struggles as a woman in a masculinist culture and a bisexual in a heteronormative world, but H.D.'s feminism, however foundational to her work and to my thinking about her, is not the point of my argument. What draws me to her writing is the intricacy, connectivity, strangeness, and stamina of her thinking. In the pages that follow, I interpret her poetry and poetic prose as acts of cognition.

"The poet," as Barrett Watten has said of Hart Crane and Larry Eigner, "thinks with his poem" ("Missing 'X'" 180). This is not to say that a poem is an exercise in logic—although, in a rare case, it might be—but rather that poetic language requires poet and reader alike to be continuously alert to the figures that construct their thought. Wittgenstein's famous warning, "Do not forget that a poem, although it is composed in the language of information, is not used in the language-game of giving information,"[12] anticipates Robert Creeley's declaration that poems are not only—perhaps even not most importantly—referential.[13] Like philosophy, in this sense, a poem is a way of thinking about how to think.

Despite her lifelong habit of passionate reading in such fields as classical literature and philosophy, anthropology, Egyptology, science, psychoanalysis, alchemical and mystical traditions, and the history of Moravian and Native American interactions in the early settlement of Pennsylvania, and despite her many autobiographical and fictional self-portraits as a researcher, critics rarely define H.D. as a thinker.[14] The work necessary to establish her as a figure of primary interest was textual, biographical, and interpretive rather than philosophical. Since the 1980s, therefore, scholars have perused reams of archival materials, composed biographies and set up chronologies of her writing, edited and seen into print a long shelf of poems, novels, plays, memoirs, film criticism, and literary and cultural writing from documents stored at Yale's Beinecke Rare Book and Manuscript Library, provided accounts of her important relationships with—among others—her companion Bryher, her daughter Perdita, and her friend and editor Norman Holmes Pearson, and developed sustained readings of even her most dense and disorienting texts. To borrow Guest's formulation, these labors of "research, detection, introspection, intuition, [and] identification" turned a figure whom mid-century reviewers represented as Pound's girlfriend, an imagist poster poet, and a minor woman writer into a major presence in the generation of modernists born in the 1880s.

As Robert Duncan was one of the first to point out, mid-century reviewers were quick to overlook in H.D.'s writing the cultural reach and ambition they so admired in the work of writers like T. S. Eliot.[15] "'I do not wish to be brutal,'" Dudley Fitts wrote in his review of H.D.'s World War II poem *The Flowering of the Rod;* "'I should be a fool to pretend that H.D.'s intentions—her conceptions, even—are other than the highest; but it does seem clear to me that her whole method in these poems is false.'" "'Queer'" and "'more than a little silly,'" added Randall Jarrell. "'[T]hin and shrill,'" said a reviewer for *The New Yorker.*[16] This spill of gender-compromised adjectives—*silly, shrill, thin, false, queer*—together with Fitts's faux-gallant "do not wish to be brutal" and his patronizing "—conceptions, even—" display the misogyny that made H.D.'s person rather than her thought the focus of early attention. The tendentiousness of these judgments made it all but inevitable that the first serious rereadings of H.D. to follow Duncan's groundbreaking essays would emerge from the matrix of feminism.

Because the oppositional narrative of feminism takes place—has to take place—on the very terrain it would correct, the wave of H.D. criticism that began in the 1980s with Susan Stanford Friedman's *Psyche Reborn* and crested in crucial essays and books by Friedman, Rachel Blau DuPlessis, Alicia Ostriker, and others established a counterportrait of an author who was strong rather than weak, serious rather than silly, major rather than minor. Because these readings coincided with an explosion of activist scholarship on compulsory heterosexuality, psychoanalytic misogyny, the gendering of modernism, and the struggle of the career of the woman artist, efforts to advance H.D.'s texts as exemplary rewritings of masculinist paradigms tended to emphasize her complicated erotic commitments, her subversion of Freudian psychoanalysis, her struggle with the overbearing masculinity of her modernist cohort, and her continuous rewriting of the story of her artistic development. "H.D.'s appeal for feminist criticism, myself included," Claire Buck writes in the opening of her book *H.D. and Freud: Bisexuality and a Feminine Discourse,* "rests on her treatment of the female self" (1).

Along with Claire Buck, critics like Deborah Kelly Kloepfer, Elizabeth Hirsh, and Dianne Chisholm followed these early readings with a series of theoretically inflected interpretations that complicated notions of authentic or alternative female identity by pursuing Lacanian or Kristevan notions of split or fractured subjectivity, linguistic slippage, oscillation, and failure. In this transition from liberal-feminist to poststructuralist-feminist readings of H.D., however, as Susan Edmunds has pointed out, "identity and fragmentation, authenticity and self-alienation, adequacy and lack have remained the governing critical dichotomies, while the relative value of their component terms has simply been reversed," and the commitment to "recuperating H.D. according to the preferred terms of each critic's chosen approach" has held steady (3).

Given this point-counterpoint structure of mid-century dismissal followed by two decades of advocacy, end-of-the-century backlash is perhaps predictable. Writing in *Representing Modernist Texts: Editing as Interpretation,* a collection of essays on the consolidation of the modernist canon, Lawrence S. Rainey dismisses H.D. as an overrated coterie writer, a poster poet for the feminists, and a pawn in the wars of identity politics. "What still remains to be established, though," he writes, drawing a bow at the opening of his essay, "is whether she was a great poet" ("Canon" 101). "She was," he concludes, shooting the arrow at the end of his essay, "a figure interesting for the life of her times, but not a major force 'in the history of twentieth-century poetry,' and certainly not 'one of the most original poets . . . in our language'" (118).[17] The "great poet" bull's-eye is a tiny, contested, tendentious target, however, of interest mainly to those attempting to get a writer back into print, into select anthologies, or, more simply, into—or out of—the conversation. H.D.'s originality, I argue here, lies in a radicality in language use that both instigates and carries her thinking, not a quality that consolidates into poetic mastery under conventional lyric definitions.

In shifting the focus from H.D.'s person to the cultural links generated within her poetic language, I move away from psychological or psychoanalytic debates about the formation of H.D.'s subjectivity, moral debates about the integrity of her character, and aesthetic debates about the "greatness" and/or "originality" of her writing toward a wider discussion of the relationship between poetic forms and cultural meanings. In doing so, I take for granted the interdependence between gender and modernism, the interplay between language and subjectivity, and the importance of H.D.'s writing in crucial cultural discussions, all of which have been illuminated by H.D. scholars who precede me. H.D.'s poetry stands in here for a larger field of poetics constituted by socially critical perspectives that assume that neither the structure of the past nor the structure of the future is given in advance. In a century of near-apocalyptic catastrophes, the ethical work of H.D.'s texts is to put into question the possibility of "having done." This generativity and openness, this writing-in-process, is H.D.'s ongoingness.

Notes

1. "How to Live. What to Do" is the title of a poem from Stevens's 1935 volume *Ideas of Order*.

2. For Pound's interview with Mussolini in Rome on 30 January 1939, see Stock 306; for his interview with Henry Wallace and attempt to reach President Roosevelt in April 1939, see Kenner, *Pound Era* 463.

3. For H.D.'s revisionary mythmaking, see DuPlessis, "'Perceiving the other-side of everything'"; for her lesbian eroticism, see Collecott, *H.D. and Sapphic Modernism*, Friedman and DuPlessis, "'I Had Two Loves Separate,'" Gregory, "Rose Cut in Rock," and Gubar, "Sapphistries"; for her antipatriarchal poetics, see especially Friedman, *Psyche Reborn*.

4. In the use of this term, as will be clear in part 3, I am turning a phrase used by a number of critics, among them Charles Bernstein's "radical innovations of the modernist period" ("In the Middle of Modernism" 94n.4), Donald Byrd's "radical moder-

nity" (17), Vincent Sherry's modernist radicalism, and Barrett Watten's "radical modernism" ("Constructivist Moment" 64).

5. In his discussion of the development of New Criticism in *Cultural Capital,* John Guillory identifies *The Well Wrought Urn* as the text in which Brooks found a way to drain literary works of their cultural and philosophical content "as a prolegomenon to the *reading* of the work" (158).

6. See particularly Adorno, "Lyric Poetry and Society" (1974), McGann, *The Textual Condition* (1991) and *Black Riders* (1993), and Perloff, *The Poetics of Indeterminacy* (1981) and *Radical Artifice* (1991). For an extended overview of this body of criticism, with particular attention to discussions of genders, races, and religious cultures, see chapter 1 of DuPlessis, *Genders* (1–28).

7. As many critics before me have pointed out, of course, to take "no position" is in effect to take a position in support of one or another aspect of the reigning ideology.

8. In her important book *The Poetics of Indeterminacy,* Perloff works with the larger question of the relationship between the symbolist mode of Eliot and Baudelaire and the antisymbolist mode of Rimbaud and Cage. See also Quartermain, *Disjunctive Poetics,* which emphasizes the materiality, ambiguity, and openness of modern and contemporary experimental poetry.

9. The poem comes from Cullen's first book, *Color* (1925), and is anthologized in Nelson, *Anthology* 530–31. DuPlessis's analysis should be read in full (*Genders* 17–19).

10. "A poet's motivation for such a crypt phrase," DuPlessis explains, "may range from the discovery of a shifted or deepened meaning emerging from that shadow word; a psychological revelation—not necessarily hidden or concealed; a deliberate misrepresentation for reasons of both concealment or revelation; a political encoding" (*Genders* 25). It is important to note, however, that the charged word must be detonated by an active reader.

11. See Stevens, "Extracts from Addresses to the Academy of Fine Arts," in *Collected Poems,* 252–59. In his essay "The Constructivist Moment," Watten discusses the figures the Soviet modernist El Lissitzky called *Prouns* in similar terms. "The mere fact that the *Prouns* exist as positive objects," Watten writes, "is their confirmation of political agency, which is to inculcate, as 'free radicals' of pure creativity, 'the perpetual expansion of human achievement'" (79).

12. Marjorie Perloff uses this statement from *Zettel* as an epigraph to *Wittgenstein's Ladder.*

13. The self-correcting backtrack of Creeley's sentence—"poems," he writes, "are not referential, or at least not importantly so" ("'Poems'" 490)—performs the point he makes. Peter Nicholls ties this habit of thought to Oppen's ethics by connecting Oppen's own self-reflective poetics to his revulsion against the rhetoric of totalizing vision in Pound's late *Cantos* (155–56).

14. For a representative self-portrait as a researcher, see the novel *Pilate's Wife,* in which one of H.D.'s principal characters "has studied Assyrian charts, the names of stars and star-clusters, has watched the skies, has risked her life, hidden behind curtains

at assemblies to hear what the elders proffer. She has made a business of knowledge, as some women make a pastime of love" (39). Important exceptions to the tendency to slight the reach of H.D.'s reading include the work of Susan Stanford Friedman, who carefully documents H.D.'s studies of mythology, religion, and psychoanalysis in *Psyche Reborn,* and Eileen Gregory, who has brilliantly tracked H.D.'s lifelong immersion in Greek and Latin writing in general and the classical lyric and Euripides in particular.

15. Friedman gives a parallel example of this critical double standard in her discussion of prefeminist treatments of H.D.'s early "cold," "chiseled," "passionless" lyrics: "Eliot's impersonalism," she writes, "was of course ultimately accepted as quintessentially modernist. But many of H.D.'s readers identified the living writer with the poem-as-statue and fetishized her sculpted perfection as something to both adore and reject, as if it were impossible to grant her the distilled identity of Eliot's Tiresian mask" (*Penelope's Web* 53–54).

16. Quoted in Duncan, "From the Day Book" 21–22.

17. Rainey's exemplary quotations are from Friedman's entry on H.D. in the *Dictionary of Literary Biography* and Ostriker's blurb on the back of H.D.'s *Collected Poems.*

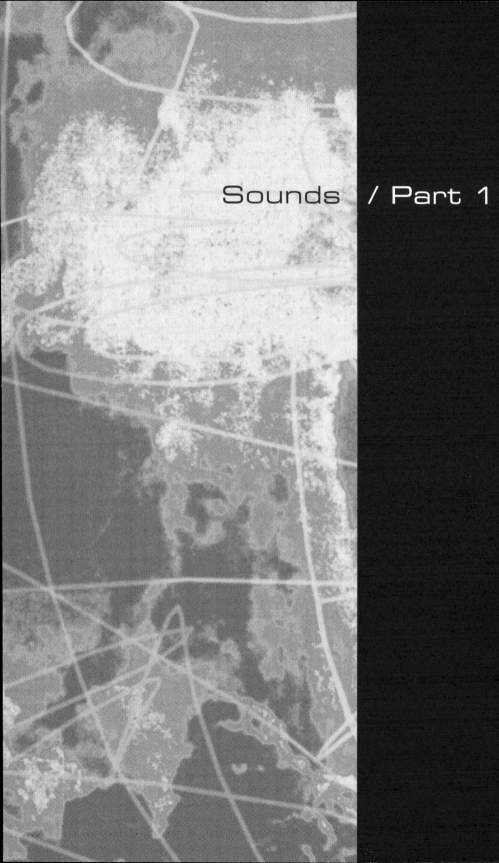

Sounds / Part 1

Wingéd Words:
H.D.'s Phonotexts and the
Configurations of Meaning

If you play James Brown (say, "Money Won't Change You . . .
but time will take you out") in a bank, the total environment is
changed. Not only the sardonic comment of the lyrics, but the
total emotional placement of the rhythm, instrumentation and
sound. An energy is released in the bank.
—Amiri Baraka, "The Changing Same (R&B and New Black Music)"

. . . the call of the phoneme, whose echoes tell of wild realms beyond the code and suggest new configurations of meaning . . .
—Jonathan Culler, "The Call of the Phoneme"

The first phrase we read on opening *Sea Garden*, H.D.'s first
book of poetry, is the title of the poem "Sea Rose." As if la-
beling a specimen in an herbarium, H.D.'s title gives genus and
species for this plant and specifies the terrain in which it can
be found. Even as the title's text sets the poem's taxonomy,
however, its sounds unsettle the syntax. In the push-pull of
H.D.'s poetics, the lexemes "sea" and "rose" hold their deno-
tations while the phonemes /sē/ and /rōz/ slide toward new
configurations: "see rose," "sea rows," "sea (a)rose," even, at
the far reaches of the echo, "z-rows" or "zeroes." As H.D.'s title
forms and reforms, adjectives turn to nouns, nouns become
verbs, and what at first appear to be whole words reconstitute
themselves as initial or terminal syllables. In these oscillations,
the title—by turns label, command, metaphor, statement, and
evaluation—releases an energy inimical to conventions of

order. This protean, transformative, generative acoustics—language's material base and fundament, rhythm, instrumentation, and sound—is the place I would like to start to investigate a poetics that aims to reach realms beyond the code.[1]

The purposes of this chapter are to open access to the sounds H.D.'s poems make, to align her writing with oral/aural traditions, and to consider the cultural work poetry performs within such traditions. In engaging these topics, I take seriously H.D.'s summary of her career in a speech written to accept the American Academy of Arts and Letters' Award of Merit in May 1960.[2] She is, H.D. says in these brief remarks, a purveyor of *"wingéd words"* (5). The Homeric epithet for language that flies from the mouth of a speaker to the ear of an audience, "wingéd words" are the swift-flying, time-based, performative medium of orators, bards, rhapsodes, and other masters of the sounded word. To appropriate this epithet centuries after the invention of writing irrevocably altered the technology of poetry is an odd and striking move.

With the exception of a few public appearances, scattered radio broadcasts, and the studio taping sessions explored in the next chapter, H.D. "spoke" primarily on the printed page.[3] In the terminology developed by the theorists of orality and literacy Eric A. Havelock and Walter J. Ong, she was neither an "oral" poet nor an exponent of secondary—or electronic—orality. In claiming "the wingéd word" as her sigil, however, H.D. makes a point that is only recently receiving its due: sounds also wing from the poet's hand through the printed page to the inner ear of the "silent" reader. As Garrett Stewart brilliantly demonstrates in *Reading Voices: Literature and the Phonotext,* writing needn't be voiced to have a voice or gain a hearing.

One register of the difficulty of talking about the acoustics of poetry is the need to develop new terminology for this dimension of a text. To make his point that the inner ear of the reader is alive to the full range of sound effects, Stewart spins the term *phonotext* off from a vocabulary developed to explore the phenomenology of reading. Related to but distinct from the "genotext," "phenotext," and "graphotext,"[4] the phonotext is the articulatory stream of sound in all alphabetic writing. Made accessible for analysis by "the kinetic, wavering tensions of phonemic reading" (28), the phonotext holds in suspension an array of sounds that is, for Stewart, richer, denser, and more various than the disambiguated articulations of any spoken text.

In the introduction to his collection of essays *Close Listening: Poetry and the Performed Word,* Charles Bernstein makes the opposite point. For Bernstein, "Unsounded poetry remains inert marks on a page, waiting to be called into use by saying, or hearing, the words aloud" (7). As an effort to undo the critical preference for marks on a page and pique the reader's ear for the fifteen essays on performed language that follow, this is good polemics, but it's not a point Bernstein or his essayists allow to banish the aurality of the phonotext. The differences between Bernstein and Stewart are, in fact, less interesting and important than the similarities that derive from their shared conviction that language is "live at the ear."[5] Given this allegiance, the enemy is neither the rigidified inflections Stewart hears in audiotexts nor the "fixed, stable, finite linguistic object" Bernstein sees in written texts but "inert" language, language not yet "called into use" by sound. "Close listening" and "phonemic reading" both aim to tune the ear to a linguistic richness, fluidity, and power muted by an age of print's fascination with visual textualities.

That Bernstein has in mind a broader category than spoken or voiced performances is the burden of the stutter in a portmanteau term from his introduction. Bernstein uses the word *a/orality,* he tells us, "to invoke a performative sense of 'phonotext' or audiotext" by joining "aurality," the sound of writing, to "orality," the sound of breath, voice, and speech (13). As the acoustical plenitude inherent in all phonetically based languages, a/orality precedes the spoken and exceeds the written. Whether in air or in ink, as the voiced spell of an audiotext or the spelled evocation of a phonotext, this mutability, evanescence, and transmissive power is the energy H.D. calls "the wingéd word." Live at the ear of the reader, it folds "Sea Rose" over "sea rows," aligns tiers of petals with lines of waves, and generates a chordal apprehension of the forces at the heart of the poem. By allowing a/orality to key my reading of poems from *Sea Garden* (1916), *Red Roses for Bronze* (1931), and *Trilogy* (1944–46) in this chapter, I hope to demonstrate some of the ways in which attention to sound provides access to the processes and convictions of H.D.'s poetry.

*   *   *

In summarizing a career of nearly fifty years before an assembly of three thousand fellow writers and artists, H.D.'s choice of the sigil "wingéd words" suggests wider ambitions than past and current conversations about her work have recognized. What is important, this rubric implies, is neither the achievement of lyric selfhood nor admission into a canon of masterworks but something more impersonal, immediate, and transmissive, which she calls the "whirr" of words, the spin and power of sound as it moves from poet to audience. "*Wingéd words,* we know, make their own spiral," she says, "caught up in them, we are lost, or found." The audience that "found H.D."—set here, like the author, in the third person—is not a collection of private sensibilities but a "collective consciousness," a community called into being by language ("Speech" 5).

H.D.'s evocation of the whirr of words shares a cultural moment with five documents that appeared independently of each other between 1962 and 1963. As Eric Havelock points out in *The Muse Learns to Write: Reflections on Orality and Literacy from Antiquity to the Present,* these documents—Claude Lévi-Strauss's *La Pensée Sauvage,* Jack Goody and Ian Watts's "The Consequences of Literacy," Marshall McLuhan's *The Gutenberg Galaxy: The Making of Typographic Man,* Ernst Mayr's *Animal Species and Evolution,* and Havelock's own *Preface to Plato*—were published in France, Britain, and the United States by authors who could not at the time have been aware of each other's investigations (25–29). Each is an attempt to understand the cultural work done by heard language.

From the perspective of the turn of the next century, these early discussions of orality and literacy have a number of disabling flaws. In their categorizing zeal, these theorists lump together and vastly oversimplify the complex cultures many of them insist on describing as "primitive." By failing to look closely enough, they miss alternative systems of recording and/or communicating information, needlessly polarize the acts of speaking and writing, and underestimate the persistence of orality following the introduction of alphabetic or phonetic writing.[6] Because they themselves reflect their own cultural moment, however, these breakthrough works—particularly the writings of Havelock and Ong—help us comprehend the importance H.D. attributed to the whirr of words and its implications for a cultural inflection of the act of phonemic reading.

For my purposes in this chapter, the three most important characteristics of a/orality—spoken or written—are transience, multiplicity, and a capacity to call into use cultural information. Ong's distinctions between orality and literacy begin in the fact that the "going on" of the spoken word is at the same time a "going away."[7] For Ong, the vitality of the wingéd word, its association with presence, depth, dimension, and fullness, its felt interiority, force, and forms all stem from the fact that voiced language is language at its quick, in the nick of time. "Sound, bound to the present time by the fact that it exists only at the instant when it is going out of existence, advertises presentness," Ong writes. "It is here, it envelops us" (*Presence* 101). Spoken language is first and foremost, for Ong, an event, a happening: we hear what is "here," close to us, in the air or, in an age of secondary or electronic orality, on the air around us.

As his thickened, dense, and dramatic descriptions of the phenomenon suggest, for Stewart phonemic reading is no less volatile an event than close listening. In the microsecond in which the phonemes /sē rōz/ generated by H.D.'s title flicker around the lexemes "sea rose," "sea rows," and "zeroes," the scriptive is transcoded into the morphophonemic. This flicker is the "here" of an ear on "hypersensitive alert" (*Reading Voices* 18), language on the fly or, as Stewart prefers to say, a/drift. Such "locutionary turmoil" (4) troubles and vivifies many aspects of language, but it is most audible in two effects that occur throughout H.D.'s writing: the slide of puns and the slosh and jostle of the effect Stewart calls the "transegmental drift."

Puns and transegmental drifts arise from an a/oral overflow caused by the wobble between lexemes and phonemes in a listener's mind or a reader's ear. A matter, in Stewart's words, of "echonomics," both of these effects arise from "the indeterminacy of graphemic shape when phonemically processed" (73): we hear "zeroes" as we read "sea rose," or alternatively, given an appropriate matrix of speech, we apprehend "sea rose" as we hear "zeroes." The production, distribution, and consumption of puns operates through a surplus in which, to borrow Geoffrey Hartman's definition of this figure of speech, two or more meanings compete for the same phonemic space, generating "too much sense for the sound," or one sound brings forth semantic doubles, generating "too much sound for the sense" (347).[8]

While classic puns—the overlap of *see* and *sea,* for example, or *rose* and *rows*—leave word units intact, transegmental drifts undo the border between words, making *zeroes* out of *sea rose* or, in one of Stewart's exuberant examples, *sound defects* into *sound effects.* Setting the *z* or the *d* in motion between two segments of speech, these transegmental drifts "zero out letters and breaks by turn, in a fluctuation of juncture that can never, by definition, be prescriptive" (25). A co-production between a text and its reader-listener, this "holding (over)" is, in Stewart's specification, a "gliding or skidding . . . slippage and blurring of a suddenly delettered lexeme which refashions adjacent diction on the sly, the slide" (179).

Like other effects of a/oral language, puns and transegmental drifts are clearly transient and multiple, but how do they call cultural information into use? Besides a groan of delight or dismay, what happens as these sound defects/effects flicker through our consciousness? The essayists in Jonathan Culler's collection *On Puns: The Foundation of Letters* suggest several answers, positioning puns—and, by extension, other a/oral overlaps—as instruments of knowledge (Culler), research strategies, philosophemes, or engines of epistemology (Ulmer), metaphors on the level of sound (Hartman), and/or devices for delaying, interrupting, or otherwise frustrating closure (Shoaf). Odd and unstable juxtapositions formed on the basis of similar signifiers open a gap the mind stretches to close by imagining contexts in which these mutually exclusive meanings can, at least for a moment, coexist. In Gregory Ulmer's terms, these "punceptual" sets, formed on the basis of similar signifiers, work as well for organizing thought as "conceptual" sets formed on the basis of similar signifieds (164). We groan because puns and transegmental drifts push us out beyond the codes we know and provoke us to conceive differently formed coherences.

In "The Aural Ellipsis and the Nature of Listening in Contemporary Poetry," the poet and psychoanalyst Nick Piombino offers two terms that help particularize the conceptual stretch sound effects generate. The first—"aural ellipsis"—points to slips, drifts, and other linguistic indeterminacies that trigger cognitive acts necessary to restore meaning; the second—"holding environment"—points to the intermediate zone such acts create, a place at once "out there" and "in here," "objective" and "subjective," fixed and free-floating.[9] "Works of poetry that can be characterized as effective mediums for the aural ellipsis," Piombino writes, "tend to be works that permit listeners and readers to discover and determine many of the structural elements of the poem for themselves, rather than foreground the narrative or didactic elements that provide the illusion of purpose, realism, or verisimilitude. . . . [T]he aural/oral ellipsis encourages listening to poetry as a holding environment within which the gaps among thought, language, and sensory experience must be bridged by the listener. Rather than only being asked to observe and comprehend a pattern of thinking, here listeners and readers, by means of a process of close, but freely imaginative, listening, are encouraged to actively participate in it" (62).

Although they both understand poems as cultural rather than personal documents, Piombino and Havelock differ radically in their notions of the audience's participation in the poetic moment. For Havelock, the listener's complete absorption is crucial. In the picture Havelock draws, the bard or reciter sends forth his wingéd words on a tide of rhythm that is at once verbal, vocal, instrumental, and physical. As the poet strums, sways, and sings, the audience—soothed, entranced, possessed—submits to the poem's spell. Such total immersion was necessary because, in Havelock's theory, Homeric poems were repositories of knowledge—handbooks, reference manuals, and treatises on ethics, politics, history, and religion—crucial to the preservation and transmission of an oral culture. If audience members were to remember the cultural codes for how to build a ship, deliver an insult, make a sacrifice, plan a feast, or face death, the story needed to be driven deep and lodged beyond the reach of reason.

Orality, for Havelock, is not only a technique of delivery but the state of mind that preceded the deliberative, abstract, self-reflexive orientation of literacy. The a/orality Piombino describes emerges from a world moving toward forms of communication that recombine the qualities Ong and Havelock divided between orality and literacy. For Piombino, even a lyric like H.D.'s "Sea

Rose"—brief, apparently private, particular, subjective, and intense—creates a "holding environment" that is neither wholly emotional nor wholly rational but "simultaneously physical and mental, objective and subjective, heard aloud and read silently, emanating from a specific self yet also from a nonspecific site of identity, coming toward comprehensibility and disintegrating into incoherence" (54). In the echonomy of the aural ellipsis, language pulls into play information from many cultural sectors at once and opens possibilities for a generative self-reflexivity. For the phonemic reader or close listener, the "zeroes" that echo out and away from "sea rose" are not ciphers but multipliers that increase its value, extend its reach, and permit it to function as a richly textured environment through which the reader-listener calls cultural information into use.[10]

*   *   *

The critical terminology employed by Havelock and Ong, Stewart, Bernstein, Piombino, and other theorists of a/orality suggests the difficulties of attending to the "wingéd word" as it traverses the technologies of orality, literacy, secondary orality, and the new digital media. Since the efflorescence of visual technologies in the early twentieth century, critics have developed a keen eye for the mirroring of perception and language in painting, photography, cinema, television, digital graphics, and virtual reality, but most of us have a dull ear for the play of sound in nonmusical texts.[11] Perhaps because of the widespread assumption that the processing of print is "silent," this neglect is particularly evident in studies of reading, interpretation, and the production and reproduction of texts.[12]

What creates this deaf spot in even the most sophisticated theories of textuality? Stewart's candidate is "a widespread (if only implicit) 'phonophobia' generated in the wake of the Derridean attack on the Logos" (*Reading Voices* 3). Derrida's dismantling of the phonocentric assumption that speech has a direct, natural, or unmediated relationship to truth and the logocentric assumption that truth exists apart from the language that records it is foundational to contemporary poststructuralism. As Stewart's phonemic readings amply demonstrate, however, neither phonocentrism nor logocentrism is foundational to processing the wordplay of the phonotext. Despite the electric fence Derrida erects around it, the urge to hear, name, and motivate sound effects remains a powerful engine of interpretation and access to meaning.

The generic variant of phonophobia is an aversion to lyric poetry, arguably the most sound-saturated of genres, and to the New Critics who made the lyric central to their practice. Like Plato and Rousseau, Derrida's primary targets, lyric poets and their New Critical exegetes make claims for and/or lay claim to the transparency of speech. The staging of romantic, visionary, and confessional poetry makes lyric language appear immediate, irresistible, and true, a spontaneous overflow uncontaminated by the mediating systems of writing. As the register and guarantee of the authenticity of the lyric moment, the "voice" of the poet thus implicitly or explicitly reinstantiates the phonocentrism and logocentrism deconstructionists aim to dislodge.[13] Poststructuralists therefore turn to the lyric rarely and with caution. Gathered to demonstrate a variety of "contemporary theoretical treatments of the lyric," the essays in the 1985 collection *Lyric Poetry: Beyond New Criticism* situate lyric poems as written documents in whose production and reception the element of acoustics is minimal or nonexistent. Here lyrophobia spills back into phonophobia, all but silencing the poems that are brought forward as exemplary lyric documents (Hošek and Parker 27).[14]

For cultural critics, the lyric is also tied to—and sunk by—the tenets of the old New Criticism. Here the problem is not the identification of the lyric with undemystified truth as much as a privileging of aesthetic issues that masks the poem's historical and sociological implications, perpetuates unexamined notions of "excellence," and obscures the variety of writing alive at any moment in culture. Although the last decades have made it abundantly clear that nothing we can say or think about a poem is free of social construction, the bifurcation of the aesthetic and the sociological continues to characterize treatments of the lyric. As Adorno insists in "Lyric Poetry and Society," however, the dimensions of the aesthetic and the sociological, active in all genres, need to be imbricated in readings of the lyric: "The tenderest, most fragile forms must be touched by, even brought together with, precisely that social bustle from which the ideals of our traditional conception of poetry have sought to protect them" (56).[15] Now that poets are employing photographic, electronic, and cybernetic technologies to broaden the range and broadcast the power of the lyric, it is particularly important to understand the cultural forces at play and at stake in poetry.

A final element that has kept critics from lending an ear to poetry is the sight-centered methodology of reading developed for early modernism by two major progenitors of imagism, T. E. Hulme and Ezra Pound. In flight from the lushness of Swinburne and the Decadents, Hulme and Pound envisioned a hard, fixed, clear-edged poetry based on images, not sounds. The "new verse resembles sculpture rather than music," Hulme declared; "it appeals to the eye rather than to the ear. It has to mould images, a kind of spiritual clay, into definite shapes. This material . . . is image and not sound" (*Further Specula-*

tions 75). Although Pound was keenly alert to poetry's appeal to the ear, which he called "melopoeia," for him, as we will see in chapter 3, poetry's "primary pigment" was *phanopoeia,* or the "casting of images upon the visual imagination" ("How to Read" 25).[16] For both men, images are not events but arrangements: the presentation, as Pound put it, of "an intellectual and emotional complex in an instant of time" ("Retrospect" 4). In phanopoeic reading, the (sea) rose is not "arose" and certainly not "a rows" because we see rather than hear not just the "cast image" but the lexeme that carries it.

In mulling over the reasons why poetry readings so often fall flat, Denise Levertov blames the imagists and New Critics, who trained readers to privilege comprehension. For Levertov, the anxiety audiences experience at a reading is, at least in part, a fear of not "getting it," which poets attempt to allay by explicating beforehand, so that, she continues, "by the time the poor poem itself gets read, it seems merely a metrical paraphrase of anecdotes already related" (47).[17] Concentration on paraphrasable content reduces information-laden, richly sensuous, oral-aural messages to taglines.[18] The unruly energies of the wingéd word—its pauses, dips, and slides, its refusal to stay put—give poems their complexity as oral-aural events. To listen to a poem is necessarily to submit to the ups, downs, curves, and quirks of its sonic path.

In a more recent meditation on audience distress at poetry readings, Jorie Graham suggests that poetry's resistance to paraphrase is not a flaw but something closer to a law. At the reading Graham describes, the novelist went first. "People changed or didn't," she says. "You felt at home." Then the poet ascended the podium and "resisted the very desires that the fiction, previously, had satisfied. . . . [T]he motion of the poem as a whole resisted my impulse to resolve it into 'sense' of a rational kind. Listening to the poem, I could feel my irritable reaching after fact, my desire for resolution, graspable meaning, ownership. I *wanted* to narrow it. . . . It resisted. It compelled me to let go" (xv, xvi). The audience's distress registers the difficulty of dwelling in the openness created by poetry's sound-saturated multiplicity. In the kind of modern and contemporary poetry Levertov and Graham are discussing, either/or narrative drive—"People change, or they don't"—is replaced by a both/and holding environment that functions with equal force at the level of form and the level of content.[19]

In H.D.'s early *Sea Garden* poems, her mid-career lyrics from *Red Roses for Bronze,* and the mature poetry of *Trilogy,* the agent of resistance is a/oral. Phonemes skip across the boundaries between lexemes, undecidabilities refuse to resolve into fixities, and comprehension is not a given but a challenge, even a dare. The a/orality of these poems is kinetic, unstable, and evanescent, less a "sound structure" (in Levertov's terms [51]) than a succession or, as Stewart puts it, a "*dramaturgy*" (*Reading Voices* 101). To listen well to these poems is to listen loosely to their aural ellipses, to attend to the aesthetic and cultural components of their holding environments, and to track the various cultural uses her words' play—or, in Stewart's drift, her "word-splay" (60)—makes available to the reader.

*   *   *

Although famously resistant to abstractions, imagists were not averse to ideas. For T. E. Hulme, Ezra Pound, H.D., and Richard Aldington, abstractions are concepts too inert to be called into use: "mere counter[s] to be manipulated," as Hulme puts it (*Further Speculations* 77); "the discredited, or rather the useless, logic of the Middle Ages," says Ernest Fenollosa (12); "the world of dead, murky thought," adds H.D. (*Notes* 27). An imagist idea is less a concept than a percept.[20] The two lines of Pound's "In a Station of the Metro"—"The apparition of these faces in the crowd; / Petals on a wet, black bough" (35)—constellate data of sight, movement, color, and touch into a perceptual field. "[This kind of] idea," Hulme says, "is just as real as a landscape" (*Further Speculations* 83): we call it into use by inhabiting it. Electric, transmissive, and streaming with data from sight, sound, movement, texture, smell, and taste, the poetry in H.D.'s *Sea Garden* is, in this sense, immersive rather than reflective, perceptual rather than conceptual. To read it is to dwell in it.

Although the poems in *Sea Garden* take up positions in a concept-riven world—strongly held positions on war, honor, progress, nation, history, economics, politics, and duty—ideas in this volume tend to take the form of scenes rather than comments. Like Pound's "In a Station," the poems are situated and compressed. In many of them, in fact, the agent, the act, and the object collapse into a single charged ideogram—a wreck (6), a downward slope (9), a snapped stalk (8)—that functions at once as noun and verb, actor and object. Although it is possible to decompress these ideograms narratively or thematically, H.D.'s *Sea Garden* poems work most effectively as soundscapes in which a world-constituting percept is enacted by a wash of phonemes within, across, and through its words.

Sound saturation is one of the many consequences of the imagist propensity to "[g]o in fear of abstractions,"[21] for sound is poetry's irreducible material foundation. Pound's "A Few Don'ts," published in March 1913 as a manifesto for emerging Imagistes, is strict in its instructions to the ear: reject the sequence of a metronome, Pound counsels, for "the sequence of the musical phrase" ("Retrospect" 4). This prescription anticipates a claim elaborated in the preface to the 1915 anthology *Some Imagist Poets* and resurgent in later twentieth-century models of the relation between aesthetics and assertions: the sequence of the metronome betrays a rigidified mind, the preface declares, but "a new cadence means a new idea" (54).[22] In the following phonemic reading of H.D.'s poem "Storm," I am interested in the flow, beat, and chord progression of the phonotext that Robert Creeley calls "measure" ("Measure" 290), Charles Bernstein "music and rhythm of contemplation" ("Thought's Measure" 67), and Amiri Baraka "total emotional placement of the rhythm, instrumentation and sound" (191).

The phonotext of "Storm" is dense, slurred, and impulsive:

> You crash over the trees,
> you crack the live branch—
> the branch is white,
> the green crushed,
> each leaf is rent like split wood.
>
> You burden the trees
> with black drops,
> you swirl and crash—
> you have broken off a weighted leaf
> in the wind,
> it is hurled out,
> whirls up and sinks,
> a green stone. (39)

The a/oral intensity of this modest poem is its most startling feature. Its appeal to the ear exploits the aspect of the lyric that Northrop Frye calls *melos* or "babble" (275),[23] but its acoustical display far exceeds the task of rendering the speaker's attitude or the poem's argument. Whether the poem is processed orally or aurally, the tightening and easing of its lines and the chew, pucker, and cluck of its plosives, liquids, and dentals give it a physicality that enlists, in its turn, the body of the listener. Like Havelock's wingéd word, this small lyric attempts to engage both the psyche and soma of its audience.

No small part of the pleasure of this poem is the extravagance that unmoors its phonemes from their morphemes and lexemes and floats them into the foreground. While at a semantic level the words point and exclaim, demand and describe—"You crash . . . / you crack / . . . you swirl and crash"—the phonemes ripple through graduated scales of sound. Like an infant trying out vowels, the reader-listener traverses a series of triads—*crush, crash,* and *crack; black, branch,* and *broken; swirl, hurl,* and *whirl; leaf, live,* and *-lit*—in a cascade of related sounds. Each of these triads shifts one and repeats two of three constituent phonemes, reviving for its evocalizers the archaic pleasures of syllables, breath impulsions, and intonations. The poem's too-muchness is not, in this sense, a flaw but a flowering, for its disposition is not the signified objects of an adult ego but an infant echolalia.

In Kristeva's theory, these acoustical effects carry great power because they are not symbolic but semiotic. When activated in a poem, in fact, their excess cracks the sociosymbolic order and releases from beneath its rigidities a "flow of jouissance" (*Desire* 133; *Revolution* 79). This bliss is not the same as the demanding eroticism that many critics have remarked in the *Sea Garden* poems, for H.D.'s rewritings of gender constraints are for the most part meaning effects, attempts to renegotiate the social contract by redefining feminine beauty as strength or by relocating desire from a heterosexual couple to a band of huntresses or pair of warrior-comrades.[24] The bliss Kristeva describes occurs underneath, around, across, or even despite such assertions, for it is activated not by meaning but by lip-bound, muzzle-centered movements. The aesthetic these movements generate is the praxis Barthes imagines as "*writing aloud*": the textual mobilization of "the grain of the throat, the patina of consonants, the voluptuousness of vowels, a whole carnal stereophony" that, in Barthes's orchestration, "granulates . . . crackles . . . caresses . . . grates . . . cuts . . . comes: that is bliss" (*Pleasure* 66–67).

In *Revolution in Poetic Language,* Kristeva connects this ecstasy to the anal drives that execute a kind of search-and-destroy mission against the symbolic order. The poetic language "in" which revolution resides is a process of "infiltrations," "disruptions," "shatterings," "negations," "supplantations," and "murder"—a "guerrilla war," as Calvin Bedient puts it, "against culture" (809). The effects of poetic language are complex, however, and, as Bedient goes on to argue, they are as often constructive as destructive. If semiotic bliss is generated by sound at work beyond its referential functions, listeners nonetheless—and also—take pleasure in combining phonemes into lexemes, binding them over to developing thematic imperatives, and setting them into a widening hermeneutic. While Kristeva's speculations help us hear the dissolutions in the phonotext of H.D.'s "Storm," phonemic reading alerts us to its forms-in-the-making.

The familiar devices of assonance, alliteration, and rhyme bind sounds together without dismantling the scripted words that occasion them. The effects that propel Stewart's phonemic reading, by contrast, are blurs and breakdowns occurring when phonemes spill across or fall short of the graphic signifiers that generate them. In the effects Stewart calls intralexical, interlexical, and supralexical transforms and the transegmental drift, the evocalizing reader responds to a double set of cues: the eye, as it moves along a line, marks the graphemic junctures that close off and separate words, while the ear pursues the phonemic breaks or glides that split words open or splice them together. An intralexical effect "breaks down a word without breaking it open" (55); an interlexical effect shears one word off from another to create a momentarily transformed phrasal attachment; a supralexical transform dissolves two words into the syllables of a third; and the transegmental drift, as we have seen, sets a phoneme awash between two lexemes to generate an unstable, if momentary, oscillation in the meaning.[25]

A significant part of the locutionary turmoil in "Storm" is generated by two of these four effects: the "intralexical transform," in which one word spins out and away from another at an acoustical break, and the "transegmental drift," in which a single phoneme crosses the juncture between two otherwise intact lexical units. Because it respects the borders, if not the integrity, of the words it splits, the first effect is less disruptive than the second, but it generates, nonetheless, a significant ripple. Like almost all of the *Sea Garden* poems, "Storm" is tight and spare—only four of its words have more than one syllable, only two of its lines have more than five words—but in eleven of the poem's thirteen lines one or more words undergoes intralexical fission.

"Split the atom of sound," Geoffrey Hartman says, "and you detonate an astonishing charge of meaning" (341). Intralexical breaks multiply and intensify the effect of words that are, like H.D.'s branch in the storm, cracked, crushed, rent, and split open. When "s/wirl" tightens to "whirl" and "rush" spins off from "c/rush," intralexical transforms both enact and accelerate the poem's narrative. In this word-splay, branches that are "split" are also "lit," for the gash that breaks them open lifts "white" out of "black" or even—we might say—w/height from b/lack. Although "lack" might be thought to inhere in the no-color of "b/lack" and "rack" might suggest the strain that precedes a "c/rack," the intralexical transforms in "Storm" do not so much expose entities inside or behind other entities as generate life from the flow or friction of other life.

Intralexical transforms perform a major imagist presupposition in *Sea Garden,* for the world they constitute is kinetic, not inert. The activity of "Storm" is an energy transfer that is generative rather than destructive. As Fenollosa explains this dynamic, there is in nature no negation, no possible transfer of negative force, for "all apparently negative or disruptive movements bring into play other positive forces" (14). In the vortex of "storm," all "is torn" and, through its pressures, also reborn: as "you swirl" accelerates toward "use whirl," the poem affirms a turmoil that, rather than eroding life, abrades and intensifies it.[26]

A giddy variant of the intralexical transform enacts this intensification as a prolongation that occurs when phonemic matter falls away to create not one more word but two or more. Like segmented cascades of thunder, the words "s/w/hurl" and "c/r/ash" fan out in three morphemic ripples.[27] The somatic pleasure of an effect like this is augmented when, like the "yawp" that concludes *Leaves of Grass* or the "crash" that initiates "Storm," the sounds roll from the back toward the front of the mouth. The poem's second word and first verb, "crash," begins with a voiceless, velar, plosive /k/ produced by raising the back of the tongue to the elevated soft palate, moves to an /r/ made by raising the tongue's central portion to the roof of the mouth where the hard palate ends and the soft palate starts, and ends with a /sh/ that forces a stream of breath over the flat tongue and out through the teeth.

But H.D.'s storm doesn't just "crash." The forward force of the final /sh/ propels it across a graphic juncture and attaches it provisionally to the /ō/ of "over" to make first an attenuated "crash sh/ove-" and then a briefly suspended "crash hover," echoes of the push and hush that punctuate the thunder's roll. The ligature that reshapes these adjacent lexemes is a temporary, tentative phenomenon: a suspension in which the thought "crash hover" holds even as the line's syntactical extension—"over the trees"—converts and corrects it. "No sooner said than undone," as Stewart puts it (*Reading Voices* 56), this effect makes phantom fusions throughout the entirety of H.D.'s poem: in the phrase "each leaf is rent," for example, "leaf is" slips briefly toward the hiss and sputter of "leaf fizz," while "is hurled out" flies off toward "hurled doubt" before settling back into its graphic fixity.

The poem's most striking transegmental drift dominates its last line—"a green stone"—where, after a light interlexical shift that momentarily propels "a green" toward "agree," the phoneme /s/ washes back across the juncture to pair "green stone" with "green's tone." If the poem's one stanza break marks a pause and reprise—"You crash over the trees" resuming as "You burden the trees"—what in this final transform allows H.D. to bring the poem to closure? In the whirr of the last three lines—"it is hurled out, / whirls up and sinks, / a green stone"—the poem moves "out," "up," and down, follows the /ûr/ from "hurl" to "whirl,"[28] and interjects a new pronoun, "it," which the transegmental flicker of the final phrase proceeds to complicate. As it enters—or perhaps sets off—the phonemic swirl of the last three lines, "it" seems to be simply a leaf in the act of leaving, but, ambiguated and destabilized by the last transegmental drift, "it" ends as something much more interesting: a collision and convergence of matter and energy, a kinetic pattern, one of those "things" Fenollosa called "'cross-sections cut through actions'" (qtd. in Kenner, *Pound Era* 146). Like a spot of paper riding a rapids, this leaf in the grip of gravity makes accessible to us the form of flows, the flow of forms. The phrase "a green s/tone" sets into motion at least three irreducible oscillations: in "stone" and "tone," a particle's heft and materiality alternates with a wave's sound, light, or color; in "a green," the lexeme "green" flickers from attribute to essence, from a stone's color to a phenomenon that generates tone(s); and, finally, in its shimmer across the juncture between "a" and "green," "agree" alternates with "a gree(n)" in a way that both signals and affirms these ongoing concurrences, the both/and/(and . . .) that constructs this compact and amazing line.[29]

The patterned energy of "Storm" tells at least two stories. One is written in an arboreal vocabulary that gathers to itself not only "tree," "branch," "wood," and "leaf" but the intralexical "-ash" in "crash" and the homophonic "yew" in "you." The other story branches off from the lexeme "leaf" to generate, in addition to the leaf that "sinks," a leaf "weighted" with letters, a leaf that "is inked." H.D.'s "Storm" swirls through air then "sinks" in ink: its process is the (th)inking of a leaf; its closure, a leaf's inking. Although all phrases are subject to accidents of audition, and poetic phonotexts need not exert interpretive leverage, as these morphemes sweep up, over, and across the phonemic space of "Storm," they set in motion a seemingly interminable, even an embarrassing proliferation of meanings. Through the excess, the luxuriance, the perpetual insurgence of sound, the reader comes into contact with an excessive, luxuriant, perpetually broken and re-created world, a world of fissions and fusions, flux and fertility that changes a landscape of violence into an enactment of generativity.[30]

The interpretive turmoil generated by a phonemic reading of "Storm" can be reproduced with almost any poem in *Sea Garden*. To pursue the slips and slides of these poems, however, cuts against a critical consensus that has prevailed since Pound sent the first of them off to Harriet Monroe with a note certifying it as "'the laconic speech of the Imagistes . . .—no slither'" (qtd. in Kenner, *Pound Era* 174). Even before the publication of *Sea Garden*, "H.D." was not a proper name so much as a term connoting the hard clarity, the fixed sculptural perfection that Pound and Hulme admired. The code for this clarity was the term "crystalline" or, worse, as H.D. complained to Bryher, "pure crystalline."[31] This designation discounts the opacity and shimmer—the slither, in fact—of *Sea Garden*'s poetry, and H.D. resisted it from the start. "I grew tired of hearing these poems referred to, as crystalline," she writes in her 1949 survey of her career, but then, she adds, "what is crystal or any gem but the concentrated essence of the rough matrix, or the energy . . . that projects it? The [early] poems as a whole . . . contain that essence or that symbol, symbol of concentration and of stubborn energy. The energy itself and the matrix itself have not yet been assessed" ("H.D. by Delia Alton" 184).

As H.D. implies, the matrix of a poem like "Storm" is not its fixities but its flow. Although phonemic reading provides a way to tap into this flow, it's fair to ask whether such close listening rewards the efforts it demands. Stewart introduces phonemic reading to discuss the densely patterned fixed forms of Shakespeare, Donne, Wordsworth, Keats, and other canonized English poets, but unlike sonnets or odes, H.D.'s open forms do not bring with them a long history of cultural meditations and nuanced subject positions. A poem like "Storm" is a snapshot. Focused at a peak moment in a universal landscape and closed with the click of an epiphany, it captures a moment. Just as "Sea Rose" is joined by "Sea Lily," "Sea Violet," "Sea Iris," and "Sea Poppies," such moments accumulate but do not develop or change. What's interesting in "Storm," however, is not its end but its act. As Leslie Scalapino notes of Robert Creeley's poems, the poem's "theme . . . is its form" ("'Thinking'" 44). What is exciting about "Storm" is not its commentary or its description but its demonstration: its soundscape enacts a philosophy, an epistemology, even an ethics of generativity to which H.D.'s work returns again and again.

*   *   *

Red Roses for Bronze, the volume H.D. published midway between *Sea Garden* and *Trilogy,* could not be said to be concentrated or crystalline. In its twenty-three long poems, poem sequences, and translations, the energy that charged the imagist poems seems to seep away in reiterations of a slack and distracted longing. As if to defy any effort to pin her writing to the effigy of "H.D., Imagiste," she uses the title poem to ask for relief from chiseled precision. "If I might ease my fingers and my brain," she writes,

> with stroke,
> stroke,
> stroke,
> stroke,
> stroke at—something (stone, marble, intent,
>   stable, materialized)
> peace,
> even magic sleep
> might come again. (211)

The wishful "if," the repetition of "stroke, / stroke, / stroke," the collapse into a vague "—something," the yearning for obliteration, and the wail of the /ē/ as it passes from "ease" to "peace" to "sleep" make these lines an apt introduction to the poems that follow.

Like a guest aware of being tedious but unable to stop, the speaker in these poems apologizes in advance for her "retarded rapture" (252), her "monotonous little song, / like water going over and over and on, / on, on" to "tell / and tell and tell the same thing over again, / over and over / in monotonous tone" (265–66). This is "slight verse," verse for which the speakers "make no plea" (282), verse H.D. herself drily dismisses as "not altogether satisfactory" ("Advent" 148). After this collection, apart from a few excerpts scattered through small and faithful journals like Harriet Monroe's *Poetry* and Bryher's *Life and Letters Today,* H.D. published no more poetry until 1944, when she brought forth "The Walls Do Not Fall," the first section of *Trilogy.*

Most of H.D.'s readers prefer to ignore these poems. Contemporary reviewers, who had to say something, fell back on familiar debates as to whether or not H.D.'s work was "Greek in spirit"—Eda Lou Walton thought not, Babette Deutsch thought so—whether it was "beautiful" and "accomplished," as William Rose Benét maintained, or merely, as R. P. Blackmur thought, a "pedestrian" display of the "stalest devices of poetastry."[32] The collection makes a reader want to patronize and pathologize the author, who seems to be—who must have been—sentimental, narcissistic, overwrought, hysterical, obsessive, greedy, and probably also depressed. Reaching out again and again for a "—something" she can't quite catch, the poet is "grasping," Louis L. Martz says, "for a response the words cannot command" (xxiii); the verses are, Gary Burnett concurs, "futile graspings for significance" (128). These are utterances we shrink from overhearing. "This is pitiful," Martz concludes, and it is hard not to agree with him (xxiii).

What's interesting about *Red Roses for Bronze* is not that it's unread but that it is actively, even aggressively unreadable. The petulance in the tone of many critics—the petulance in my tone—registers the frustration of codes we habitually use to decipher poems. It's possible to thematize this volume as song emerging from destruction and death, to judge its syntax "flabby" and its rhythms "fustian," and to describe its author as "a self-centered woman talking to herself,"[33] but thematic, formalist, and psychological pronouncements barely graze the surface of these odd utterances. In Barthes's sense, *Red Roses* is a *writerly* text, one "read with difficulty," Barthes explains, "unless I completely transform my reading regime" (*Roland Barthes* 118).[34] To learn from the strangeness of these poems it is crucial not to explain their oddities away.

If instead of pursuing thematic, psychological, or formalist questions, we ask what it is these utterances *do*—how do they operate? what is their effect?—it is clearly sound, not meaning, that structures them. When, in Pound's characterization, "words are charged, over and above their plain meaning, with some musical property, which directs the bearing or trend of that meaning" ("How to Read" 25), what is at work is the element Aristotle named *melos,* Pound "melopoeia," and Frye "babble" (Frye 275–78). Like nursery rhymes, jump-rope songs, and magic spells, these compositions work not because of what they say but because of how they say it. "The radical of *melos*" is, Frye explains, "*charm:* the hypnotic incantation that, through its pulsing dance rhythm, appeals to involuntary physical response, and is hence not far from the sense of magic, or physically compelling power" (278). Rhythm, rhyme, and repetition are to *Red Roses* what intralexical transforms and transegmental drifts are to *Sea Garden:* they string the words along the lines, ring the chimes that bind the parts, and ask sound to do more than referential service.

"O I am tired of measures / like deft oars," H.D. exclaims in a poem that renounces protestation, logic, and ambition, all the "brain's intricacies" (253), for a darkness and drift symbolized by Morpheus, son of sleep and shaper of dreams. "Deft oars" is a metonym for the world of warriors who rowed their triremes to Troy and for the epics that delivered their deeds to posterity in long, metrically regular lines that progress down the page in smooth isochronic strokes. The poetry of "deft oars" celebrates linearity, conflict, progression, and might. It is the cadence that obsesses the poet Ray Bart in H.D.'s story "Murex": the "metres in her head that beat and beat and beat" (*Palimpsest* 159); the "feet, feet, feet, feet, feet" (155) not only of the soldiers' lockstep march but also of pentameter lines rehearsing their glories (their each, as it were, glorious feat); the "tick, tick like some insistent metronome" of clock-driven, agonistic time (148); the "beat and beat of metres. Feet, feet, feet" (155). The contempt behind the phrase "deft oars" renders it one of few effective transegmental drifts in the *Red Roses* poems, for "measures / like deft oars" seem also to be, in the poetry of this period, "deaf doors," even, perhaps, "deft whores."[35]

Between 1924 and 1931, throughout her writing but particularly in the *Red Roses* poems, the fiction and embedded lyrics in *Palimpsest,* and the novel *HERmione,* H.D. sought rhythms counter to the cadences of strife, efficiency, and accomplishment.[36] The speakers of these texts supplant the "stroke" of oars with the swoon of drugs, the trance of erotic satiety, the ecstasy of sacred dancing (*Collected Poems* 224–25). "O I am tired," "O let me rest," her speakers say again and again, "I'm ill; I want to go away / where no one can come" (253, 275). The "magic sleep" the poems pursue through kisses, wine, and "the subtle fruit" of the lotus or poppy (253) is the same "snuffed-out . . . twilight of the spirit" and "cocoon-blur of not-thinking" (*Palimpsest* 95–96) that Ray Bart seeks in her daily life in London and Hermione finds in the fever that concludes the poetic apprenticeship of *HERmione.* If the "stroke" of sickness, madness, fasting, drugs, or prolonged arousal do not in themselves create poetry, this writing implies, they at least prepare for it by transporting the aspirant into a liminal territory, a "borderland of consciousness" (*Collected Poems* 263) where the rhythms of active rationality recede.

In her essay "On Being Ill," Virginia Woolf glosses this state in a way that clarifies its connection with the intensified a/orality of the *Red Roses* poems. "People write always of the doings of the mind," Woolf remarks, "the thoughts that come into it; its noble plans; how the mind has civilized the universe," but in sickness, "with the police off duty," we think once again somatically, through our bodies (194).[37] In health, Woolf continues, "meaning . . . encroache[s] upon sound. Our intelligence dominates over our senses," but in the swoon of illness "meaning . . . come[s] to us sensually first" (200). When a third kind of stroke succeeds, then—the "stroke, / stroke, / stroke" of the pen—the result, at least in *Red Roses for Bronze,* is a poetry that contains only enough referential content to occupy our minds while it solicits and soothes the body through rhythm, rhyme, and repetition.

Rhythm in the *Red Roses* poems falls into the broad patterns Andrew Welsh identifies as song-melos and charm-melos (162–65). Although both oppose the lockstep of rationality, these sound-patterns generate different aural effects. The opening lines of the poem "Wine Bowl" are typical of song-melos: "I will rise / from my troth / with the dead," the poem begins, "I will sweeten my cup / and my bread" (241). The anapestic predictability of these lines and their bland archaic speech give them the lilt of words rendered for music.[38] Charm-melos, the more prominent pattern in *Red Roses,* creates a stranger and more striking effect. Instead of following pregiven patterns, charms use irregular rhythm to mobilize magic spells. In these lines from H.D.'s "Choros Sequence from *Morpheus,*" the choros chants:

> out of sleep and sleep,
> the fringe of consciousness is lined with bright
> wild,
> wild,
> wild,
> wild,
> white arums
> and the night-lily. (262)

These lines, which seem stuck and frantic when read briskly for content, enact an eerie spell if we let their line breaks pace our attention. The first line sets a standard of five syllables, subsequent lines double it to ten, hold it to one syllable across four consecutive lines, jump it to three, then, finally, restore it to five. Read isochronically, moment by moment, these aural permutations strain to recapture the archaic power of the spoken word.

At their best, the poems of *Red Roses* have the "'coefficient of weirdness'" that the anthropologist Bronislaw Malinowski identifies as the crucial component in charm language (qtd. in Welsh 152). What separates charm-melos from ordinary speech is not only irregular rhythms but unpredictable rhymes amplified in incremental echoes. The choros from *Morpheus* seeks to call a "fringe of consciousness" into being through hypnotic reiteration of related sounds. The poppies, arums, and night-lilies of this borderland are "lined"— turned into lines—by the repetition-with-a-difference of assonance: framed by the short /ĭ/s of "fringe" and "lily," the long /ī/ cascades across the rhymes "bright," "white," and "night," echoes through the off-rhymes "lined" and "wild," then slows down to begin again (and again) in the series "wild, / wild, / wild, / wild."

Repeated with insistence—as, for instance, in the witches' chants from *Macbeth*—rhyme seems to come not so much from as through the speaker.[39] In this liminal state, chiming leads the mind through connections that seem both startling and predetermined. In chains like "lined," "bright," "wild," "white," and "night," aural overlaps bind objects, states, and events into a hidden system of relationships, a system the charm not only activates but appears to control.[40] H.D.'s account of Ray Bart's poetic seizures in "Murex," the second of the three overlapping autobiographical stories in *Palimpsest*, foregrounds exactly this effect as, in her fits of composition, she picks her way through stepped series of signifiers toward a rule that binds their signifieds: "This was the absolute answer," Ray Bart surmises in a typical moment, "that 'hour' rhymed with 'flower.' . . . This was the answer, the law, that 'dower' went with 'flower'" (165).

If, as Debra Fried has observed, the habit of making coincidences of rhyme serve meaning "robs them of some of their wildness and shimmering contingency" (99), repetition, the third effect at work in the poems of *Palimpsest* and *Red Roses for Bronze*, more than makes up for lost outlandishness. Repetition is a structural component of all rhythm and rhyme, but its predominance in *Red Roses* lies in the habit of saying the same word over and over and over again. This can occur within a single line, as in "O why, why, why" from "Halcyon" (270) or "gone out, out, out" from "Calliope" (286); across a series of lines, as in the fivefold "stroke" from "Red Roses for Bronze" (211) or the fourfold "wild" in *Morpheus;* or through a refrain such as "Give me your poppies" from *Morpheus* (252–70) or "Let them not war in me" from "Triplex" (291). Repetition is, as Welsh points out, "the basic structural principle of melopoeia. It stands in the same relation to melopoeia as spatial juxtaposition does to phanopoeia. . . . Repetition is a temporal structure of what we have called the aural imagination" (136).

In the *Red Roses* poems, repetition generates three quite different effects, not all of them successful. The first, registered by Martz's "pitiful," is an air of unbearable neurosis. Here repetition seems not just sloppiness or failed invention but a desolate and ungovernable compulsion that forces the poet—and the reader—over and over the same unmastered events or ideas.[41] Draining the material and exhausting the reader, this is, in Bruce F. Kawin's useful distinction, not repetition but "repetitiousness." A second effect—which Kawin calls "repetitiveness"—is created when words repeat with equal or greater force at each occurrence, as in Lear's "never, never, never, never, never" or, arguably, H.D.'s "stroke, / stroke, / stroke" (4). When repetition is most successful in the *Red Roses* poems, however, it works in a third fashion as a kind of mantra. Here repetition does not increase force so much as suspend it, releasing the reader from rational, ordering, interpretive thought and producing a state that is at once concentrated and still. In these poems, words repeated again and again float free from their lexical meanings to soothe and charm the mind.

Readers of the lines organized by the repetition of the words "stroke" and "wild" may experience a series of reactions. The most negative is dismissal of the verse, of H.D., of women's writing, or all of the above, all at once. The most positive is probably a partial and incremental series of reactions in which if at first a reader feels trapped inside a mind struggling to free itself from its own fixations, slowly, almost imperceptibly, repetition detaches the sounds from their referential content until finally, and again more or less imperceptibly, repetition generates enough energy to propel poet and reader toward some new idea or information. In "Red Roses," the repetition of "stroke" evokes the odd series "stone, marble, intent, stable, materialized," while in "Choros Sequence from *Morpheus,*" the repetition of "wild" generates the hallucinatory "white arums / and the night-lily." In an imbrication of all three aural devices from *Red Roses,* these lines move the reader forward through hypnotic repetitions, uneven "wave-lengths" of rhythm (236), and sporatic surges of rhyme.[42] In such moments, we are as far as it is possible to get from the regimentation of "deft oars."

At their best, the poems of *Red Roses* and the drawing room banter of *Palimpsest* have the oblique and weary sophistication H.D. admired in Euripi-

des' antiwar dramas. As Eileen Gregory argues in *H.D. and Hellenism*, Euripides stood in relation to H.D. as Aeschylus to Eliot or Homer to Pound: faced
with the "deft oars" ethos of his time, Gregory explains, "[Euripides] consistently disintegrates the intellectual and moral *nomos* of the heroic world and
simultaneously reveals the intensity of isolated lyric moments and the loneliness of partial heroisms enacted within fragmented contexts" (25).[43] H.D.'s
inclusion in *Red Roses for Bronze* of translations of choros sequences from *The
Bacchae* and *Hecuba* are, in this sense, not ornament but underpinning. Her
directions for the performance of these pieces specify poppies and lotus flowers, bowls, craters, and vats of wine, a "sacred dance-beat" (225), "stringed
lyre" (242), and "festival" dress and decorations (277–78), all the props Havelock's oral poets mobilized to drive their wingéd words—their formulas of
"mystic lore" (286), "law, / [and] . . . the mysteries true" (305)—deep into the
psyche of their listeners.

The revulsion many readers feel for the poetry of *Red Roses for Bronze* supports Ong's point that writing has restructured consciousness away from a
participatory, formulaic, and repetitive orality toward the more rational, dis-
tanced, and abstract discourse characteristic of literacy (*Orality* 78–116). By
staging some of the poems in *Red Roses* as drama and apologizing in advance
for the monotony of others, H.D. seems to acknowledge that even the most
aurally alert reading can't turn these repetitions and exclamations to the service of "magic sleep" or visionary transformation. Song-melos and charm-
melos may work for spells and curses, operatic arias, and, as we will see in the
next chapter, the amplified and broadcast oratory of the fascist state, but after
Red Roses for Bronze H.D. abandoned this concatenation of rhythm, rhyme,
and repetition for a more productive assault on the "deft oars" of war. The
poetry she wrote in the midst of the World War II bombing of London turns
the energies of a/orality from escapism to the intellectual, cultural, and emotional work of realigning a culture gone awry.

*   *   *

In *Trilogy,* sound is neither phonemic enactment, as it is in *Sea Garden,* nor
song- or charm-melos, as it is in *Red Roses for Bronze,* but a kind of research
strategy or material for thought. The transforms at work in *Sea Garden* yield
in *Trilogy* to a series of transformations that align the terrors of World War II
with larger mythological, historical, and spiritual patterns; the spells of *Red
Roses for Bronze,* in a similar manner, give way to a "spelling out" or decipherment that offers the poet an opportunity to think for or on behalf of her culture. "I suppose," H.D. wrote her friend Norman Holmes Pearson in mid-

composition, "this book is 'philosophy'" (*Between History* 33). "The Walls Do Not Fall," the title of the first section of *Trilogy,* announces the premises of her inquiry, and the poem's forty-three sections play out its strategies.[44]

The pattern for language in "The Walls Do Not Fall" is the Egyptian hieroglyph. In use in Egypt for over three thousand years and still legible across the millennia on the stone of temples and tombs and the papyrus of cultural records and documents, hieroglyphs make their initial appearance in the first section of H.D.'s poem:

> An incident here and there,
> and rails gone (for guns)
> from your (and my) old town square:
>
> mist and mist-grey, no colour,
> still the Luxor bee, chick and hare
> pursue unalterable purpose
>
> in green, rose-red, lapis;
> they continue to prophesy
> from the stone papyrus. (3)

In the complex system of ancient Egyptian writing, a hieroglyph can be read as a pictogram, a phonogram, or a determinative. As a pictogram, it stands for the object, being, or event represented by the picture: here, a bee, a quail chick, a desert hare. As a phonogram, it represents the consonantal structure of word roots: in this case, *bt, w, wn.* As a determinative, finally, it indicates which of a number of words with similar structures is intended in a certain context. A wingéd word in a new and complicated sense, then, the Luxor bee functions as a pictogram for a bee and/or a phonogram for the consonant structure *bt;* followed by the determinative of a pot, it means *honey,* while followed by the determinative for a god or king, it means *King of Lower Egypt.*[45]

On her trip to the Valley of Thebes with Bryher in 1923, H.D. had been deeply struck by the enigma and beauty of the hieroglyphs on the walls and columns of the Temple of Karnak at Luxor. Attempting to convey their hold on her in "Secret Name," the third narrative in *Palimpsest,* she sets the characters' visit to the temple in moonlight. In the drift of this moment in H.D.'s story, as in the sensuous receptivity Woolf describes in her essay, "The intellect was . . . off guard, benumbed" (203). Bathed in moonlight, the visitors, their driver, the guards, palms, sphinxes, and gates appear as dark forms filled with shadow, writing set amidst writing. "In the stark light," the narrator tells us, "the hieroglyphs stood forth . . . clear demarcation of chick and giant bee, squares of crochet-like wave pattern, of broken line" (206). The opening of "The Walls Do Not Fall" aligns the ruins of London—"your (and my) old town square: / . . . / mist and mist-grey"—with the temple courtyard, open to the sky. This juxtaposition of London and Luxor reiterates and reverses the syntax of the poem's epigraph—"*for Karnak* 1923 / *from London* 1942"—positioning the two pictographs as mutual determinatives. Throughout the poem, H.D.'s syntax instructs us to read these charged chronotopes as reciprocal hieroglyphs, each an inflection and interpretation of the other.[46]

Deeply incised into the walls and columns of the temple in Luxor, the hieroglyphs of the bee, chick, and hare are, in one sense, as "unalterable" as the sculpture Hulme and Pound idealize for imagism. Hulme admired sculpture because "it appeals to the eye rather than to the ear" (*Further Speculations* 75), but the hieroglyphs in *Trilogy* appeal to the ear as well as the eye.[47] In addition to visual glyphs like the bee, the chick, the hare, and the town square, "The Walls Do Not Fall" contains aural glyphs or phonograms on the model of *b-t* or *w-n*, each composed of one or more consonants.[48] Like the sound patterns in *Sea Garden* and *Red Roses,* these phonograms function as metaphors at the level of sound, but unlike H.D.'s earlier transegmental drifts and repetitions, their patterns are both mutable and unalterable. Although they are open to change because of their variant vowels, their aural architecture—their "walls" or consonantal structures—do not fall.

The opening stanzas of H.D.'s poem offer a lesson in reading these phonograms by demonstrating, three times over, sequential variations on a consonantal matrix. In the first example, the phonogram *p-r-p-s* generates the variants *purpose/prophesy/papyrus,* as if forming a sentence that announces the writer's intent to use these skeletal frames to give flesh to past, present, and future. A word root or consonantal matrix, in this sense, can cast forward or predict an effect from a cause or read a purpose into or out of seemingly random recurrences. Section 1 continues, supplying two further examples,

> there, as here, ruin opens
> the tomb, the temple; enter,
> there as here, there are no doors:
>
> the shrine lies open to the sky,
> the rain falls, here, there
> sand drifts; eternity endures. (3)

Like Fenollosa's Chinese written characters, Egyptian hieroglyphs are "alive and plastic," able to generate all parts of speech, "as flexible as possible, as full of the sap of nature" (17). In these lines, the first example is a simple noun-for-noun equivalency in which the root *t-m-b* generates the words *tomb* and *temple;* the second, more complex transformation cuts across lexical borders and grammatical categories to turn the root *n-t-r-s* into the sequence *enter/no doors/endures.*[49]

Had the ancient Egyptians restricted themselves to uniliteral or one-letter signs, they would have had alphabetic writing, but the "bone-frame" of most phonograms is a consonant chain like *b-t* or *n-t-r-s.* Many readers have noted the way in which *Trilogy* mobilizes figures that have "the same—different—the same attributes, / different yet the same as before" (105)—Ra, Osiris, and Christ (25); Maia, Mary, Mother (71); Thoth, Hermes, Mercury, and the angel Michael (17, 63); and many, many others—but the fact that these reiterations of sameness and difference can play out for the ear as well as the eye points toward yet another important strain of meditation in H.D.'s poem.

The primary example of this process in "The Walls Do Not Fall" amplifies the triplet Ra, Osiris, Christ through transformations of the word *Amen-Ra,* a variant spelling of a variant name for the Egyptian sun god. Generally depicted as a human with the head of a ram, Ammon-Ra was a composite deity devised by the priests of Ammon, the patron deity of the city of Thebes, in an attempt to link New Kingdom worship of the god Ammon with the older solar cult of the god Ra. In a union of this sort, the power represented by Ammon is thought to manifest itself through the person of Ra, merging these two deities as H.D.'s poem will try to merge Amen and Christ (25). Because the reader supplies the vowels for a hieroglyph, the god's name can be translated with equal accuracy *Ammon, Amon, Amun,* or *Amen.*[50] In H.D.'s poem, the phonogram retains the *a-m-n* structure to appear as *amen* and *a man* as well as the anagrams *name* (21) and *mean* (16), each variation bringing with it a dense array of connotations. "Take me," H.D. writes toward the end of "The Walls Do Not Fall," "home"

> where the mantis
> prays on the river-reed:
>
> where the grasshopper says
> *Amen, Amen, Amen.* (32)

"We have always worshipped Him," H.D. writes, "we have always said, / *forever and ever, Amen*" (26). "Now," she continues, reasoning through this repetition with a difference, "it appears obvious / that *Amen* is our Christos" (27). This combination of the unalterable and the mutable plays out the lesson that is *Trilogy's* gist and pith.

The plot of "The Walls Do Not Fall" is a kind of epigraphy: a reading of the runes in London's ruins.[51] In this labor, the poet stands in the position of the Egyptian scribe whose cultural work was to write and read hieroglyphic script, while the reader stands in the position of the poet who writes and reads the hieroglyphs that compose *Trilogy*. Variance is built into the series, as is a certain interpretative bravado, for, H.D.'s claim notwithstanding, few of these decipherments are "obvious." Not given but made, meaning in "The Walls Do Not Fall" is a collaboration, a co-creation, in an ongoing community of "rune-maker[s]" (*Between History* 32). In the reading I am creating here, three related uses of these forms become important to the plot of the poem.

The first use is the poet's alignment of phonograms in order to meditate on and motivate their similarities. The poem's second line, for example, reads "and rails gone (for guns)" (3). Here desolation is brought about not by an external enemy but by an internal decision to turn cultural assets into armaments. In an act equivalent to beating ploughshares into swords, the railings around the town square have been torn up, melted down, and transformed into weapons: "*gone* (for *guns*)." The phonogram *g-n* is amplified by a second phonogram—*c-r-t-ch* or *c-r-t-/dg*—which soon follows:

> yet give us, they still cry,
> give us books,
>
> folio, manuscript, old parchment
> will do for cartridge cases;
>
> irony is bitter truth
> wrapped up in a little joke,
>
> and Hatshepsut's name is still circled
> with what they call the *cartouche*. (16)

The word *cartridge,* designating a heavy paper case for gunpowder, is a variant of the word *cartouche,* the oval or oblong in hieroglyphic script that encases the names and epithets of such royal or divine figures as Hatshepsut, Queen of Egypt.[52] From the aural overlap of *cartridge* and *cartouche,* the poem reasons its way toward a bitter truth detonated by wordplay. On the death of her husband in 1504 B.C., Queen Hatshepsut bestowed upon herself the title and powers of pharoah, but on her death in 1482 B.C., her successor, Thutmose III, erased the hieroglyphs from her royal cartouches. H.D.'s point is that even if a culture pulps its books and rubs out its heritage, traces of its history will linger in its language. "Great literature," in Pound's variant of this trope, "is . . . language charged with meaning to the utmost possible degree" (*ABC* 36). The irony is that even when pulped to package gunpowder, books and manuscripts remain explosive, just as the blank in Hatshepsut's cartouches tells a story no power can obliterate. *Scripts* may degenerate into *scribbles,* as yet another example suggests, but the walls of these words—in this case, *s-c-r-p/b-s*—preserve the power of the *scribes* (17, 42).

The consonants—or constants—in a series like *purpose/prophesy/papyrus* pull the words into a cluster that the poet reads by aligning their meanings. As Frederick M. Ahl demonstrates in *Metaformations: Soundplay and Wordplay in Ovid and Other Classical Poets,* the assumption that words that sound or look alike are related in meaning fills Greek and Roman writing with puns and implied etymologies, some verifiable and others concocted. The words in H.D.'s triplet *script/scribe/scribble* all derive from the Latin *scribere,* while the pair *tomb/temple* derive from two different words, the Latin *tumba* and *templum.* The efficacy of these clusters, however, comes not from their etymological accuracy but from the poet's ability to convince us of the rightness of teachings that derive from their similarity of structure.[53]

A second use of phonograms in "The Walls Do Not Fall" draws on the mutations rather than constancies in word structure. Allowing variants to pull away from each other, vowels and liquid or allophonic consonants are, in this sense, not walls but doors: they open word roots—the radicals of words—to change. Phonogrammic series of this sort are centrifugal rather than centripetal, evolutionary rather than conservative. Instead of foregrounding constancy across difference, they allow for a gradual pluralization through which different, more complex, or more adaptive forms can emerge.[54] As we will see, not only is this use of words a powerful corrective to imagist idealizations of crystalline fixity but it also gives H.D. a way to think through the causes and effects of war.

Relinquishing the role of hypnotist or medium, which she had assumed in *Red Roses for Bronze,* H.D. in *Trilogy* accepts the role of thinker. In this section of the poem, her meditations on sound participate in a quest initiated by the experience of surviving the Nazi firestorm: "the frame held: / we passed the flame: we wonder / what saved us? what for?" (4). "Now here it is," H.D. explained to Pearson, "very stark and written at the last—a sort of vindication of the writer, of the 'scribe'" (*Between History* 31). Epic composers inhabit public space—the space of "your (and my) old town square"—addressing their auditors in their capacity as citizens with the conviction that events have rendered their words not ornamental but crucial. This is a bold assumption for any poet to make, but it is perhaps especially so for a middle-aged woman in wartime, "[t]oo old to be useful," as the poem wryly comments, "not old enough to be dead" (24), a woman unconnected to power and unaccustomed to public speech.

For all their showmanship, imagists did not hail their readers in their capacities as citizens, nor did they claim space in "your (and my) old town square."[55] By 1942, H.D. was three decades beyond "H.D., Imagiste" and keenly aware of the limits of her World War I persona. Section 4 of "The Walls Do Not Fall" returns to the setting of the *Sea Garden* poems to generate a new and more effective stance. Deploying a series of hieroglyphs, which are both visual and aural, the section begins

> There is a spell, for instance,
> in every sea-shell:
>
> continuous, the sea thrust
> is powerless against coral,
>
> bone, stone, marble
> hewn from within by that craftsman,
>
> the shell-fish:
> oyster, clam, mollusc
>
> is master-mason planning
> the stone marvel. (8)

The mollusc—"firm in [its] own small, static, limited // orbit"—closes against the "invasion of the limitless" to create a "pearl-of-great-price" (9). Supplementing this fable of the self generating from within a more precious and permanent incarnation of itself, a more important story unfolds through incremental permutations of the phonogram *s-l*. Using difference to pry the icon open and generate the next stage in its evolution, H.D. generates the series *spell, sea-shell, shell-fish, shell-jaws, egg-shell* (8–9). As if hatching the hieroglyph of the chick, the rest of "The Walls Do Not Fall" works open the wedge between sea-shell and egg-shell, producing, one after another, a series of repetitions-with-a-difference: brain in its skull case, mollusc in its shell, the Genius in the jar, the worm in its shroud, the caterpillar in its cocoon, and, finally, in Section 25,

> *Amen,*
> only just now,
>
> my heart-shell
> breaks open,

though long ago, the phoenix,
your *bennu* bird

dropped a grain,
as of scalding wax. (35)

In this series, which continues to evolve through the next two parts of *Trilogy,* the plot shifts from unification and closure to metamorphosis and change.[56] The radical suggestion in this series—its implication—is not that dramas of unification, closure, and power inevitably generate war, although that is part of the story, but a more complex conviction that a capacity to break or break open is crucial to the evolution of life. Like sequoias whose cones must pass through fire to germinate, cultures, H.D.'s hieroglyphs suggest, must break—or be broken—to evolve.

In its most concentrated use, the phonogram in "The Walls Do Not Fall" is the grain or seed of renewal. Like the *bennu* bird—the Egyptian sun-bird, symbol both of the rising sun and of the dead sun god, Osiris, from whom it sprang and to whom it was sacred—the poet is the seed carrier. The word the poet drops into the heart-shell or skullcase of her audience mutates in ways she does not claim to control but can, nonetheless, read out for her listeners. The most sustained and stunning example of this process is a guided meditation on the phonogram *s-r-s,* which concludes "The Walls Do Not Fall."

"Osiris equates O-sir-is or O-Sire-is," H.D. begins, moving the series past the star Sirius, which represents Isis coming to wake her brother from death in the annual inundation of the Nile, to the ritual questions concluding "O, Sire, / is this union at last?" through the implied anagrams of Sire—*eris* or strife and its aftermath *rise*—toward a final naming of the whirr and roar in the high air above London, the *zrr-hiss* that seeds death and resurrection (54–59). The poem's final hieroglyph is this phonogram spoken by the Nazi rockets falling on the city and heard by the epigrapher who takes upon herself the responsibility to find a purpose for such destruction, to prophesy by aligning history and mythology, and, finally, to commit these charged words to the cartridge of her poem.

*   *   *

Several critics have taken up the issue of generativity as it plays out in H.D.'s life and writing through traumas of childbirth and dramas of blockage and breakdown.[57] Although it can be assimilated to these plots, *Trilogy* is built on different architectural principles. "The Walls Do Not Fall" opens and closes in the national and international sociopolitical climate of World War II. Its first words mimic contemporary news reports that referred to Nazi air attacks as "incident[s] here and there" (3) in order to avoid specifying their locale but also, importantly, to calm a populace suffering the consequences. The poet's job, by contrast, is to place disaster in a larger framework through the kind of thinking Bernstein describes as "the investigation/creation of human culture." "[N]ot just an interest in expression of 'my' thoughts," Bernstein writes in his essay "Thought's Measure," "thoughts think the world" (68). H.D.'s ambition in *Trilogy* is to think the world forward by using word-shapes, sounds, and determinatives to understand events anew. To hear the aerial "incident" give its name in its oral trace—"zrr-hiss"—positions it as a world-destroying, world-generating event that takes place under the aegis of Osiris, Amen, Ra. The rocket is the poem's final embodiment of the wingéd word.

H.D.'s point, Havelock's point, and Pound's and Bernstein's point is that the keepers of language—its scribes, poets, and readers—are the structural engineers of culture. As H.D.'s language assimilates historical events to mythic paradigms, she reiterates with a difference the work of the poets Pound translated and Havelock and Ong investigated. As Milman Parry and Albert B. Lord demonstrate in their studies of the oral epic, the "repetition with a difference" at play in repetition, rhythm, and rhyme is crucial to performers whose cultural work is to memorize a vast array of materials and recast them for successive generations. Prefabricated hexameters are cartridges packed with cultural themes and thought patterns. As Parry and Lord confirmed in their work with Serbo-Croatian epic composers, such formulas not only guarantee effective preservation of knowledge but also provide an efficient means of adjusting that knowledge to meet a crisis or catastrophe.[58] In this kind of composition, the composer's originality resides in an ability to repeat a series of formulas with a difference that brings them to bear on the needs of a particular audience at a specific moment in time.

Invited to teach a seminar at Bryn Mawr after the war, H.D. surveyed a broad group of friends and acquaintances to ask each for a list of ten to twelve lyrics held in their minds. "Suppose you had a RATION of memory," she asked May Sarton, "what would you choose to remember?" "I do not want BOOK lists," she adds, "[but] things that are in your head now—and maybe, not all special or high-brow selections."[59] What H.D. is after is "poeticised memory," the faculty identified with Mnemosune, the mother of the muses: this is neither written memory nor memory as a mental phenomenon but rather a re-minding, recalling, memorializing, or memorizing achieved through the acoustics of poetry.[60] To play out the metaphor H.D. used again and again in her letters of request, it is as if each culture has a limited but sustaining store of seed-phrases kept alive by scribes whose task is to preserve, refresh, renew, and redistribute the wisdom of the group.

The close listening in this chapter is an attempt to hear the resonances of H.D.'s wingéd words not in order to redress the eclipse of stylistics in contemporary literary discussions nor to reconstitute H.D.'s personal history and intentions but to lay some foundations for an understanding of how a poet can use words to think culture away from catastrophe toward more generative structures of community and collectivity. This chapter has worked outward from words on the page to words in the air over World War II London. The next chapter begins with sounds on the air—sounds amplified by twentieth-century acoustical technologies—and their effect on the repetition-with-difference of the Homeric materials in *Helen in Egypt*.

Notes

1. Gertrude Stein caricatures the poetics of the code as the "elaborated argument," the "hovering for instance" of "forensics" ("Forensics" 385; see also "Patriarchal Poetry"). Kristeva's poetics, famously, also start from a separation between the realm of the echo and the realm of the code.

2. Although the final draft of this speech appears to have been ghostwritten for H.D. by Norman Holmes Pearson, it was presented in—and under—her name and stands as one of few public summations she made of her career. A first draft of the speech, which H.D. sent to Pearson, was published under the title "Speech of Acceptance to the American Academy of Arts and Letters" in the *H.D. Newsletter*. For more details about the composition of this speech, see the introductory paragraphs written by Eileen Gregory ("Speech" 4–5).

3. In addition to her appearance before the American Academy of Arts and Letters, H.D. took part in a "Reading of Famous Poets" given at the Aeolian Hall before the Queen Mother, Queen Elizabeth, and her daughters Princess Elizabeth and Princess Margaret in April 1943. For a contemporary description of this event, see "Poets in Public." See also Guest, *Herself Defined* 263–64.

4. For definitions of these terms, see Barthes, *Pleasure* 66.

5. *Live at the Ear* is the title of the first audio-anthology of postmodern Language Poetry, digitally remastered by Charles Bernstein from taped performances at Manhattan's Ear Inn.

6. For further discussion of this topic, see the essays collected by Elizabeth Hill Boone and Walter D. Mignolo in *Writing without Words*.

7. For a sustained version of this argument, see Ong, *Presence*, chap. 3 (111–75).

8. For additional definitions of the pun, see Attridge, "Unpacking the Portmanteau," and Culler, "Call of the Phoneme."

9. Piombino's terms draw on Walter Benjamin's formulation of the "aura," Roman

Jakobson's and Krystyna Pomorska's notion of "elliptical perception," and especially D. W. Winnecott's theory of "transitional objects." Winnecott uses the term "holding environment" for contexts that hold in suspension modes of paying attention to external and internal experience.

10. A/orality's hybrid appeal to the eye and the ear is captured by the retained archaism of the written phrase "wingéd word." The diacritical mark that expands "winged" into "wingéd" inserts a trough between two strongly alliterated stresses in a pulse that mimics the beat and flap of bird flight.

11. The introductory paragraph of Martin Jay's *Downcast Eyes* deploys, by Jay's own count, twenty-one visual metaphors in a spectacular display of "how ineluctable the modality of the visual actually is, at least in our linguistic practice" (1). For sound and art, see Kahn, *Noise.*

12. In his study of "the textual condition" from Byron to Pound, for example, Jerome McGann focuses on "the deployment of a double helix of perceptual codes: the linguistic codes, on one hand, and the bibliographical codes on the other" (*Textual Condition* 77). Similarly, "[o]ur primary concern," Jay David Bolter and Richard Grusin announce in their study of the effects of the process they call "remediation" on the new digital media, "will be with visual technologies, such as computer graphics and the World Wide Web" (14). For examples of excellent work on sound in cinema, see Lawrence and Silverman.

13. There is, of course, no logical tie between listening for a "voice" behind a lyric inscription and attending to a poem's generative acoustics. In practice, more often than not, the contrary seems to be the case, so that to listen for a voice in a poem muffles what Baraka might call the "total emotional placement of the rhythm . . . and sound" (191). In both the imagist aesthetic within which H.D. emerged and the New Critical aesthetic that surrounded the publication of her mature work, the lyric's echoing energies were controlled by the presumption of a coherent voice behind the poem.

14. Marjorie Perloff makes this point in her essay "Can(n)on to the Right of Us, Can(n)on to the Left of Us" (14–23). See also the essays collected in *Contemporary Poetry Meets Modern Theory,* edited by Antony Easthope and John O. Thompson.

15. This sentence serves as the epigraph for the introduction to Christopher Beach's *Poetic Culture.* Beach argues that neither aesthetics nor sociology alone can answer the question, "What contribution does contemporary American poetry make to contemporary American culture?" (1). For another demonstration of cultural forces operative within lyric aesthetics, see Noland.

16. For melopoeia, see the discussion of *Red Roses for Bronze* later in this chapter.

17. The critics Levertov names in her indictment include Hulme, Pound, Eliot, I. A. Richards, F. R. Leavis, Allen Tate, and John Crowe Ransom.

18. In an argument for treating oral history as poetry, Dennis Tedlock laments the information lost when ethnographers transcribe interviews into alphabetic writing then toss the tape away, an act equivalent to making a sketch from a photograph then

destroying the photograph ("Learning to Listen" 712). See also Tedlock, "Toward an Oral Poetics."

19. Poems resist "a demand for boundaries, for containment and coherence," as Lyn Hejinian argues in another context, in favor of "a simultaneous desire for free, unhampered access to the world prompting a correspondingly open response to it" ("Rejection" 41).

20. In "Thought's Measure," Charles Bernstein calls these percepts "world creating / perceiving idea[s]" (71). Bernstein's distinction separates "'thinking' as an activity of 'self'" and thinking that generates or constitutes a world. H.D.'s imagism has been persistently read for its efficacy in constructing a self; here I read it, by contrast, as creating a world.

21. See Pound, "Retrospect" 5. Pound's manifesto goes on to label abstractions "perdamnable rhetoric" (11) and "poppy-cock" (12).

22. Although subsidized by Amy Lowell, this anthology—and probably its preface—was the product of a joint collaboration between Lowell, H.D., and Richard Aldington.

23. For more on Frye's *melos,* see Culler, "Changes" 40.

24. See, for example, Gregory's reading of "Storm" as an address to Eros in *H.D. and Hellenism* (155–56) and her reading of the *Sea Garden* poems as re-creations of sustained spiritualized lesbian eroticism in "Rose Cut in Rock," Friedman's analysis of their carefully constructed "genderless" persona in *Penelope's Web* (50), and DuPlessis's charting of their erotic plot in *Career* (12–13). Additional poems that engage these themes include "Sheltered Garden," "Huntress," and "Loss."

25. For full descriptions of these effects, see *Reading Voices* 55–57.

26. This is not only the aesthetic but also the ethics of *Sea Garden:* see "Sheltered Garden" for H.D.'s polemic against the wadding that, in the name of protecting (particularly) women from life, chokes life out of them; see "Sea Iris," "Sea Rose," and "Sea Lily" for the beauty that emerges from exposure to elemental forces.

27. When these words are spread across a poem as end rhymes, they create an analogous effect that Stewart calls "rhyming pares," citing as his examples the triadic eroding rhymes "CHARM"/"HARM"/"ARM" and "START"/"TART"/"ART" in George Herbert's "Paradise" (*Reading Voices* 78).

28. See Robert Duncan's discussion of the effect he calls "the tone-leading of vowels and the variation of consonant groupings" in the second part of H.D.'s poem "Garden" ("Beginnings" 13). Duncan's reading is a model of close listening to H.D.'s sounds. For other texts that construct one or another path through these /ûr/ or /ûrl/ sounds, see the poems "Oread" (*Collected* 55) and "Halcyon" (*Collected* 270) and the novel *HERmione.* As Duncan explains, such rhymes as these are "finely conditioned, felt along the track of some inner impulse" (13) that connects, for example, "her" to "whirr" to "whirl." Another fruitful way to discuss the transformations of "Storm" is to think of them as variations on an acrostic structure that repeats consonant groupings: cr-sh, for example, fanning out as "crush" and "crash," or s-w-r-l appearing as both "swirl"

and "whirls." In a third pertinent sound effect, a pattern Kenneth Burke calls "augmentation," the *br* of "branch" is stretched into the "bur-" of "burden" then contracted again in "broken." For a nuanced discussion of these and other sound techniques, see Burke.

29. H.D. returned to the focusing image of "Storm" four years later in composing *Notes on Thought and Vision & the Wise Sappho:* "Is there," she wonders, "a beauty greater than the white pear-branch which broke so white against a black April storm sky that Zeus himself was roused from his sacred meditation?" (32–33).

30. In this connection, see Modris Eksteins's *Rites of Spring.* "Here again," Eksteins writes of pre–World War I depictions of sexual themes in literature and art, "the fascination with violence represented an interest in life, in destruction as an act of creation, in illness as part of living" (83).

31. H.D. to Bryher, 13 May 1936 (H.D., Letters). See Friedman on the petrification of the signature "H.D. *Imagiste*" and the struggle the writer herself waged against it (*Penelope's Web* 33–99).

32. Walton 264; Deutsch 12; Benét 461; Blackmur 97, 95.

33. For examples of these approaches, see Burnett 123–25; Blackmur 96; Quinn 91. The best—and most sustained—treatment of this volume is Burnett, chap. 7 (113–39).

34. The distinction between readerly and writerly texts comes, of course, from Barthes's *S/Z.* In *Roland Barthes,* Barthes suggests a third term, the *receivable,* to designate an "unreaderly text which catches hold" (118). Because of the resistance it generates in its readers, *Red Roses* is not, in these terms, a receivable text.

35. In theory, intralexical transforms and transegmental drifts partake in what Stewart calls the "pronounced defects" (*Reading Voices* 35) of all speech and should be found more or less randomly through disparate linguistic formations, but in poetry these effects seem to flare and dwindle. The attempt to find transegmental drifts and intralexical transforms, so fruitful in *Sea Garden,* yields only desultory results in *Red Roses.*

36. "Secret Name," written in spring 1923, and "Hipparchia" and "Murex," started in 1924, were published in 1926 as part of *Palimpsest; Red Roses,* begun in 1924, appeared in 1931; *Her,* composed in 1926–27, was published in 1981 under the title *HERmione.* For a chronological table of the composition and publication of H.D.'s writings, see Friedman, "Chronology."

37. The phrase "think through our bodies" alludes not only to Woolf's argument but to the ruminations of Adrienne Rich (284) and Jane Gallop (*Thinking through the Body*). I am grateful to Stewart for alerting me to Woolf's essay (*Reading Voices* 22–23).

38. For song-melos in H.D.'s work from this period, see, in *Red Roses,* the first eight lines of "Trance" (244), the first five lines of "Wine Bowl" (241), and the sequence H.D. called "Songs from Cyprus" (277–81), and, from "Murex," the metrically regular quatrains of Ray Bart's long poem sequence (*Palimpsest* 150–72). Practicing this art as early as the lyrics of "Hymen" from 1921 (101–43), H.D. enjoyed writing songs and did it well. In the thirties three of the "Songs from Cyprus" were set to music for voice and flute by Eric Walter White (see his *Images of H.D.* 17).

39. This is true even of the witches' chatter. See, for example, the lines, "But in a sieve I'll thither sail, / And, like a rat without a tail, / I'll do, I'll do, and I'll do" (I.3.8–10).

40. John Hollander observes that rhyme may "do some of the work of metaphor by associating words through their sounds alone, and by thus juxtaposing them with some of the same strength as an actual image" (157).

41. For Freud's discussion of "repetition compulsion," see *Beyond the Pleasure Principle*.

42. For an analogous dynamic in Gertrude Stein's writing, see Marianne DeKoven's analysis of repetition in *Three Lives* (27–45). In her essay "Portraits and Repetition," Stein compares her use of repetition to the shot-by-shot reiterations of cinematic frames, a technique that became familiar to H.D. both through her work with POOL's avant-garde productions and through such theorizations as Sergei Eisenstein's two-part study "The Fourth Dimension in the Kino."

43. For extended analysis of H.D.'s readings and rewritings of Euripides, see Gregory, *H.D. and Hellenism*, chap. 6 (179–231).

44. Because *Trilogy* mulls many of the questions central to this book, discussion of it is dispersed through the chapters. Chapter 1 looks at part 1, "The Walls Do Not Fall"; chapter 6 considers part 2, "Tribute to the Angels"; and part 3, "The Flowering of the Rod," is discussed throughout. Excellent companion volumes to *Trilogy* include Bryher's wartime memoir, *Days of Mars*, and H.D.'s correspondence with Norman Holmes Pearson, *Between History and Poetry*.

45. For information about hieroglyphs, see Gardiner. According to the catalogue of H.D.'s library at the Beinecke Rare Book and Manuscript Library, Yale University, H.D. possessed copies of E. A. Wallis Budge's *Easy Lessons in Egyptian Hieroglyphs* (1902) and *A Hieroglyphic Vocabulary to the Theban Recension of the Book of the Dead* (1911). Since *wn,* the phonogram of the hare, also stands for the verb *to exist* or *to be,* it is possible that the bee and the hare are two signifiers occupying the space of one signified: a multilingual pun on being or, perhaps, bee-ing. In her story "Secret Name" (in *Palimpsest*), based, like "The Walls Do Not Fall," in Luxor, H.D. returns again and again to the figure of the bee, imagining her main character as an insect and the temple as an enormous flower "heavy with pollen, stable, yet sure with the slightest variation of wind or summer breeze to spill its just hovering, just clinging dust" (209, 211). H.D. defines the determinative as "the picture that contains the whole series of pictures in itself or helps clarify them" (*Tribute to Freud* 56).

46. For Mikhail Bakhtin's discussion of the chronotope or space-time figure, see "Forms of Time and Chronotope in the Novel" and "The *Bildungsroman* and Its Significance in the History of Realism."

47. This orality is thematically instantiated in *Trilogy* through messages that arrive in the form of wingéd words addressed to the listener's ear: Amen-Ra whispers (30), the Pythian "pronounces" (4), Samuel prophesies (3), John speaks (65), and the poet's interlocutor commands and questions (76); Thoth, Hermes, Mercury, and the seven angels to whom H.D. pays tribute rush between realms carrying messages in "a voice,

a breath, a whisper" (78); and over the terrifying "whirr and roar in the high air" comes "a Voice [that is] louder, / . . . / though its speech was lower / than a whisper" (19).

48. Stewart's term for the aural expansion of a word matrix is "paraphone." This term plays off Michael Riffaterre's "paragram," which designates the expansion of a matrix in the form of words linked together grammatically (*Reading Voices* 41).

49. The consonant patterns H.D. devises in the poem make use of allophones or predictable phonetic variants of a phoneme. In these examples, typically, the stops *b* and *p* and the dentals *t* and *d* are treated as equivalents.

50. See *Helen in Egypt,* which takes place, H.D. tells us, in "*[t]he great Amen, Ammon, or Amŭn temple*" (11).

51. H.D. told Norman Holmes Pearson that she began to write part 2 of *Trilogy,* "Tribute to the Angels," "on top of the bus [to Putney] brushing through . . . chestnut trees" (*Between History* 44). This view from above, reduplicating the view available from H.D.'s fifth-floor flat in Lowndes Square, would have made London's bombed-out buildings resemble hieroglyphic squares framing iconic objects of debris. "We pass on," H.D. writes, including the reader of "The Walls Do Not Fall," "to another cellar, to another sliced wall / where poor utensils show / like rare objects in a museum" (4). DuPlessis's argument that "Helen's major activity [in *Helen in Egypt*] is decoding and remembering" (*H.D.* 110) amplifies this theme of decipherment.

52. Edmunds points out that E. A. Wallis Budge made this connection in his book *Easy Lessons in Egyptian Hieroglyphics:* "'the cartouches,'" Budge writes, "'are so called because they resemble cartridges'" (16).

53. Other examples of etymological series in "The Walls Do Not Fall" include the famous riffs on the names of the angels and the Bona Dea in "Tribute to the Angels." For an excellent analysis of this and other soundplay in *Trilogy,* see McCauley. Other useful treatments of sound in H.D. include Boughn ("Elements"), Kerblat, Ostriker, and Stricker.

54. The changes can also, of course, track cultural degradations or desublimations. "Knaves and fools // have done you impious wrong, / Venus," H.D. writes, "for venery stands for impurity // and Venus as desire / is venereous, lascivious" (74). In this section, however, I will concentrate not on devolution, which H.D. attributes to "them"— knaves, fools, rogues, the smug and fat—but to an evolution in which poets and readers play a part.

55. "Cities," the final poem in *Sea Garden,* makes an attempt to speak out more directly against the culture that created World War I, but its extended conceit of the poet as bee renders it pale and stiff in comparison to the poems that precede it.

56. A crucial variant of this trope is, of course, the bundle of myrrh that Mary holds in her arms. The poem's last two words, "her arms," reiterate the root h-r-m, which also generates the words "Hermes" (63) and "Hermon" (113) and the anagram "myrrh."

57. For discussion of the trope of childbirth in H.D.'s work, see Friedman, *Penelope's Web,* Kloepfer, *The Unspeakable Mother,* and Hollenberg, *H.D.: The Poetics of Childbirth and Creativity.* For discussion of her various breakdowns and her analysis with

Freud, see Friedman, *Psyche Reborn,* Guest, *Herself Defined,* and Buck. For an exemplary sociopolitical reading of H.D., see Susan Edmunds's interpretation of *Helen in Egypt* in light of postcolonial liberation struggles in Egypt in the 1950s, when H.D.'s poem was written (95–148).

58. For a summary of the work of Parry, Lord, and other students of the techniques of oral memorization, see Ong, *Orality and Literacy* 57–68.

59. H.D. to Sarton, 7 January [1946] (Letters). For H.D.'s requests, see also her letters of 27 December 1945 to Norman Holmes Pearson (*Between History* 48–50) and of 26 November 1945 to Marianne Moore. Among others whom H.D. asked for lists were Edith Sitwell and Logan Pearsall-Smith. Although her postwar breakdown prevented H.D. from conducting this course, she took her notes to Switzerland with her, where she continued to work on them (see letter to Pearson, 11 June 1946, in *Between History* 56).

60. The term "poeticised memory" comes from Havelock, *Preface to Plato.*

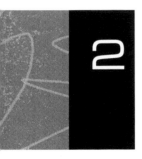

2

H.D. on the Air:
Acoustical Technologies,
Virtual Realities, and
Helen in Egypt

H.D.'s *Trilogy* is not the only noisy modernist epic. Hart
Crane's *The Bridge,* T. S. Eliot's *The Waste Land,* William Carlos Williams's *Paterson,* Ezra Pound's *The Cantos,* and H.D.'s
Helen in Egypt reverberate with subway rumbles, rolls of thunder, snatches of song, knocks, horns, even the "whhsssh, t ttt"
of a buzz-saw (Canto 18/83) and the "breathless silence" following the fall of a city (*Helen* 123). "'What is that noise?'"
Eliot's neurasthenic asks, alerting us to the poem's surround

of sound. "'What is that noise now?'" (*Waste Land* 57). In epics composed, read, recited, and recorded between 1917 and 1960, sounds cut in, rise, then fade away as other sounds intrude, as if we were tapping into a party line on a municipal phone exchange, spinning down a radio dial, or sampling a stack of records. Sound technologies enter *The Cantos, The Waste Land, The Bridge, Trilogy,* and *Helen in Egypt* sometimes as things, sometimes as themes, and sometimes as models or types of communication, but their most important effect is generative: the acoustical technologies that grew up with the generation of poets born in the last decades of the nineteenth century created conditions that supported a brief but intense resurgence of epic ambitions in the first half of the twentieth century.

Whether orally or aurally, in air or in ink, the epic has been, from its beginnings, a noisy affair. First vocalized by bards reciting to an audience, then evoked by poets writing for readers, the epic solicits the ear of the public. Epic composers speak as citizens to other citizens, engaging a tribe, community, nation, or alliance in order to move it through a moment of crisis. The term *modernist epic* signals a handful of poems written in response to two world wars, global economic collapse, and the development of nuclear armaments. Although these poems are by no means identical, they have in common an ambition and urgency, a set of ancestors, and an array of allusions, tropes, and gestures that invite us to consider them together. However dependent they are on capaciousness and continuity, these are not "long" or "serial poems": their reach is prerequisite to the magnitude, eloquence, and structural complexity they need to mobilize a culture's historic, spiritual, and/or mythic heritage and suggest a route toward durable release.[1]

Like their predecessors, modernist epics have an aural opulence that produces, in Garrett Stewart's pun, not only "semantic excess" but "somatic access" (*Reading Voices* 2). Their sounds appeal to the body. Eric Havelock's proposition in *Preface to Plato* is that epics of primary orality, composed and recited before acoustically sophisticated audiences, directly engaged the body's vibratory field: as the bard intoned and strummed, auditors hummed, clapped, and swayed, partially hypnotized by the intricately coordinated verbal, vocal, instrumental, and physical rhythms that surrounded them (152). Stewart's proposition in *Reading Voices* is that silent readers also process sound through the body's vibratory fields, for the act of reading sets in motion not only the organs of sight but also the diaphragm, throat, mouth, and tongue, all the organs of vocal production (1). In this sense, as poets from Virgil to Whitman insisted all along, literary epicists also "sing": they produce an articulatory stream of sound—a "phonotext"—that takes its place within the body of the reader. In recited epics, sound traveled from the mouth of the bard to the ears of his auditors; in written epics, sound travels from the poet's sensorium through the spaced letters of a phonetic alphabet to the body of the reader. The poem's phonotext makes the reader a sounding board for the poem's language.

The acoustical technologies developed in the first half of the twentieth century enticed and enlivened the ear of a print-saturated audience. Filling the airwaves with sounds, telephones, radios, loudspeakers, and tape recorders created a territory of the voice that early media theorists termed "secondary orality" (Ong, *Orality* 11). Technologized sounds, no matter how pervasive and insistent, can never recreate the conditions of primary or preliterate orality: secondary orality is not, as Havelock emphasizes, "a reversion to a primeval past but a forced marriage, or remarriage, between the resources of the written word and of the spoken, a marriage of a sort which . . . reinforce[s] the latent energies of both parties" (*Muse* 33). The epic of secondary orality—the modernist epic—engages the newly energized ear of its audience with a phonotext that is jagged, peculiar, insistent, and insinuating. Crane's bridge is an acoustical instrument, a harp of "*choiring strings*" (44). Mr. Paterson's "thought is listed," Williams informs us, "in the Telephone / Directory" (18): to ring it up is to initiate a decisively aural interchange. "What is that sound high in the air?" Eliot asks toward the close of his poem (*Waste Land* 67). "Hear me," Pound commands at the opening of his (Canto 4/13). "[D]o you hear me?" H.D.'s Helen asks. "Listen," she whispers, "it is no matter" (*Helen* 175, 177).

How has the no-matter of sound come to matter so little in discussions of the modernist epic? Leading critics of these poems for the most part ignore their shifting, speeding, slurring, sliding, and slowing phonotexts in order to pay attention to a more stable set of visual analogs and antecedents. Joseph Frank was the first to argue that *The Cantos* and *The Waste Land* are "based on a space-logic that demands a complete reorientation in the reader's attitude toward language" (13): these epics are, he concludes, poems for the eye rather than the ear. In the thirty years since this reorientation, Marjorie Perloff has placed the poems of Pound and his contemporaries "in the context of the 'documentary' collages, Futurist as well as Cubist, that were its exact contemporaries" (*Dance* 34), Hugh Kenner has situated *The Waste Land* as an imitation of newsreel quick-cutting (*Mechanic* 9) and *The Cantos* as an array of written ideograms (*Pound Era* 447–54), and Jerome McGann has located the visible language of modernist poetry as "a direct function and expression of the Renaissance of Printing that began in the late nineteenth century" (*Black Riders* xi). As these and other critics have shown, typewriters, linotype machines, photographs, paintings, cinema, and video all provide useful entries into modernist poetic structures and strategies, but what happens if we close our eyes and attune our ears instead to the ring of a phone, the crackle of the radio, or the creak of a capstan driving a tape?

*   *   *

"Brrrr-rrr." "'Ye-e-e-e-*es.*'" In H.D.'s fictionalized autobiography *HERmione*, the twenty-three-year-old apprentice poet and author-to-be of two modernist epics lifts a receiver outside Philadelphia to hear "tin pan noises, little tin pan against my ear and words striking, beating on it." It's the twenty-four-year-old author-to-be of *The Cantos* calling. Tympanums vibrating with their tin-pan phone connection,[2] these two young poets play out a logic of sound across distance through a series of aural overlaps that start with deictic sparring: "'I didn't know you were here,'" she opens. "'I'm not here,'" he retorts (41–42). The chime of "here . . . here" opens out into the homonyms "hear" and "ear," announcing the theater of these poets' interaction. In the realm of the eye, previous to the development of film and video transmission, it was impossible to be at the same moment "here" and "not here," but in the realm of the ear at the turn of the century newly available technologies routinely transported voices, as H.D. put it, "[f]ar and far . . . out of something, out of nothing, holding something, holding nothing" (41).[3] Like the puns the young H.D. and Pound deployed to make this paradox audible, telephones are all about unexpected connections.[4] Because, as Marinetti suggested, the tin-pan noises of early twentieth-century communication technologies had a decisive influence on the psyche of the modernists who first used them, this call between poets resonates with their call to be poets.

By the 1930s, as Pound and H.D. reached middle age, a series of inventions made it possible, at least in theory, for "[a] single voice addressing a single audience on a single occasion" to be heard by "the entire population of the earth" (Havelock, *Muse* 31). This fact was not lost on Pound in the 1940s as he shouted again and again into the microphones of the Italian Broadcasting System, "'EUROPE CALLING! EZRA POUND SPEAKING!'" "'If yew hadn't bin such *mutts,*'" he yelled into living rooms across the United States, Canada, the Pacific, New Zealand, and Australia, "'you woulda *heerd* me . . . long before now!'" (qtd. in Carpenter 588). Extending the range of transmission and generalizing the audience of address, radio gave poets like Pound and H.D. an opportunity not only to invade the homes of strangers but to imagine a global audience for their work.[5]

During her visit to Manhattan in 1937, H.D. had a similar experience of being, in its several senses, "heerd": "I was called to the telephone," she tells Norman Holmes Pearson. "'Your island[s] were on the air,' I was informed 'and read beautifully.' 'Where?' I asked. 'Radio City, just a few minutes ago'" (*Between History* 10). The poem on the air, "The Islands," chanted the names of Rhodes, Samos, Chios, Paros, Milos, Crete, and other Greek islands that H.D. identified with Calypso's Island in the Lehigh River near Bethlehem, Pennsylvania, where she grew up, and the Casco Bay islands off the coast of Maine, where she vacationed as a child (*Collected Poems* 124–27; *Between History* 9). To hear of its broadcast as she arrived "here in this island" (10) from the island of England offered evidence for an intuition that sustained not only many of H.D.'s lyrics but her two epics as well: the sense that all space and time converge in a vast "here" and "now," a cosmic matrix, a global Radio City, a web of information intermittently accessible through dream, vision, and the reach of aural technologies.

By the 1950s, as Pound and H.D. entered old age, the development of inexpensive tape technology made it as easy to preserve sound across time as it had become to transmit it through space. In January 1955, at the urging of Norman Holmes Pearson, the sixty-nine-year-old H.D. leaned into the microphones of a studio in Zurich to record for posterity portions of *Helen in Egypt*. Just as Pound chose to begin his *Cantos* with a rendering of Odysseus's visit to the shades in the underworld, H.D. opens her reading with a meditation on the theme of disembodied presences that are, like voices on the air, both "here" and "not here." Now, more than three decades after her death, by sliding a cassette into a player, it is possible to hear her voice, thin as a reed, retelling the events at Troy: "Do not despair," she says, "the hosts / surging beneath the Walls, / (no more than I) are ghosts" (1).[6]

Modern and contemporary technologies helped to shape the literary production and continue to shape the literary reception of H.D.'s poem *Helen in Egypt*. In an introduction composed for the poem's first publication in 1961, Horace Gregory identifies it as "a semidramatic lyric narrative" (viii); in *H.D. and Hellenism* Eileen Gregory argues that it resembles Euripidean drama (218–31); most critics, however, have read this poem as an epic. Based on obscure variants of Greek legend, the poem narrates the intertwined destinies of Helen, Achilles, and Paris in the aftermath of the Trojan War. Following Susan Stanford Friedman's interpretation in *Psyche Reborn,* sustained readings have parsed the poem as H.D.'s attempt to rewrite her personal story, an enterprise that led her to recast Freudian psychoanalytic theories and recalibrate the foundational structures in Western mythology.[7] The poem is difficult and dense, strained and strange, so much so that most critics have felt it necessary to disentangle and thereby normalize its narrative before proceeding with an analysis. In this chapter, I want to return some of the strangeness to H.D.'s tale by resituating it within the auditory networks in which it was first produced and the virtual storyspaces it now joins.

"'Beneath' the metaphysical structure of the unifying logos, the word of reason, the idea and institution of definitive speculation," Dianne Chisholm writes in her interpretation of this poem, "[Helen] uncovers a different form of thinking, perceiving, feeling, and communalizing which cannot be translated into readerly discourse, cannot be intellectually absorbed without a radical reconfiguration of mind" (168). My argument in this chapter is that this form of thinking, perceiving, feeling, and communalizing belongs to a cultural moment made available to H.D. and her contemporaries through the acoustical technologies invented at the turn of the century, perfected in the aftermath of World War I, and globally instantiated by the onset of World War II.[8] The unifying logos and word of reason that undergird the age of print are foundational neither to the primary orality that preceded it nor to the secondary orality that succeeds it. The epistemological inquiries of *Helen in Egypt* that strain the resources of the written word correspond to the power of words transmitted on the air.

The rise, flourishing, and fading of the modernist epic coincided with the rise, dominance, and supersession of telephones, radios, loudspeakers, and tape recorders. Epic commitments do not emerge from thin air: Pound, Eliot, H.D., and Williams had ample models and motives for their labors.[9] Their educations prepared them to reverence the poems of Homer, Virgil, Dante, and Milton; they lived in a time of sustained political, social, and spiritual crisis; they held poets responsible for cultural continuities; and, finally, as colleagues and rivals for over half a century, together they prepared an audience to receive their difficult writings. There was, however, a final factor that nourished these poets' epic ambitions: in the years between 1917 and 1960, telephones, radios, and tape recorders restored some of the conditions of primary orality by linking sound to vivid imaginings, enriching and expanding rituals of listening, gathering a vast potential audience for cultural pronouncements, and making perceptible a cosmos in which voices routinely emerged "out of something, out of nothing, holding something, holding nothing" (H.D., *HERmione* 41).

In *Discourse Networks, 1800/1900*, Friedrich A. Kittler presents a dense and compelling argument for the constitution of literature in and through technological media. Because literature is a means of processing, storing, and transmitting data, Kittler maintains, it changes according to the material and technical resources at its disposal. According to Kittler, in the thirty years on either side of 1900, Edison's two great inventions, film and the gramophone, decisively altered the nature of poetry and literature. In 1912, toward the end of this thirty-year period, Marinetti welcomed "the complete renewal of human sensibility" through the new optical and acoustical technologies. Although he was excited by cinema, he reserved his greatest enthusiasm for the "[m]ultiple, simultaneous consciousness" of the "wireless imagination" and the "art of noise" (45, 47).

In their fascination with film, television, video, and the emerging media of virtual reality and cyberspace, most cultural critics have overlooked—or underheard—the wireless imaginings of the first half of the twentieth century.[10] The phonotext of the modernist epic is one of the most sustained and ambitious experiments in the art of noise. What were the effects—positive and negative—of the newly organized sense ratios of secondary orality? What approaches to world crisis emerged from the ghostland or dreamland of the wireless imagination? If, as Kittler argues, "[m]edia determine our situation" (*Gramophone* xxxix), what can H.D.'s encounter with acoustical technologies teach us as we learn to live with the digital technologies that have emerged in the wake of World War II?

*   *   *

One of the earliest recorded acoustical machines was a golden bird that sang in the boughs of a gold and silver tree (Davies 15). Metalworkers in ninth-century Baghdad are said to have fashioned this device for Abbasid Khalif Abdallâh al-Ma'mûn, but it is, of course, familiar as one of the signal images of modernism: the "[m]iracle, bird or golden handiwork" presiding "[i]n glory of changeless metal" over William Butler Yeats's Byzantium (243). The bird's golden tones announce an indefinitely remote realm of perfection to which listeners are summoned with songs, calls, and gongs. The summons comes to the ear as the most attenuated of the senses, the least contaminated by "complexities of mire or blood" (243). In 1930, the year this poem emerged, the ear of the public was still astonished by transmissions streaming through the airwaves from afar. For most of the Western world, radio transmissions now as routine as phone calls seemed only slightly less miraculous than the singing of a golden bird on a golden bough.

Although many of the devices used to capture, save, send, and/or receive sound were conceived in the decades flanking the birth of Yeats, Eliot, Pound, H.D., and Williams, it wasn't until after World War I that acoustical technology became a feature of daily life.[11] During the 1920s, tens of thousands of radios were produced, distributed, purchased, and installed in places of honor in homes across the Western world. News photos, cartoons, sketches, and advertisements taught consumers a vocabulary for naming this technology, a set of customs for its use, and an array of ways to conceptualize its peculiar combination of art, technology, and power. The paradoxes these popular documents take up are the same paradoxes H.D. and Pound excited in their play on the puncept "hear" and "here." Contemporary advertisements and cartoons again and again worried the enigma of disembodied presence: how can what we hear be at the same time both here and not here? In sketch after sketch, musical instruments, dance bands, entire symphony orchestras, song lyrics, political speeches, and advertising slogans ride the sound waves out of radio speakers into bourgeois living rooms. Dogs perk up their ears, teenagers kick up their heels, couples spoon, matrons sew, and old men snooze in their armchairs, all enveloped in the wavy lines that came to represent radio signals.

Cartoons of the period register both excitement and anxiety about the intrusiveness of radio. In one cartoon, a little girl asks her mother, who bends and stretches to the commands of an invisible announcer, "What will he say if you don't do it?" In another, a mother tosses a tea tray into the air, a baby screams, and a boy, dog, and cat, all with bristling hair, rush from a room as a lion's "G-R-R-R" spills out of a radio speaker (Hill 67; see figs. 1 and 2). The little girl assumes—not incorrectly—that an apparatus that receives can also be used to transmit; the mother, baby, boy, dog, and cat assume—again not incorrectly—that sound precedes and announces presence. As Michael David-

Figure 1. "What will he say if you don't do it?" (1940s cartoon)

Figure 2. "Listenin'!" (1923 postcard)

son points out, these and other aspects of acoustical technology became crucial factors in the surveillance ideology of the cold war. When bugging devices
of all sorts—among them, martini olive transmitters, detectaphones, and spike
mikes—invade the privacy of households and workplaces, the suspicions these
early cartoons position as infantile or hysterical return as ghostly premonitions
of a government that no longer needed to be "here" to "hear" (200).

Habits formed through the cartoons, advertisements, and news stories of
the 1920s joined the nightly routines necessary to maximize reception of ra-

dio signals to transform the physiological act of hearing into a series of culturally charged rituals of listening. As James A. Connor reminds us, in the early days of broadcasting, before frequency stabilizers and more advanced tuning devices, at least one member of each family had to spend the evening arranging and rearranging batteries, crystal detectors, vacuum tubes, and antennae to coax signals through the chatter of thousands of amateur and commercial stations (19). As acoustical technology improved, however, increasingly sophisticated receivers set into podium-sized, "Temple Style" cabinets allowed the whole family to sit back while components with names like "Beam-a-scope" and "Dynapower" made "all barriers of time and space seem to fall away" and "the unseen curtain of distance" lift.[12]

The General Electric advertisement from which this copy comes is captioned "Don't Cry Mother . . . It's *Only* A Program!" An opulent, full-page, illustrated spread on the inside cover of *Life* magazine, the advertisement shows a family gathered in its living room on either side of a GE "Golden Tone" cabinet-style receiver. "What a wonderful thing this radio is!" the text exclaims. "Its magic conjures people, nations, castles and kings right out of the air! It carries you on thrilling journeys to exciting places—brings colorful people to call who become closer friends than the folks next door. Summons interesting guests . . . brings countless bits of radiant color to weave into the pattern of gray days" (see fig. 3). The illustration is, among other things, a lesson in the art of listening: in it the unknown fits so snugly into the known that no one needs to run from the room. The family is anchored by Father, who sits to one side of the podium reading his paper; Mother, at the opposite side, moved by what she hears, puts down her mending to dab at her eyes with a handkerchief; leaning over her shoulder, her golden-haired daughter, reminding her of the differences between representation and reality, murmurs, "Don't Cry Mother." Simply by listening, all members of the family have entered "another dimension," one in which "all barriers of time and space seem to fall away." Although the transmission may be, as the copy says, "*only* a program," the radio sits at the center of the scene as if it were another member of the family, a storytelling grandparent or neighborhood bard. On its gleaming surface, doubled by a golden mirror suspended behind it, stands a bouquet of six large white blossoms.

On dashboards, sport headsets, bedside tables, kitchen counters, and even in the shower, radio in the twenty-first century is a music delivery system, timekeeper, weather monitor, exercise pacer, and commercial bulletin board. Early radio, however, had higher aspirations. In 1936 to Rudolf Arnheim and many others, radio was no less than "the great miracle of wireless": an extraordinary

Figure 3. Advertisement for General Electric Radio, from *Life*, January–February 1940, inside front cover. (Used by permission of James R. Harmon, General Electric Corporation)

event, an ethereal intervention, a cause for pride, excitement, wonder, and fear, available day and night through "forty million sets . . . scattered over the world" (Arnheim 14). The hold of radio technology on the public imagination was due not only to its novelty and rapid improvements but to the utopian dreams it suddenly made plausible: "the omnipresence," in Arnheim's list, "of what people are singing or saying anywhere, the overleaping of frontiers, the conquest of spatial isolation, the importation of culture on the waves of the ether, the same fare for all, sound in silence" (14). And not only this. In his survey of radio art in the wireless age, Gregory Whitehead enumerates a series of even grander dreams: "communication with alien beings, the establishment of a universal language, instantaneous travel through collapsing space," even "the achievement of a lasting global peace" (254).

Just as in the unrevised version of his first Canto Pound declined to "sulk and leave the word to novelists" ("Three Cantos" 118), he and his cohort refused to leave utopian dreams to radio. With Yeats, Eliot, Joyce, Wyndham Lewis, Gaudier-Brzeska, and numerous other artists of the 1920s and 1930s, Pound and H.D. described their art in terms borrowed from the new technologies of reception and transmission of sound. For Pound, artists were "the antennae of the race"; for H.D., more elaborately, they had "the right sort of brains" to act as "receiving station[s]" and "telegraphic centre[s]" relaying "lightning flashes of electric power" across "the world of dead, murky thought."[13] "[The artist] draws," Pound says, "from the air about him," for "the best of knowledge is in the air."[14] The spirits these modernist poets invoke to superintend their transmissions are the epic messengers of primary orality, to be sure, but they are also, more strikingly, the emblems of Western Union, RCA, Ekco, and Gramophone, the corporations that built and marketed the acoustical technologies of secondary orality: Hermes with his winged sandals, Mercury with his lightning bolt, the nymph Echo, and Gramophone's angel etching a message on a wax tablet.[15] When Edison named his invention the "phonograph" and Emile Berliner called his the "gramophone," their coinages conveyed the same idea as Stewart's compound "phonotext": "sound-writing," "writing-sound," "sound-writing."

Bell's telephone, Edison's phonograph and "aerophone," Cros's "paleophone," Bell's "photophone," Edison's "kineto-phonograph," the marconiphone, microphone, paleophone, dynamophone, aetherophon, and phonoautogram are only a few of the many acoustical devices invented, patented, improved, and distributed between 1880 and 1960.[16] Although the trope of "silent reading" and a persistent critical privileging of the image, the gaze, and other aspects of the visible have occluded its workings, the phonotext is an aural technology as ancient as phonetic writing itself. The technologies of secondary orality, which created a new environment of structured and meaningful sound and resituated the ear as an active processor of information, put us in a better position to apprehend and analyze the phonotext as a system for the storage and delivery of sound.

Like a record or tape, a phonotext is an acoustical track or trace activated by the process of scanning. As we saw in the previous chapter, phonotexts are not simply background sound for content—euphony or cacophony to complement meaning—but engines that generate and complicate meaning. The acts of writing and reading, storing and scanning, recording and replaying give words that are "inked-in"—to listen to a telling transegmental drift from *Helen in Egypt*—the power of ink-din (23).[17] Viewed in a span that stretches from primary orality through the ages of print and secondary orality into the digital media of the post-print age, writing is an episode in the history of discourse. New communication technologies constantly redefine and resituate the old. With the coming of computers, Kittler writes, "Homer's rosy-fingered Eos changes from a Goddess into a piece of chromium dioxide that was stored in the memory of the bard and could be combined with other pieces into whole epics. 'Primary orality' and 'oral history' came into existence only after the end of the writing monopoly, as the technological shadows of the apparatuses that document them" (*Gramophone* 7).

The audience for the dense, jagged, and powerful phonotext of the modernist epic was trained by an incessant flow of fact, intention, and persuasion over the international airwaves between World War I and World War II. Among early radio's most avid listeners were not only the writers who devised the modernist epic but the scholars who first theorized its oral ancestry. What Pound, H.D., Williams, Eliot, Lévi-Strauss, Jack Goody and Ian Watt, Ernst Mayr, Marshall McLuhan, Eric Havelock, and Walter Ong all had in common was immersion in rituals of technologized listening. "We had all," Havelock says, "been listening to the radio" (*Muse* 30).

In an example with overtones to which I return at the end of this chapter, Havelock recounts a memory from October 1939 when he heard a speech that could have been—and, given the tensions of the moment, probably was—simultaneously audited in England, Italy, Switzerland, and New Jersey by Eliot, Pound, H.D., and Williams. "I recall standing on Charles Street in Toronto adjacent to Victoria College," Havelock writes,

> listening to an open air radio address. We all, professors and students, as by common consent had trooped out to listen to the loudspeaker set up in the street. It

was broadcasting a speech from Hitler, with whom we in Canada were, formally speaking, at war. He was exhorting us to call it quits and leave him in possession of what he had seized. The strident, vehement, staccato sentences clanged out and reverberated and chased each other along, series after series, flooding over us, battering us, half drowning us, and yet kept us rooted there listening to a foreign tongue which we somehow could nevertheless imagine that we understood. This oral spell had been transmitted in the twinkling of an eye, across thousands of miles, had been automatically picked up and amplified and poured over us. I have sometimes wondered whether McLuhan as a young man in Toronto at that time would have heard the same speech, shared the same experience. (*Muse* 32)

Radio made a new type of demand on the attention, exercised a new kind of power on the mind. If, as Havelock speculates, the effort to understand the personal and political effects of this demand led these scholars to generate their theories of orality and literacy, these theories also, in their turn, help us comprehend the ambition, buoyancy, and address of the epics that emerged and faded during radio's glory days. As the ink-din of H.D.'s *Helen in Egypt* and the "radio . . . noise" (Pound qtd. in Terrell 75) of Pound's *Cantos* reach out to the reader's ear, what styles of thought, what social and subjective configurations, what apprehensions of the cosmos do they create? What "tunings," what attunements, were made possible by the wireless imagination? As the poet David Antin asked in "whos listening out there," a radio piece broadcast on KPBS in California, what price do we "pay for being able to go through [this medium] or transmit through it   or receive" (278)?[18] How does the no-matter of sound matter in the making of meaning?

*   *   *

Published in 1961, H.D.'s *Helen in Egypt* is the last modernist epic composed under the spell of the wireless imagination. The least familiar and arguably the most elusive of these epics, it is also the most extreme in its creation of an inclusive field of resonance, a rapt attention—a tension—of the ear. Although H.D. was typical of her generation in her fascination with the new acoustical technologies, she had more occasion than most to reflect on their impact: as a critic for the cinematic journal *Close Up,* she reviewed an early demonstration of the Movietone sound machine; as a translator and poet, she had several of her works put on the air from London and New York; and, finally, her sound-studio taping of several sections of *Helen in Egypt* significantly altered the course of its composition by giving her the idea to add prose captions to introduce each of the cantos.[19] A careful reading of the aesthetics, cosmology, and politics of this epic should help us audit some of the ef-

fects—both positive and negative—of the new sense ratios set up by the technological dilation of the ear.

Sound in *Helen in Egypt* is more than melopoeia, onomatopoeia, or echo:
it is a form of primary attention, an orientation, a concentration. Many factors in H.D.'s background encouraged aural acuity: among them, the centrality
of hymns in Moravian ritual, her family's passion for music and storytelling,
and her many years of residence abroad.[20] Listening in *Helen in Egypt*, however, is more than a predilection or a skill: in H.D.'s epic, sound opens directly into memory, desire, and meaning. When Achilles is ferried into the afterlife, what he remembers is not the smell of the smoldering city, the last glimpse
of his ship, or the disorientation in his body but "only the sound of the
rowlocks" (57); Thetis lures Helen from the temples of Egypt with a promise
that a forest tree's "whispering . . . holds subtler meaning / than this written
stone" (108); Helen backs her claim that the defeated Trojans still exist by saying not "I see their bodies" but "I hear their voices" (2). The crucial scenes of
H.D.'s epic occur on a beach at night, in a candlelit bedchamber, a "winter-
dark" room (157), or a dim mountain hut, dusky settings that isolate and sharp-
en the sense of hearing. As in a radio drama, H.D.'s audience joins her characters in a near-total orientation through sound.[21]

To a large extent, sound is the scenery of this epic. Each character has a sound
motif, and every shift of scene is signaled by a shift in sound, so that, to return to H.D.'s telephone punning, we know we are "here" or "not here" by
what we do or do not "hear." The action of the epic is arrayed across four distinct acoustical planes: the masculine world of Achilles, which rings, rasps,
cracks, and clangs with the machinery of war (39); the feminine world of Helen,
which echoes with laughter, murmuring, lyre music, and footsteps in a hall or
on a turret; a divine world that manifests through disembodied oracular en-
ticements and summations; and, under and throughout it all, the "*beat and
long reverberation, / [the] booming and delicate echo*" of the sea, the matrix from
which sounds emerge and into which they subside (304).[22] As characters from
different planes meet, interact, recede, and reminisce, the epic takes its form
as a kind of Eisenstein for the ear: an acoustical collage, a montage, a fading,
clashing, and blending of sounds. In the last stage of composition, H.D. gave
each section of the poem a headnote that functions as a kind of voice-over,
an introduction to and meditative guide through the mix of sounds to come.
Like an avant-garde radio play, H.D.'s epic emerges from the workings of the
acoustical imagination.

The separation of hearing from seeing in H.D.'s epic is as startling and
powerful as the separation of seeing from hearing in silent film. Such drastic

alteration of normal sense ratios produces an eerie, intimate, elusive effect, an effect that led H.D. to prefer silent film to Movietone sound cinema. To see as in a silent film or, by extension, to hear as through radio induces a concentration keen enough to propel us out of the everyday world into a "super-normal or . . . sub-normal layer of consciousness" ("Cinema and the Classics III" 116). While the projection of voice and the projection of image "[e]ach alone [leaves] us to our dreams," together they are "too much": too crude, too realistic, too materialistic to provide more than a caricature of day-to-day experience (115). In 1956, the year after she completed *Helen in Egypt*, H.D. ran across reviews of the global release of a movie that realized her worst fears for sound cinema: this film, she complained to Pearson, reduces Helen of Troy—a Spartan, a goddess—to a talking doll, a "cutie" (Letters, 31 January 1956).[23] For H.D., the concentration of attention in a single sense—eye or ear—facilitates access to the layers of the mind identified with myth, dream, and the unconscious.

One of the best guides to the importance of listening in a period of technologized orality is, appropriately enough, the model for one of the characters in H.D.'s epic. After leaving Egypt, Helen visits the philosopher-hero Theseus, who settles her on a low couch near a small stove in the late afternoon dusk to recount her story. This staging replicates the scene of H.D.'s analysis with Freud and demonstrates a point Freud elaborated in his recommendations to physicians. For the same reasons H.D. preferred silent film to Movietone sound, Freud advises analysts to place themselves behind—and therefore out of sight of—their analysands. Using an analogy from acoustical technology to elaborate this recommendation, Freud argued that the analyst, deprived of sight clues, "turn[s] his own unconscious like a receptive organ towards the transmitting unconscious of the patient . . . adjust[ing] himself to the patient as a telephone receiver is adjusted to the transmitting microphone. Just as the receiver converts back into sound-waves the electric oscillations in the telephone line which were set up by sound waves, so the doctor's unconscious is able, from the derivatives of the unconscious which are communicated to him, to reconstruct that unconscious, which has determined the patient's free associations" ("Recommendations" 115–16).[24] Like an archaic Greek attending to a bard, like Havelock in Toronto listening to Hitler, like Mother entranced by GE's golden tones, the analyst is an ear in thrall to a voice.[25]

Unlike her imagist poems, which were "written to be seen," *Helen in Egypt*, H.D. told Pearson, must be "dramatized" (Letters, 25 February 1955). Whether in print or on tape, she insisted, this poem needs to be processed as acoustical data. The centrality of the phonotext became clear to H.D. through the act of taping. As she reports to Pearson, this ecstatic, even transformative experience made a composition in space into an event in time, connected it with performative traditions of the epic, and restored its address, at least in theory, from a small number of eyes to a collective ear. "[I]nstead of confiding my tale, my song, my saga, confidentially, to the few," she explained to Pearson, "I seemed to be 'lecturing' a multitude" (Letters, 27 January 1955). From this point forward, memorizing its lines, murmuring them to herself like a chant or mantra, H.D. insisted on the dual nature of her composition: for her, henceforward, it was in equal parts aural *and* oral, graphotext and phonotext, "inked-in" and ink-din.[26]

Like other successful epics, H.D.'s poem is a revision—or, perhaps better, a reaudition—of a tale familiar enough to constitute a community: "*We all know the story,*" the poem begins, "*of Helen of Troy*" (1). H.D.'s rendition of this story is as disembodied as a narrative told over the phone or on the radio: to engage it is to enter the place GE's advertising copy calls "almost . . . another dimension." In this strange territory, the narrator speaks, Helen speaks, Paris speaks, Theseus speaks, and Achilles and his mother Thetis speak not to each other, except in memory, but, it seems, directly to us. Rhythmic, repetitive, intimate, eerily familiar, H.D.'s language repeats—or re-creates—a moment when we were all, first and foremost, oralists. As the conventionally gendered structure of the advertisement suggests, this moment is tied to the Mother/Daughter dyad, not to the realm of the Father.

As many critics have pointed out, the territory of the voice is a preoedipal ghostland or dreamland, at once sensuous and dematerialized, erotic and disembodied.[27] While Father sits to the side reading his newspaper, the voice on the radio transports Mother into another realm. Connections in this territory are no less instantaneous than phone transmissions or radio relays: to think of a person is to reach her, to conceive of a place is to go there, to recall an event is to relive it. Helen feels she "draw[s]" Achilles to her on the beach in Egypt (5); Thetis "*calls Helen out of Egypt*" to Leuké (208); Helen's memory calls her back to the walls of Troy (232). To ask if the real Helen is here or there—on the ramparts in Troy or in the temples of Egypt, back in Egypt or still in Leuké—is to miss the point. Like the conundrum that obsesses Achilles—"'Helena, which was the dream, / which was the veil of Cytheraea?'" (36)—these distinctions come from another register of consciousness: truth in *Helen in Egypt* is a matter not of distinctions but of conflations.

The both/and structure of thought that Achilles and Helen move toward in the progress of H.D.'s poem is characteristic of the habits of thought Ong and Havelock associate with primary orality. Like an oral epic, H.D.'s poem is copious, elaborative, and participatory. "*There is more to it,*" a headnote proclaims, summing up the story of Paris (112). "There was always another and another and another," Theseus says, setting up his own story (167). Additive rather than analytic, thinking in this poem moves by means of formulas and clusters, parallel terms, phrases, and clauses. The poem's hinges are paratactic rather than hypotactic: "and" and "then," not "however," "because," or "therefore." If the voice-over in a headnote asks a question—as it almost invariably does—the section that follows presents not an answer but a series of echoes that proliferate and complicate the query. "*[W]ho caused the war?*" a headnote inquires. A rational question. "Paris . . . Thetis . . . Eris," the section chimes, starting a rhyme that cascades through the rest of the epic (111). In this clustering of sounds, Paris is at once Eros and Eris, love and strife; he seduces Helen, an act that allies him with Eros, but he also shoots the arrows that kill Achilles, an act that makes him the double of Ares, the brother of Eris, the nymph who sought revenge when Thetis excluded her, alone of all deities, from her marriage feast. "[D]id Ares bequeath his arrows / alike to Eros, to Eris?" H.D. asks (183) in a spin of sounds that functions as a kind of aural *mise en abîme*, an M. C. Escher for the ear. The answer, of course, is both/and or, better, as Rachel Blau DuPlessis suggests, "both/and/*and*" (*H.D.* 113).

The replications of H.D.'s language pluralize meaning by folding the many into the one and exfoliating the one into the many.[28] This simultaneous proliferation and condensation performs a structuring law of H.D.'s epic, a cosmic principle embodied by its heroes and deities, who are, she tells us, "One," even though, she continues, "the many // manifest separately" (78–79). When Osiris is torn into pieces, is he singular or plural? Are Isis, Osiris, and their child Horus three-in-one, one, or many? How about Helen, Achilles, and their child Euphorion, in whom are reborn, H.D. tells us, the slain hero-warriors of Greece? When the souls of these warriors rise in a cloud of sparks from the funeral pyre at Troy to surround the union of Helen and Achilles by the fire on the beach in Egypt, are they one or many? Are love and death, L'Amour and La Mort, two signifieds occupying the space of one signifier or one resonant sign (288)? The unstable phonotext of H.D.'s epic, its aural flux and swirl, makes questions such as these—questions of the logical, rational, scientific mind—seem not only unanswerable but, in some fundamental sense, beside the point.

Slipping across the permutations of H.D.'s language, the reader learns to think in a communal, aggregative, undifferentiated manner, a manner that is closer to orally based thought and expression than it is to consciousness structured by writing.[29] In this state of mind, families, tribes, and nations cohere like a cluster of bees, a swirl of snow, a Galaxy, "an infinite number," in H.D.'s

summary, "yet one whole" (43). Violations of this aggregative way of thinking are the eruptions of hierarchy and competition that power the story of the
Trojan War: the challenge of the apple inscribed "*to the fairest*" (111), the decision made by the Greek "Lords of the Hierarchy" to back Odysseus rather than
Achilles (95), Agamemnon's choice of the fortunes of his army over the life of
his daughter, Iphigenia (72–73).

   Although there are disquieting implications to this condemnation of the
dynamics of choice, implications to which I will return, within the poem the
stakes of unity are raised by the charged terms H.D. uses to describe the effects of the war: it is "a holocaust," she says three times over (5, 38, 229), one
that ends in a "*flash in the heaven at noon that blinds the sun*" (160):

> brighter than the sun at noon-day,
> yet whiter than frost,
> whiter than snow,
>
> whiter than the white drift of sand
> that lies like ground shells,
> dust of shells—
>
> —dust of skulls. (160–61)

This flash—identified elsewhere in the poem with the "Meeting" of Helen and
Achilles on the sands of Egypt (100)—doubles in the poem's mythological
matrix as the destruction of Troy. Like the word *holocaust*, however, the blind-
ing flash in the heavens at noon has unavoidable resonance in the poem's contemporary matrix, not only as the flash of the atomic bombs dropped by the
Allies on Hiroshima and Nagasaki in August 1945 but also as the flash of the
hydrogen bombs detonated by the United States on 1 November 1952 at the
Eniwetok proving grounds in the Pacific and on 1 March 1954 at the Bikini Atoll
in the South Pacific. *Helen in Egypt,* written after five years of poetic silence,
was begun in September 1952, just before the shock of the first hydrogen bomb,
and concluded in August 1954, soon after the second sent up a fireball that
measured more than three miles in diameter and a mushroom cloud that extended more than thirty miles into the stratosphere.[30]

   The puncepts of H.D.'s epic give resonance to her meditations on the hieroglyph of the thousand-petaled lily by presenting Ares, Paris, Eris, and the
arrows of Eros as the splitting into parts—the fission—of one lexical nucleus.
In this sense, the phonotext of *Helen in Egypt* recasts the empathic, communal, ritualistic imagination of primary orality with an urgency fueled by the
genocidal actions of both the Nazis and the Allies in World War II and by the

development of weapons hundreds of times more lethal for use in a possible World War III. In contrast to Homer's epics, in which the engine of plot is the honor of nation states and the outcome is the destruction of one state by another, in H.D.'s epic, the engine of the plot is aggregation. By refusing to allow Greece to set itself apart from Troy, *Helen in Egypt* imagines a community that is global, not national. Thetis, the sea-mother, mother of Achilles and guide of Helen, "*mourns 'for Hector dead'*" (299); Helen, mother of Hermione with Menelaus, becomes with Achilles not only the mother of Euphorion, a child who is many yet one, but also, improbably, the mother of her Trojan lover, Paris. The bending of time, the twisting of cause and effect, and the breakdown of differentiations is caught in the epithet for Thetis, the female double of the shape-shifting god Proteus: Achilles' mother, the "sea-mother," is, like every character and event in this epic, also a "seem-other." Out of this fission and fusion, war crosses over into love: La Mort, as H.D. puts it in another one of her acrostic permutations, becomes L'Amour.

If "writing restructures consciousness," as theorists of orality and literacy argue (Ong, *Orality* 78), the poet's bet in this text is that the reverse could also be true: the resurgence of an aural imagination in a time of strife might be able to mitigate the rigidities and divisions of a linear and hierarchical print culture. The modernist epic's glossolalia, echolalia, puns, transegmental shifts and drifts—all the sound effects, the sound defects, of a charged poetic phonotext—are amplified by the convergence of a moment of historical crisis, the flourishing technologies of secondary orality, and a public ear newly attuned to a flow of sound. The inventions that allowed a World War II speech delivered in Germany to resound in real time through the streets of Toronto meant that the world was once again sufficiently small to submit to a single strong storyteller, a politician or poet able to weave a spell into which "all members of the community [could be] drawn" (Havelock, *Preface* 140).[31]

In the postwar years during which H.D. composed *Helen in Egypt,* a divided Germany, the cold war, the rapid disintegration of empires, Egypt's struggle for independence, and, above all, the threat of nuclear warfare testified to communities torn to pieces.[32] It is not surprising, then, that H.D. would turn all the resources of her epic toward the task of cohesion. The phonemes that collapse one into another reverse the current of dissolution, pull the fragments back toward each other, and ask a center to hold. With the swift and startling economy of the first photographs of the earth from the moon, H.D.'s acoustics bring together gods and warriors, Greeks and Trojans, men and women, adults and children, the living and the dead. In the aural overlaps of H.D.'s epic, we return full circle to Arnheim's utopian dreams for radio: "the omnipresence of what people are singing or saying anywhere, the overleaping of frontiers, the conquest of spatial isolation, the importation of culture on the waves of the ether, the same fare for all, sound in silence" (14), even, perhaps, the establishment of a universal language, instantaneous travel through collapsing space, and the achievement of a lasting global peace.

The voice that suggested to Havelock and others the power of the oral epic, the voice that reverberated through the public space of Toronto in 1939, belonged, however, not to a generative, shape-shifting, variously manifesting godforce like H.D.'s Thetis but to Hitler, a fact that ought to give us pause about the ghostland of the wireless imagination. Plato ejected the bards of orality from his Republic in the name of values that intellectuals critique but nonetheless continue to endorse: among them, rationality, discrimination, and critical distance. Like the Homeric epic, radio, loudspeakers, and other sound technologies charged the air with electricity: they cast a hypnotic spell. Because they asked the audience to engage with or even submit to the sounds of a speaker, they were less a spectacle apart than a resonance within, less an exercise of our faculties, perhaps, than a kind of possession. As Alice Yaeger Kaplan has shown in her compelling study of Fascist France, these were the technologies that served—and continue, in other sites, still to serve—as instruments for xenophobia, anti-Semitism, fundamentalist diatribe, and other seductive group-mind ideologies. The force Arnheim and others wanted to appropriate for peace has also been turned to indoctrinate, intimidate, and infantilize its audience.

If the wireless imagination sometimes lost sight of the many in its vision of the one, the predominantly specular imagination of the later twentieth century could be said to err in the opposite direction: in our fascination with difference, that is, we lose sight of binding similarities. Both extremes of the continuum are vexed—few would want to have to choose between coercive community and balkanization. The history of acoustical technologies in the first half of the twentieth century indicates the ways in which media provide new opportunities and new ideological vulnerabilities. The tie between acoustical technologies and the flaws and virtues of the modernist epic suggests it would be a mistake to abandon either our skepticism or our utopian dreams in the processes of engaging the new mediations of virtual reality.

*   *   *

In the uneven process of change that N. Katherine Hayles calls "seriation," new media technologies "emerge by partially replicating and partially innovating upon what came before" ("Condition" 202). The gramophone, film, and typewriter that stored and separated sound, sight, and writing at the beginning of the century converge in the communication networks of the twenty-first century, where standardized transmission frequencies and bit format carry streaming audio, visual, and print information through fiber optic cables into homes, libraries, and workplaces. In a process Marshall McLuhan was the first to identify, old media supply the content of the new media: silent films and audiotape provide the content of cinema, records and tapes the content of radio, cinema and radio the content of television.[33] The digitized world of instant interchanges and mobile interfaces folds together aspects of orality, literacy, and secondary orality to produce "virtual reality," just as virtual reality, in its turn, produces newly configured subjects for the ghostland of the fiber optic imagination.

The record of critical readings of H.D.'s epic suggests how difficult it has been to align *Helen in Egypt* with the values and structures of liberal humanism. Fixed boundaries, a stable and coherent self, a self-identical subject, and a plot consisting of rational either/or choices—the conventions of the written subject in the age of print—can be located in H.D.'s poem by reading it as a narrative of the growth of feminine self-sufficiency and self-esteem or by identifying it as a record of the persistence of colonial mentalities in a post-colonial world, but such readings require that we bracket, suppress, or explain away the strangeness of her text: its multiplicities, fluidity, extensions, and disruptions, its creation of a fourth dimension of space and time, its acoustical echoes and aural maze. It is in many ways easier to back-read *Helen in Egypt* from the standpoint of a virtual world than it is to situate it securely in a world of print.

As this chapter has argued, aspects of the oral subject described by Havelock and Ong return in H.D.'s refashioning of the story of the Trojan War to meet the crises of the Holocaust, Hiroshima, Nagasaki, and the nuclear arsenal lying in wait for World War III. To understand H.D.'s Helen, Achilles, and Paris, however, it is useful to look forward toward the era of virtual reality as well as backward to the age of primary orality. In concluding this chapter, therefore, I would like to align H.D.'s characters with an aspect of the virtual subject Hayles describes in *How We Became Posthuman: Virtual Bodies in Cybernetics, Literature, and Informatics.* In the seriation characteristic of mediated discourse, H.D.—like many other modernists—anticipates configurations to come at the same time as she recalls configurations that have passed. Among the strangest of her innovations in *Helen in Egypt* is the structuration of her characters as information patterns rather than embodied beings, a decision that has ethical and political implications for our reading of this text and for its bearing on the future.[34]

Although most of the science fiction narratives Hayles takes up in her book imagine their subjects as hybrids or cyborgs—amalgams of humans and machines, conflations of "meat" and silicon, six-million-dollar men or robotic women—the defining characteristics of the configuration she calls "posthuman" involve the construction of subjectivity rather than the presence of nonbiological parts. For Hayles, the marks of the posthuman are a downplaying of consciousness as the seat of human identity, the conceptualization of the body as a prosthesis we learn to manipulate, the development of functional interfaces between human beings and intelligent machines, and the privileging of informational patterns over their material instantiations (1–5).[35]

As Hayles explains at length, the theories of the American electrical engineer Claude Shannon mark the first important steps in the separation of information from the substrates that carry it. Shannon's theory of information, developed during his years at AT&T's Bell Laboratories, formalized the mathematical laws governing the transmission, reception, and processing of signals through telephone, teletype, and radio channels. The need for these formulations arose from the increasing complexity and crowding of acoustical channels, but information theory also encompasses other forms of information relay and storage, including images transmitted by television and pulses transmitted by computers. As anyone who adjusted a crystal set to receive radio transmissions in the 1920s, fiddled with rabbit ears to capture television transmissions in the 1950s, or lost a signal on a cellular phone in the 1990s knows all too well, messages transmitted through a channel or medium are susceptible to interferences that distort and degrade the signals. Two of the major concerns of information theory are the reduction of noise-induced errors in communication systems and the efficient use of total channel capacity.

The formulas Shannon created to address these concerns defined information as a probability function with no dimensions, no materiality, and no necessary connection with one or another specific embodied context. "[Information] theory is formulated," Hayles emphasizes, "entirely without reference to what information means" (*How We Became* 53). Among the most important consequences of this decision to bracket meaning is a shift in orientation from the binary opposition of presence and absence that drives the thinking of print-bound theorists like Derrida to the opposition between pattern and randomness that preoccupies communication theorists like Shannon and Norbert Wiener. Information theory takes for granted the disembodiment that sent H.D. and Pound into their spin on the homonyms *hear, ear,* and *here* and set off their riffs on "voice[s] out of something, out of nothing, holding something, holding nothing" (*HERmione* 41). In telephone calls, as in the other transmissions that concern Shannon and Weiner, Hayles dryly observes, "Questions about presence and absence do not yield much leverage" (*How We Became* 27).

Just as a mind jacked into a computer network is at once inside and outside the screen, Helen, called by Thetis to Leuké, is also and at the same time in Egypt, Greece, and Troy. The lure of Achilles' either/or conundrum—was the Helen who appeared on the ramparts at Troy a phantom or a presence?—is the idea that if Helen never went to Troy she would be innocent of complicity with the Trojans. This chain of reasoning, however, is neither a promise nor a preoccupation in *Helen in Egypt* but, in a literal sense, its "pretext."[36] Embodiment—and therefore presence or absence—counts for little in a poem in which all the characters are, at one point or another, dissociated from their physical instantiations, beamed up, teleported, translated, or bilocated from one context to another in a flicker of time. What determines their identity and provides the poem's plot is not presence or absence—whether they are here or there, living or dead, real or imagined—but their constitutive patterns, the information that is, in a fundamental sense, their identity.

This switch from the axis of presence and absence to the axis of pattern and randomness helps to explain one of the oddest dynamics in this odd poem: the recurrent whisking of characters through switchpoints between contexts. Such transfers occur in a spark or a flash: the glance exchanged by Helen and Achilles at Troy (54), the blast as Helen vanishes down a set of spiral stairs during the fall of Troy (127–28), the flash in the heavens on the beach in Egypt (185). In each of these moments, we are asked to imagine the transmission of patterns from one context to another. In the first, Achilles moves from the world of death to a world of generativity; in the second, Helen turns from action to contemplation; in the third, Achilles and Helen metamorphose from enemies into lovers whose momentary union engenders both Euphorion, who ushers in the next era, and Paris, who ushered out the last.

In the nonlinear moment of these switchpoints, time folds in on itself in such a way that events "that had not yet happened, / had happened long ago" (55).[37] Borrowing a term from a lecture by the mathematician René Thom, Susan Howe calls such moments "singularities." As Howe explains, "a singularity is the point where plus becomes minus. On a line, if you start at x point, there is +1, +2, etc. But at the other side of the point is -1, -2, etc. The singularity . . . is the point where there is a sudden change to something completely else. It's a chaotic point. It's the point chaos enters cosmos, the instant articulation" ("*Talisman* Interview" 173). The event that preoccupies Howe in the poems gathered under the title *Singularities* is the switchpoint of North American history constituted by the European "settling" of the wilderness and the wilderness's "unsettling" of European colonialists. Like the Japanese bombing of Pearl Harbor and the American bombings of Hiroshima and Nagasaki, moments Howe addresses in other texts, singularities are the "[m]ortal particulars / whose shatter we are" ("Thorow" 50).

Moments in H.D.'s poem that are at best unlikely—an assault that is at the same time an embrace, a lover who is suddenly a son, a baby who becomes "*not one child but two*" (288)—can be wrenched toward plausibility with the help of Freudian or Kleinian psychoanalytic theories, but it is simpler to think of them not as events between embodied beings or developed characters so much as transfers of information between disparate contexts. In this sense, Helen, Achilles, Paris, Euphorion, the Greek and Trojan hosts, and the gods who shift among them are codes, information patterns, bearers of cultural DNA. Their relations are not so much narratives as catastrophes and mutations. In this light, explanations in H.D.'s poem that seem preposterous, grandiose, or repellent on a romantic, psychological, or personal level—the imputation, for example, that thousands died at Troy so that Helen and Achilles could embrace in the afterlife (20)—regain some semblance of significance.[38]

In moments of singularity, slight shifts generate significant ruptures. Biologists have applied Thom's theories in *Mathematical Models of Morphogenesis* and *Structural Stability and Morphogenesis* to explain what happens when non-native species enter an ecosystem or genes mutate to produce newly configured organisms. The moment of singularity is at once a disintegration and a new formation: a "blast"—to borrow the puncept the Vorticists used to title their short-lived journal—that is both a violent tearing apart and an embryonic coming together.[39] In this much larger, more impersonal interpretation, the disintegration of Greek and Trojan hosts also and at the same time opens an opportunity for reconfigurations and reintegration across dividing lines. It is, however, not possible to think this thought—or, to be more candid, to think this thought so blithely—if we imagine the dead as more than "hosts" for the configurations of information they carry, as people, that is, rather than codes.

H.D. insists on codes at every turn in *Helen in Egypt:* the actors are hieroglyphs (17), Helen is the writing (22), her task is to read the script or discern the pattern (264), and, in the end, she judges "*[t]he pattern in itself . . . sufficient*" (32). Like Watson and Crick, Helen is in search of a kind of DNA she imagines to be at work at the level of cultures or civilizations. The reason not to follow H.D. into this ghostland is, of course, the racist trap that awaits us there—it is, after all, but a short step from notions of cultural coding to the ideas that fed the Holocaust and continue to nourish strains of American bigotry and European ethnic cleansing. Only if information retains its body can it also retain sufficient complexity and holistic focus to thwart this line of thinking.

"The best possible time to contest for what the posthuman means," Hayles writes, "is now, before the trains of thought it embodies have been laid down so firmly that it would take dynamite to change them" (*How We Became* 291). If the danger of the posthuman is disembodiment, its opportunity lies in its assumption that the boundaries of the human subject are constructed rather than given. H.D.'s epic insists that information patterns play out variously in different circumstances or contexts—Helen in Sparta is not the same as Helen of Troy, nor is Helen of Troy the same as Helen in Egypt. At each turn of the spiral, there is hope that humanity can avert its own collapse by altering its configurations. The urgency behind *Helen in Egypt*, like the urgency behind *Trilogy*, is the intuition that the moment for intervention may soon be over.

*   *   *

If, as H.D., Pound, Williams, and Eliot hoped, poets function as antennae for their cultures—transmitting stations, as H.D. supposed in her work of the 1920s, or filaments in a web, as she imagined in the 1950s—the idea that poems can make a difference in culture is not as feeble as it sometimes seems in the years following the heyday of the modernist epic. If, as Marinetti surmised in the epigraph to this chapter, the technologies that configure and convey information route themselves through our speech and our psyches, they are not opposed—cannot be opposed—to poetry. "On the contrary," Carrie Noland argues in her study of French modernists and American postmodernists, "the technologies depicted as menacing poetry's existence—from the printing press to electronic communications—have turned out to be vital, rather than fatal, to poetry's evolution as an aesthetic form" (14).

Contemporary dreams for digital technologies repeat Arnheim's aspirations for "the great miracle of wireless," aspirations that in turn repeat a previous generation's ambitions for the comprehensive information network created by the telegraph: omnipresence of information, overleaping of frontiers, conquest of spatial isolation, instantaneous travel through collapsing space, and, not least, an infrastructure capable of supporting global peace and prosperity.[40] The events that came between Arnheim's dreaming and our own—the rise of fascism, World War II, and the development of heretofore unimaginably destructive armaments—were, as it turned out, facilitated by the technologies that were to obviate them.

If there is a middle way between optimism and the necessary asperities of pessimism, it might become evident through close observation of cultural patterns that can keep us from blowing ourselves and each other to pieces. This, I will suggest in part 2 of this book, is the work H.D. attempted through her stories of moments in which embodied human beings discern and reinforce cultural patterns of generosity and generativity. The patterns of projection, the gift, and post-Newtonian science—the topics of the next three chapters—run counter to entrenched assumptions and habits of Enlightenment humanism and late market capitalism. In her work they appear "out of something, out of nothing, holding something, holding nothing." Whether they bear on the future is, it seems, up to us.

Notes

1. In this concept of the epic, I am indebted to Jeremy Ingalls, "The Epic Tradition: A Commentary" and "The Epic Tradition: A Commentary II," and Michael André Bernstein, *The Tale of the Tribe.* For a capacious definition of the category "modern epic"—one that includes not only "the many structural similarities binding it to a distant past" (2) but also the many structural discontinuities in such exemplary texts as *Moby-Dick, Ulysses, The Cantos,* and *The Waste Land*—see Moretti.

2. H.D.'s pun, of course, is on "tympanum" and "tin pan," but one of its referents—the name of New York's "Tin Pan Alley"—provides yet another instance of acoustical blur. Responding to complaints from neighbors, the songwriter-publisher Harry Von Tilzer stuffed newspapers in his piano to reduce its volume. When the songwriter-journalist Monroe H. Rosenfeld commented, "It sounds like a tin pan," Von Tilzer replied, "Yes, I guess this is tin pan alley," a phrase Rosenfeld repeated in his *New York Herald* music columns from 1903 ("Music, 1903"). H.D.'s use of the phrase no doubt alludes to her interlocutor's Uncle Sam Tin Pan Alley showmanship and horseplay.

3. In his essay "The Voice in the Machine," focusing on the electric telegraph as a relay of intelligence through sound, Jay Clayton points to a similar dynamic in which "the telegraph seems to bring distance inside the subject, allowing it to incorporate two positions without contradiction" (227).

4. Among the earliest acoustical technologies still in use, the telephone is by now so ubiquitous most people no longer think of it as a technology. For far different reactions when telephones were new, see Marvin.

5. On the global reach of the modern epic and its status as a "world text," see Moretti 2.

6. Tape available from the Writers' Center, Order Number C-1158. For H.D.'s descriptions of the act of taping and Norman Holmes Pearson's reaction to the recordings, see their interchanges in *Between History and Poetry* 176–79.

7. For an excellent summary of the way in which the feminist recovery of the psy-

chodynamics of H.D.'s poetic career is entangled with themes from psychoanalysis, history, and mythology, see DuPlessis, *H.D.* For sustained analysis of *Helen in Egypt,* see especially Friedman, *Psyche Reborn* 59–67, 253–72; chap. 9 of Kloepfer, *The Unspeakable Mother;* chap. 4 of Chisholm; and chap. 2 of Edmunds, *Out of Line.*

8. The invention of the most salient of these technologies, the radio, is credited to the Italian electrical engineer Guglielmo Marconi, who developed an improved coherer and connected it to a rudimentary form of antenna in 1895. In 1896 Marconi transmitted signals over the distance of one mile and applied for his first British patent. In 1899 he established commercial communication between England and France that operated in all types of weather.

9. Born in 1899, a decade after Pound, Eliot, H.D., and Williams, Crane died in 1932, two years after the publication of *The Bridge.* Because of the differing arc of his career, his work falls outside the following analysis.

10. Exceptions to this generalization include the essays collected in the "Radio-Sound" issue of *Continuum* (1992), edited by Toby Miller; the essays collected in "Radiotext(e)," published by *Semiotext(e)* (1993), edited by Neil Strauss; and, especially, the essays in *Wireless Imagination* (1992), edited by Douglas Kahn and Gregory Whitehead. Catalogues of such prestigious publishing houses as Routledge bear out the disparity of interest in media of sight and media of sound: against a plethora of historical, theoretical, and critical studies of film and TV, to date Routledge has published only three studies of radio: the second edition of Andrew J. Crisell's brief overview of British radio, *Understanding Radio,* Pete Wilby and Andy Conroy's *The Radio Handbook,* and Tim Crook's *International Radio Journalism.*

11. See Davies for a convenient timeline of acoustical legends, musical instruments, automata, technologies, and treatises from before c.1150 B.C. to 1977.

12. For detailed descriptions of early radio, see Czitrom, especially chap. 3. Frank A. Biocca tells us that in 1922 America was gripped by an audio "purchasing craze," "a veritable epidemic," "bombs bursting in the air." "According to the most conservative estimates," he writes, "the number of radios by late 1923 jumped by an astounding 660 percent though a number of contemporary writers placed that estimate as high as 2500 percent. The number of broadcasting stations increased by 1850 percent" (65–66). For the evolving shape of radio cabinets, see Hill.

13. For Pound, see *Literary Essays* 58, 297; *ABC* 73, 81. For H.D., see *Notes* 26–27.

14. Pound, "I Gather the Limbs of Osiris [IV]," 179, and "I Gather the Limbs of Osiris [II]," 130. For more on this topic, see Nänny.

15. Kittler reproduces a picture of the writing angel that Emile Berliner used as the trademark for his gramophone in *Discourse Networks* 232. Hermes, the Greek prototype for Mercury, haunts both *The Cantos* and *Trilogy.* For angels, see H.D.'s series of invocations in "Tribute to the Angels," part 2 of *Trilogy.*

16. See Davies for dates and brief descriptions of these inventions.

17. As if to underscore their secondary orality, modernist epics were, from early on, performed, recorded, and/or taped—Pound read his on his radio broadcasts, H.D.

taped parts of one of hers, and Eliot and Pound read theirs for Caedmon Records. It is not, however, crucial to my argument that these poems be read aloud.

18. For further elaboration of the term *tuning,* see Antin, *tuning* 130, 169, 170. For Antin, "tuning" is the coming together of artist and audience in the moment of performance, an effect available through vocalized sound in an auditorium or on the air and through evocalized sound in the "somatic access" (Stewart, *Reading Voices* 2) of reading. H.D.'s taping of *Helen in Egypt*—its transformation from evocalized to vocalized sound—made available to her, at least in theory, the collective audience for her performance. Antin's term draws on Stockhausen's *Stimmung* or attunement, which suggests Heidegger's notion that our moods are our basic attunement to being-in-the-world.

19. For H.D.'s discussion of these introductory captions with Norman Holmes Pearson, see *Between History* 176–79.

20. For the aurality of her Moravian background, see her memoir *The Gift*. Moravian traditions included a trombone choir, in which her grandfather Francis Wolle played, and, in the early days when the community contained native speakers of numerous different languages, polyglot hymn-singing. Her uncle, Fred Wolle, established the annual Bach festival in Bethlehem, Pennsylvania, and her mother was for many years a music teacher. From 1911 until her death in 1961, she lived in England and Switzerland, traveled in Germany, France, Italy, Greece, and Egypt, and translated from the Greek and Latin.

21. See Cory, "Soundplay," for a similar use of sound in radio drama.

22. As Friedman has observed, the masculine world of war in *Helen in Egypt* is also "imaged by the darkness, cold, metal, weapons, clanging sounds, and fortresses repeatedly associated with it" (*Psyche Reborn* 258).

23. In "The Work of Art in the Age of Mechanical Reproduction," Walter Benjamin makes a similar point by linking the advent of sound to the "artificial build-up of the 'personality' outside the studio" that turns "the unique aura of the person" into "the 'spell of the personality,' the phony spell of a commodity" (231).

24. See also Freud's reprise of these instructions in "On Beginning the Treatment." "[P]sychoanalytic texts," Kittler points out in a discussion of this recommendation, "are haunted by the absolute faithfulness of phonography" (*Gramophone* 89).

25. In his essay "Listening," Roland Barthes links the posture of hearing to "an attitude of decoding what is obscure, blurred, or mute, in order to make available to consciousness the 'underside' of meaning" (249). The power of listening to bring "two subjects into relation" (251) seems to hold even when the listener is a crowd lending an ear—or, as the transegmental drift would have it, "a near"—to the speaker.

26. "I have been happy with the *Helen,*" H.D. reported to Pearson, "—the only poems I ever wrote that I memorized in part, and say over and over" (Letters, 24 December 1955; qtd. in part in *Between History* 181). The rhythm of these poems is, she told him, "hypnotic. . . . I have never felt so happy about my work, before" (*Between History* 177).

27. See, for example, Kloepfer's argument that "decades before structuralism, post-structuralism, and deconstruction, women, partly through their absorption of modernism and partly through their private vision and despair, *were* viewing the mother-child dyad outside the structure of the father, even though what they viewed was often loss" (*Unspeakable Mother* 2). "The maternal gift," Kittler argues in *Discourse Networks,* "is language in a nascent state, pure breath as a limit value from which the articulated speech of others begins" (27).

28. The hieroglyph that teaches this method of thinking is the lily, the Egyptian representation of the number 1,000, which initiates a flurry of embodiments in H.D.'s text: the thousand feathers of the hawk Horus, the sails of the thousand ships that set out for Troy, the thousand souls of Achilles' elite troops, the thousand-petaled rose (25), all expressing the same conundrum of the many that are nevertheless one.

29. For an enumeration of the habits of thought that are characteristic of primary orality, see Ong, *Orality,* chap. 3 (31–77).

30. In a letter to Pearson (3 August 1954), H.D. wrote, "I did do the last *Helen,* which I love very much" (*Between History* 159). As Susan Stanford Friedman was the first to point out, the notebooks in which H.D. collected her thoughts for *Helen in Egypt* contain references to the development and testing of nuclear armaments contemporaneous with the composition of her poem. As if in associative free fall, an unnumbered page of the red, spiral-bound *Helen in Egypt* notebook in the H.D. Papers at the Beinecke reads in whole: "Los Alamos— / atomic energy base— / A-bomb tests in Nevada— / Radarscope— / saucer lights flashing / red-green + white—." For more on H.D.'s awareness of H-bomb testing and the international protests it provoked, see Crown.

31. "Chesterfield is merely the nation's cigarette, but the radio," Adorno and Horkheimer proclaim, "is the voice of the nation" (377). Part of the power of World War II broadcasts by Hitler, Mussolini, Roosevelt, Churchill, and DeGaulle was the claim made by these leaders to speak in the voice of a collective entity.

32. For a discussion of the political context into which H.D. inserted her meditations on Egypt, see Edmunds.

33. "[T]he 'content' of any medium is always another medium," McLuhan writes. "The content of writing is speech, just as the written word is the content of print, and print is the content of the telegraph" (*Understanding* 8).

34. In *How We Became Posthuman,* Hayles founds her arguments in the definitions of information formalized by Claude Shannon and Norbert Wiener as part of U.S. techno-scientific culture during and immediately following World War II. Although H.D.'s composition of *Helen in Egypt* is contemporaneous with the work of Shannon and Wiener, it is not my intent to suggest that she knew of the developing discipline of cybernetics and informatics, much less that she anticipated its developments or implications. As I will argue at greater length in chapter 5, the relationship between science and literature is not a unidirectional flow but a complex crossing of currents. Models of influence are of much less interest to this analysis than notions of simultaneous or concurrent cultural work. Because culture circulates through science just as

science circulates through culture, ideas in literary texts are never merely passive conduits for scientific ideas. As Hayles has forcefully shown in her work with literature and science, imaginative texts and readers' interpretations of them actively shape what technologies mean in cultural contexts.

35. For a similar argument in a different context, see Lury.

36. "*We all know the story of Helen of Troy,*" H.D. begins, listing her sources as Homer's *Iliad* and *Odyssey*, Stesichorus's *Pallinode,* and Euripides' *The Trojan Women.* Achilles brings the question of presence and absence, guilt and innocence, with him from the classical world, but it is a question that fades as he begins to fit into the ghostly terrain of Helen's Egypt.

37. In such moments of "timeless-time" (39), H.D. elaborates, "*Time values have altered, present is past, past is future*" (57). "*[T]here is,*" she continues, holding on to the hybridity of this infinite-finite, "*no before and no after, there is one finite moment*" (301).

38. "*Is it possible that it all happened,*" H.D. asks, "*the ruin—it would seem not only of Troy, but of the 'holocaust of the Greeks,' of which she speaks later—in order that two souls or two soul-mates should meet?*" (5) The queasiness of such a suggestion is, of course, augmented when *Helen in Egypt* is read as an autobiographical fantasy in which H.D. plays the part of Helen, Sir Hugh Dowding the part of Achilles, Dowding's Royal Air Force fighter pilots the part of Achilles' dead warriors, and, presumably, the airmen and civilians who died in the Battle of Britain the part of those who died at Troy.

39. The etymology of the word *blast*—from the Greek *blastos* or bud—also aligns it with H.D.'s hieroglyph of the thousand-petaled lily bud.

40. In "The Voice in the Machine," Jay Clayton quotes a report on Samuel Morse's invention written by the Congressional Commerce Committee in 1837. The telegraph, this report assures us, will "'amount to a revolution unsurpassed in moral grandeur by any discovery that has been made in the arts and sciences, from the most distant period to which authentic history extends, to the present day. With the means of almost instantaneous communication . . . space will be, to all practical purposes of information, completely annihilated. . . . The citizen will be invested with . . . the [attributes of God], in a degree that the human mind, until recently, had hardly dared to contemplate'" (213). "The rhetoric of cyberspace," Jay David Bolter and Richard Grusin write, "is reminiscent of the manifestos of Filippo Tommaso Marinetti and the futurists. Moreover, the cyberspace enthusiasts have a similar relationship to technologies of representation that Marinetti and the futurists had to technologies of motive power (race cars, airplanes, etc.)" (54).

Mana-Words / Part 2

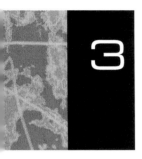

3 Projection:
A Study in Thought

In an author's lexicon, will there not always be a word-as-mana, a word whose ardent, complex, ineffable, and somehow sacred signification gives the illusion that by this word one might answer for everything? Such a word is neither eccentric nor central; it is motionless and carried, floating, never *pigeonholed*, always atopic (escaping any topic), at once remainder and supplement, a signifier taking up the place of every signified.
—Roland Barthes, *Roland Barthes*

You need not be a chamber to be haunted, nor need you own the Roxy to let loose the spirit of cinema on yourself. You can hire or buy or get on the easy system, a projector. You then have, on the occasions on which it works, people walking on your own opposite wall. By moving your fingers before the beam, you interrupt them; by walking before it your body absorbs them. You hold them, you can let them go. When the projector stops, they stop.
—Robert Herring, "A New Cinema"

A POOL film. A study in thought.
—advertisement for *Wing Beat*

Like transegmental drifts and Fenollosa's Chinese written character, mana-words are alive and elastic. Although the lexicon of these words will differ for each author, even for each reader, the function of these words is similar: mana-words are words that lead thought forward across time, sustain its openness and generativity, and maintain its relevance to events at work within a culture. The three chapters of part 2 examine three such signifiers in H.D.'s lexicon. As markers for the acts of throwing forward, circulating, and theorizing, the words *projection, gift,* and *science* engage her attention because they point toward ways in which cultures continue to evolve. Appearing throughout H.D.'s writing, these words put forward for consideration continuously mutating patterns of generosity and generativity.

This chapter focuses on a term from the technologies of "light writing" that joined technologies of "sound writing" to reorganize perception in the early decades of the twentieth century. Chapters 1 and 2 listen to telephone, radio, and tape technologies and the phonotexts they echo and amplify; chapter 3 looks at photographic and cinematographic technologies and the thought processes they concentrate and reflect. Just as the sound cluster *hear, here,* and *ear* makes audible dilemmas of presence and absence, an array of meanings around the term *projection* makes visible beliefs, experiences, and aspirations that shaped H.D.'s lifelong habits of thought.

As a focus of "ardent, complex, ineffable, and somehow sacred signification," the mana-word *projection* is slighter, more precise, and less predictable than pre–World War I abstractions like "History," "Truth," or "Honor." For Barthes, however, the power of a mana-word lies not in its heft but in its magnetism: its ability to pull information into pattern and constellate fields of meaning. The patriotic rhetoric of World War I drained the abstractions that organized Enlightenment systems of thought and value, rendering their exponents, in Pound's view, as hollow and brittle as their own rhetoric:

> Thin husks I had known as men,
> Dry casques of departed locusts
>   speaking a shell of speech . . .
> Propped between chairs and table . . .
> Words like the locust-shells, moved by no inner being. (Canto 7/26)

"[N]either eccentric nor central," as Barthes puts it, mana-words are subject neither to the fantasy that they exist at the margins of meaning nor to the illusion that they are unmoved movers at meaning's center. At once everywhere and nowhere, these "thought-words" act as reservoirs and relays of meaning throughout a textual network (*Roland Barthes* 145). Their primary trait, however, is neither their capaciousness nor their versatility but their generativity. As acorns make oaks, mana-words make worlds: "they are," as H.D. puts it, "anagrams, cryptograms, / little boxes, conditioned // to hatch butterflies" (*Trilogy* 53).

The slogan "A POOL film. A study in thought" that provokes this chapter's subtitle comes from an advertisement featured in the first issue of *Close Up*, the journal of avant-garde cinema collaboratively produced by Bryher, Kenneth Macpherson, and, at first but to a lesser extent, H.D.[1] POOL is the name of their production company, newly formed to disseminate not only *Close Up* but also avant-garde writings like Macpherson's novel *Poolreflection* and innovative films like *Wing Beat,* the "study in thought" that the advertisement describes at some length (see fig. 4).[2] In contrast to the Hollywood films excoriated in *Close Up* essays, reviews, and editorials, *Wing Beat,* we are told, does not aspire to be a novel, chronicle, fantasy, play, or epic: neither a vehicle of plot nor an exploration of personality, it is a "free verse poem" made up of "dimensions in dimensions . . . chains and layers." As a study in thought, it is "[o]f minds and spirits," the advertisement concludes, "not of persons."

ON THE WAY

WING BEAT!

A POOL film. A study in thought. The screen has had all these equivalents :

the epic,
the novel,
the chronicle,
the fantasy,
the play.

But no free verse poem. WING BEAT is the first. Telepathy and attraction, the reaching out, the very edge of dimensions in dimensions, the chemistry of actual attraction, of *will* shivering and quivering on a frail, too-high, too inaccessible brink.

WING BEAT shakes and trembles from its first moment, wings beating, ploughing wet clouds ; sky and space at it were, chains and layers of interminable journey, wings driven, tired but desperate. Of minds and spirits, not of persons.

Figure 4. "On the Way WING BEAT!" (advertisement from *Close Up,* July 1927)

Analogous to wingéd words, which fly from mouth to inner ear via print on paper, *Wing Beat* is a series of pictures that move through a projector to the eye of the viewer by way of images on a screen. The fragment of *Wing Beat* that remains is a carefully edited cross-cut sequence of three shots leading to a triple superimposition of a man reading, a younger man dancing, and a spinning phonograph disk (Friedberg, Introduction 212). If this sequence is representative, as it would appear to be, *Wing Beat* was composed in segments of varying lengths, like free verse lines or musical phrases, measured out in beats.[3] Although it can be read for plot or character—the man reading is disturbed by the phonograph record, the man dancing is inconsiderate, etc.—its more interesting implications are self-reflexive and paratactic: by giving equivalent time to machine and human, Macpherson suggests that the phonograph plays its listeners as much as it is played by them. In this, the sequence comments astutely not only on early twentieth-century media technologies but on POOL's own enterprise, which was, from the beginning, dependent on an array of equipment described in detail in *Close Up*'s advertisements, reports, comments, discussions, and debates.[4]

"[N]or need you own the Roxy," POOL's ally, the writer, editor, and amateur actor Robert Herring, reminds *Close Up*'s readers in July 1929, "to let loose the spirit of cinema on yourself" (54). To view a film shot by shot—stopping on images that speak to you, adjusting the speed of shot sequences with a hand-crank—you need only purchase an Agence Debrie "Jacky" projector, a box on a tripod "available on the easy system" for education and home use (see fig. 5). Like General Electric's golden-tone radio, "priced to fit all purses," the Jacky sets up in your living room to make images walk across your own opposite wall. Because it erodes the borderlines between real and imagined, external and internal, the projector is, like the radio, at once magical and intimate, strange and familiar. "It's *only* a program," but, GE's ad copy continues, "it's real and the people in it live!" "You hold [the projected images], you can let them go," Herring says. "When the projector stops, they stop." By walking in front of the beam, you absorb the images onto your own body, just as Mother, listening to GE's golden tones, takes in "the heartbreak of a girl who is hundreds of miles away—yes, farther than distance itself."

In the *Borderline* pamphlet, H.D., struggling to register film's new demands on the artist, turns to a hybrid category she calls the "mechanical-creative." Leonardo da Vinci is one exemplar of "mechanical efficiency, modernity and curiosity allied with pure creative impulse"; Kenneth Macpherson is another. In H.D.'s description of Macpherson at work on *Borderline,* "He stands, after any human being would drop dead of fatigue, casually with his elegant Debrie,

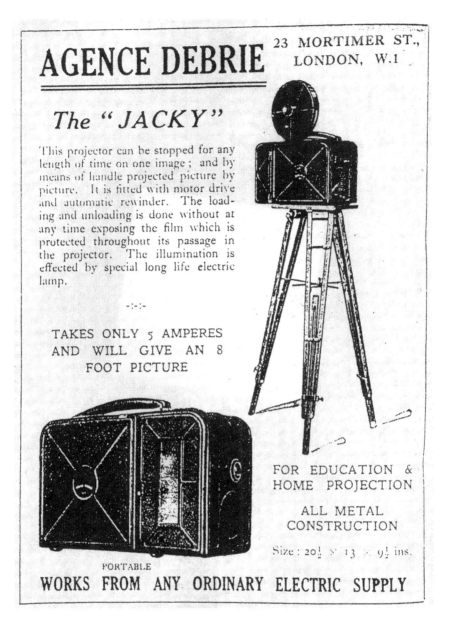

Figure 5. Advertisement for the "Jacky" projector. (*Close Up*, March 1930)

machine man with it" (224–25). This portrait of the artist as cyborg, part human and part mechanical apparatus, is a trope in play among the avant-garde
of the twenties,[5] one H.D. had used before and would use many times again.
As a sigil of creativity, this hybrid apparatus makes visible important aspects
of H.D.'s conception of the artist's visionary power.

∗   ∗   ∗

Almost a decade before her cinematic ventures, while staying with Bryher in
a hotel on the island of Corfu in April 1920, H.D. had a vision that positioned
her as a hybrid human-machine projector and viewer. Marking and measuring the rest of her life, this experience set the aims, announced the means, and
disclosed the dimensions of her most compelling work: the poems *Trilogy* and
Helen in Egypt and the prose meditations *Tribute to Freud* and *The Gift*. It
would be twenty years from the Corfu vision to the poems and prose that
grasped its promise, however, years of drift and anxiety in which H.D. wrote
and rewrote the story of her vision. By the time the event achieves its final
formulation in the first part of *Tribute to Freud*, it is clear that, however charged
the vision's imagery, the plot we are to follow, the *mythos* of the matter, is its
method: the "mechanical-creative" projection of the images.

    As H.D. explains in *Tribute to Freud*, the images she witnessed had the clar-
ity, intensity, and authenticity of dream symbols and yet took shape not inside her mind but on the wall between the foot of her bed and the washstand.
Because it was late afternoon and their side of the hotel was already dim and
because the images were outlined in light, the shapes that appeared could not
have been cast shadows. Neither accidental nor random, they formed with a
stately, steady purpose, one after another, and seemed inscribed by the same
hand. Their abstract, impersonal, conventional notation—a head in profile, a
chalice, a ladder, an angel named Victory or Niké—made them seem part of a
picture-alphabet or hieroglyphic system, a supposition reinforced by their
orderly succession, their syntax. For these reasons and because of the eerie
portentousness of the moment, H.D. calls this experience the "writing on the
wall" (*Tribute* 3).

    When Belshazzar witnessed the writing on his wall, he glimpsed along with
the letters a part of the hand that wrote them. The origin of H.D.'s writing is,
if equally mysterious, less simply formulated. The agent, it would seem, is not
a hand but a projective process: the casting of images onto a wall or screen.
The earlier images, which appear entire, are like magic lantern slides; the later
ones, which draw themselves in dots of light elongating into lines, resemble
primitive "moving pictures."

The path from mind to wall is direct. It at first seems to follow what H.D. calls her "sustained crystal-gazing stare" (*Tribute* 47), a concentration that propels the image outward on her eyebeam. Because the vision rides on will, she must not flag: "if I let go," she thinks, "lessen the intensity of my stare and shut my eyes or even blink my eyes, to rest them, the pictures will fade out" (49). When, however, she drops her head in her hands, exhausted, the process continues, and Bryher, who has until now seen nothing, witnesses the final image. What she sees—H.D.'s Niké elevated into the sun-disk—is so consistent with the preceding figures that H.D. compares it to "that 'determinative' that is used in the actual hieroglyph, the picture that contains the whole series of pictures in itself or helps clarify or explain them" (56). With the power of a poet, H.D. has apparently not only materialized the images of her psyche but cast them into the consciousness of another, who in turn now projects them forward onto the wall.

The images of the vision are described as flowing from or at least through H.D.'s psyche, yet their origin is obscure. What creates these slides or magic transparencies? Where do they come from? The answer given in *Tribute to Freud* is ambiguous. On the one hand, the images seem little different than the clips from memories or dream scenes that H.D. had earlier compared to "transparencies in a dark room, set before lighted candles" (35). In this sense, however extraordinary, they would be "merely an extension of the artist's mind, a *picture* or an illustrated poem, taken out of the actual dream or daydream content and projected from within" (51). On the other hand, in an interpretation H.D. clearly prefers, one sanctioned by the classical belief that the gods speak through dreams and oracles, the images seem "projected from outside" (46), messages from another world, another state of being.[6]

Images as signs and warnings from her own subconscious, images as signs and wonders from another world; the artist as moving-picture machine, the artist as psychic, the artist as message transmitter: what gives this combination of attributes coherence, positions it within H.D.'s development, and makes it pivotal in any interpretation of her work is the concept of projection. All the more apt for its abundant ambiguities, projection is one of H.D.'s leading intuitions. Its operations connect the material, mental, and mystical realms and enact her belief that there is no physical reality that is not also psychic and spiritual. Without the energies of projection, H.D.'s work stalls and thins; with them, her writing has strength and brilliance. It is this excellence that the "projected pictures" at Corfu seem to promise.

The word *projection* appears throughout H.D.'s work. Although its meaning alters subtly and sometimes confusingly, the term always marks a key moment in her creative process. From the verb meaning *to throw forward*, projection is the thrust that bridges two worlds. It is the movement across a borderline: between the mind and the wall, between the brain and the page, between inner and outer, between me and you, between states of being, across dimensions of time and space. The concept of projection informs H.D.'s transitions from imagist to clairvoyant to film theorist, analysand, and prophetic poet. What does it clarify at each stage? How does it change between stages? What light does it throw on the overall strategies and strengths of H.D.'s work? These will be the questions that guide the inquiry of this chapter.

Projection: The Act of Throwing or Shooting Forward

"[C]ut the cackle"! "Go in fear of abstractions"! "Don't be 'viewy'"![7] Most memorable imagist statements are prescriptions against a poetic tradition conceived as rigid, overblown, and unoriginal. Cackle is the chatter of conventional verse. It fills long lines with flourishes that Pound calls "rhetorical bustuous rumpus": platitudes, circumlocutions, and rolling, ornamental din (*Literary Essays* 202). To theorists like Pound and T. E. Hulme, these flourishes are self-generated and self-sustained, cut off from the world they purport to present. In its eagerness to pronounce upon the world and in the vaporous grandeur of its pronouncements, cackle goes in fear neither of abstractions nor of viewiness.

The cure for cackle is contact. Imagist theory privileges sight as fresh, accurate access to the exterior world. Sight is the acid bath that dissolves the sticky sludge of rhetoric. It connects us directly, so the imagists argue, with the things of this world. Bad art, for Hulme, is "words divorced from any real vision," strings of conventional locutions, abstractions, or counters that, like x and y in an algebraic formula, replace six pounds of cashews and four Florida oranges. Formulaic words, like algebraic symbols, can be manipulated according to laws independent of their meaning. Hulme's test of good poetry is whether the words turn back into things that we can see (*Further Speculations* 77–79).

The imagists and their allies echo each other on this point. "Each *word* must be an image *seen,* not a counter," Hulme legislates (*Further Speculations* 79). "Language in a healthy state," T. S. Eliot insists, "presents the object, is so close to the object that the two are identified" (*Selected Essays* 285). For Pound, "the very essence" of a writer's work is "the application of word to thing" (*Literary Essays* 21). It was Pound who found, through the work of Ernest Fenollosa, the ur-pattern of the word-thing: the Chinese ideogram, which was assumed to be direct, visibly concrete, natural rather than conventional, a picture language within which, as Fenollosa put it, "'Thinking is *thinging*'" (qtd. in Chisolm 168).

The image of a thing set into a poem becomes for the imagists the innocent word, the word that somehow escapes the conventional, abstracting, mediating nature of language. The assumption of transparent expression is a correlate of the Bergsonian faith in the artist's direct intuition of the object. Where contemporary theorists hold that we see what we know, imagists insist we know what we see. They find in vision a release from a shared system of signs into spontaneous, intuitive, unmediated apprehension of essences. Whatever her subsequent elaborations—and they are many and strange—this belief in the possibility of essential intuitions, so central to imagism, remains at the core of H.D.'s projective practice.

Projection is the act of throwing or shooting forward. Though the imagists don't use the term, they depend on the concept. In the genesis of the imagist poem, a thing in the world projects its essence onto the poet's consciousness; the poet imprints the image, or record of the thing, in a poem; and the poem, in turn, projects the image onto the reader's consciousness. The model for this, the simplest form of projection, is the magic lantern show. It is Hulme's concrete display of images that "always endeavours to arrest you, and to make you continuously see a physical thing" (*Speculations* 134); it is Pound's *phanopoeia,* the technique by which "[y]ou use a word to throw a visual image on to the reader's imagination" (*ABC* 37).

H.D.'s *Sea Garden* is full of phanopoeia. The reader's visual imagination is bombarded by sand, tree bark, salt tracks, silver dust, wood violets, and thin, stinging twigs—objects in a world of clear, hard-edged, gritty particularity. The images have an almost hallucinatory specificity. The view is tight, close up, almost too bright: on the beach, "hard sand breaks, / and the grains of it / are clear as wine"; in the late afternoon sun, "each leaf / cuts another leaf on the grass"; night, when it comes, curls "the petals / back from the stalk / . . . under till the rinds break, / back till each bent leaf / is parted from its stalk" (41, 17, 35). These moments are doubly projective, for H.D.'s images, forcibly cast onto the reader's imagination, themselves record moments in which one thing, thrown onto another, opens, releases, or transforms it. In *Sea Garden,* objects are perpetually twisted, lifted, flung, split, scattered, slashed, and stripped clear by rushing energies that enact the impact the poet wishes to exert on the reader's imagination.

The rushing energies are the sea, the sun, and the night, but in H.D.'s world these are more than fierce weather: they testify to a sacred power and promise in the universe. Both H.D. and Pound conceived of essence as god-stuff. For

Pound, visionary light—"The light now, not of the sun" (Canto 17/76)—usually heralds the appearance of a god or goddess such as Artemis, Dionysos, Hermes, or Athena. Both in the early *Cantos* and in *Sea Garden,* each charged landscape enshrines a god or demigod. Thus, in *Sea Garden,* dryads haunt the groves, nereids the waves; Priapus transfuses the orchard, Artemis courses the woods; Hermes marks the crossroads, and the mysterious Wind Sleepers roam in search of their altar. The world glows with sacred energy.

This aura, however, like a Derridean sign, usually marks a presence that has vanished or is just now departing. Gods do not manifest directly to mortals— "It was *de rigueur,*" as H.D. puts it, "for an Olympian not to appear to a mortal direct" (*Notes* 38)—but they do, like Apollo at Delphi, leave signs, a kind of afterglow of presence. The speaker in *Sea Garden* is a supplicant in search of deities that are everywhere immanent in the landscape: they beckon, stand tense, then surge away, leaving behind heel prints, snapped stalks, and a charged silence. The poet, like a skilled tracker, moves from sign to sign in rapt, sagacious pursuit.

As embodiments of essence, H.D.'s deities might seem mere metaphors, relics of the kind of claptrap the imagists despised. H.D.'s work, however, is spare, stripped, "objective," as Pound insisted, "—no slither" (*Letters* 11). The gods function not as a poem's ornament but as its absent center. The deities are both cause and condition of this poetry; the poems do not work if the reader doesn't posit the reality of the presence they yearn toward.

The poems in *Sea Garden* are thrown out as bridges to the sacred. They project themselves toward the gods with a plea that the gods will in return appear to the speaker. Poems like "Sea Gods," "Hermes of the Ways," "The Helmsman," and "The Shrine" address the gods directly, compelling them from immanence to manifestation: "For you will come," H.D. presses, "you will come, / you will answer our taut hearts, / . . . and cherish and shelter us" (32). Projection as phanopoeia, a poetic technique, here, in H.D.'s first important modification, broadens into a technique of meditation or prayer: an imaging used to summon a being from another plane.[8]

Projection: A Representation on a Plane Surface of Any
   Part of the Celestial Sphere

Except for three brief reviews in *The Egoist,* H.D. took little part in the barrage of imagist manifestos and treatises. Contrasting strongly with the polemics she later wrote for avant-garde cinema, this silence had several sources. She was a new poet, unused to literary disputation, and, until the arrival of Amy

Lowell, the only woman in a contentious group of men. In addition, she occupied a constricted position in the movement: if, as John T. Gage has argued, Hulme was its principal theorist and Pound its chief publicist (Gage 6), H.D. was from the first the Imagiste extraordinaire, the movement's foregrounded practitioner. Her poems stimulated and exemplified positions held by others.[9]

A third, more significant source of H.D.'s silence, however, may lie in hesitations about imagist doctrine intimated in her *Egoist* review of John Gould Fletcher's *Goblins and Pagodas.* In this review, H.D. makes an obligatory bow to imagist principles but is compelled by something else. "[Fletcher] uses the direct image, it is true," she writes, "but he seems to use it as a means of evoking other and vaguer images—a pebble, as it were, dropped into a quiet pool, in order to start across the silent water, wave on wave of light, of colour, of sound" (183). Fletcher attempts, H.D. specifies, "a more difficult and, when successfully handled, richer form of art: not that of direct presentation, but that of suggestion" (183). As the title's invocation of goblins and pagodas intimates, Fletcher's poems pursue not physical things so much as the exotic enigmas around them.

The next stage of H.D.'s development furthers her own shift from pebbles to their radiating rings: from the objects of this world to phantasms of light, color, and sound; from isolate phantasms to the phantasmagoria of fevers, dreams, and ritual pageants;[10] from the three dimensions perceived by the average person to a fourth dimension available to the enhanced vision of a few. In 1919, after her bonds with Pound, Aldington, and the other imagists had cracked, after her alliance with Bryher had begun and her daughter, Perdita, had been born, H.D. had a series of intense psychic experiences. The visions of 1919 and 1920 undid any remaining traces of imagist empiricism, affirmed a privileged role for the woman poet, and strengthened H.D.'s faith in her own clairvoyant powers. Applied to these experiences, the term *projection* registers not the poet's design on a reader or on the gods but rather the dynamics of clairvoyance. To this end, the term takes on a meaning that comes from geometry and cartography.

In the language of mapping, projection is the representation of a sphere on a flat surface. Like all figuration, projection is a simplification, in this case the reduction of three dimensions to two. Two methods of charting the skies clarify the distinction between the general use of this word and its cartographic meaning. In the first sense, as Robert Duncan observes, we make the night "a projected screen" by casting our mythologies into the heavens and rendering "the sky-dome above . . . the image of another configuration in the skull-dome below" ("Nights and Days" 101–2). This is projection in the sense of throwing one's own imaginary onto a neutral or indifferent surface. In their sky charts, astronomers reverse the direction of projection to bring intersecting coordinate lines of a celestial sphere down into their maps. This entry of another dimension into familiar figurations is the equivalent in H.D.'s work of the process by which material from a celestial or astral plane manifests on an earthly plane. It is this movement between dimensions that haunts and compels H.D.

H.D. experienced what she felt was an inrush of material from other dimensions at least four times in 1919–20, all after surviving her near-fatal illness and childbirth and all in the company of Bryher. The first, in late spring 1919, involved "the transcendental feeling of the two globes or the two transparent half-globes enclosing me" (*Tribute* 168); the second was an apparition she witnessed on the voyage to Greece in 1920; the third and fourth, in the hotel room at Corfu, were the projected pictures and a series of dance scenes conjured up for Bryher. Each of these experiences seemed, as H.D. affirmed, "a god-send" ("Majic" 150): an irradiation of the world of ordinary events and rules by material from another dimension.[11]

The first of these experiences is described in *Notes on Thought and Vision,* a document composed for Havelock Ellis, whom H.D. and Bryher had been consulting and who subsequently accompanied them to Greece. Though rough and sometimes contradictory, these notes describe a matrix of creativity she calls the "jelly-fish" or "over-mind" state (19). As H.D. describes them, there are "[t]hree states or manifestations of life: body, mind, over-mind" (17). Although all three states are necessary and interdependent, it is also possible to think of them as stages. The artist-initiate begins, like a neophyte in the Eleusinian mysteries, with the body's desires and the brain's sensitivities, but her aim is to maximize the over-mind, the receptacle of mystical vision.

Like Ellis, H.D. begins her exposition with sexuality. All humans need physical relationships, she argues, but creative men and women crave them "to develop and draw forth their talents" (17). The erotic personality, suffused with sympathetic, questing, and playful energies, is the artistic personality par excellence, a hypothesis Ellis and H.D. both exemplify by evoking Leonardo da Vinci (Ellis, *Dance of Life* 113; H.D., *Notes* 18). Ellis, however, separates sexuality's primary reproductive function from a secondary spiritual function of "furthering the higher mental and emotional processes" ("Play-Function" 117). H.D. counters this separation with a theory derived partly from the Eleusinian mysteries and partly from her own recent childbirth.

Complementing the "vision of the brain" is a force H.D. calls "vision of the womb or love-vision" (*Notes* 20). The term underscores the artist's receptive/procreative role. In the womb-brain thoughts from another realm are received, nourished, and brought to form, then projected out into the barrenness H.D. calls "the murky, dead, old, thousand-times explored old world . . . of over-worked emotions and thoughts" (24). This model rewrites conventional phallic metaphors for creativity by depicting visionary consciousness as "a foetus in the body" that, after "grinding discomfort," is released in the miracle the mysteries celebrated as Koré's return.[12] "Is it easier for a woman to attain this state of consciousness than for a man?" H.D. asks. Though both sexes possess this capacity, her formulation privileges her own particularly biological experience of generativity (19–20).

Notes on Thought and Vision provides many explications of visionary consciousness, but the most pertinent to H.D.'s developing notion of projection are three ocular models. H.D.'s fascination with optics—a fascination revived in her portrait of Kenneth Macpherson as a man-camera—came from hours spent in childhood watching her father the astronomer and her grandfather the botanist gaze through lenses into a teeming world where before there had been only a blank. Each of her optical models in *Notes on Thought and Vision* postulates two kinds of vision, womb vision and brain vision, and each invents a way to adjust them so as to generate plenitude out of an apparent void.

H.D.'s initial formulation describes the jellyfish state as enclosure in two caps or diving bells of consciousness, one over the forehead and one in the "love-region" (19). Each is a sort of amniotic sac, "like water, transparent, fluid yet with definite body, contained in a definite space . . . like a closed sea-plant, jelly-fish or anemone" (18–19). This sac holds and nurtures the delicate, amorphous life of the over-mind, but it has a further function. Like a diver's mask or aquarium glass, the over-mind makes visible the elusive inhabitants of the watery depths: here, H.D. elaborates, "thoughts pass and are visible like fish swimming under clear water" (19).[13]

The second formulation transforms these caps into dual lenses for a pair of psychic opera glasses. These lenses "properly adjusted, focused . . . bring the world of vision into consciousness. The two work separately, perceive separately, yet make one picture" (23). What they see is the whole world of vision registered by the mystic, the philosopher, and the artist.

In the last and most evocative formulation, these lenses merge into a complexly constituted third eye. "The jelly-fish over my head," H.D. explains, "had become concentrated. . . . That is, all the spiritual energy seemed concentrated in the middle of my forehead, inside my skull, and it was small and giving out a very soft light, but not scattered light, light concentrated in itself as the light of a pearl would be" (51). Like a crystal ball, this eye both receives and emits the force H.D. calls "over-world energy" (47). It draws in, concentrates, then projects outward "pictures from the world of vision" (50). This receptive/transmissive eye is the gift of vision, the pearl of great price.

The jellyfish eye opens the skull-dome. Into, out of, and through this rupture pours the prophetic energy scientific materialism would deny but H.D. believes her visions and visionary poetry affirm. Archetypal memories, dreams, the Corfu pictures all exemplify this projected vision, but a more excessive, startling instance is the sudden apparition of Peter Van Eck at the shiprail of the *Borodino.* For more than twenty years, H.D. struggled to tell the story of Van Eck, her code name for Peter Rodeck, an architect, artist, spiritualist, and her fellow passenger on the voyage to Greece. This story formed the heart of a much rewritten novel entitled *Niké,* finally jettisoned in 1924. The most ample remaining accounts are in the short story "Pontikonisi (Mouse Island)," published under the pseudonym "Rhoda Peter" in 1932; in the analysis notebooks of 1933, published as part of *Tribute to Freud;* and in the still unpublished autobiographical novel "Majic Ring," written in 1943–44.

It was sunset, neither day nor night, and the ocean was suffused with a soft violet-blue glow. The ship was approaching the Pillars of Hercules, between the outer-waters of the Atlantic and the inner-sea of the Mediterranean. "We were crossing something," H.D. explains—a line, a boundary, perhaps a threshold (*Tribute* 156). Alone at the rail of the *Borodino,* she felt she stood "on the deck of a mythical ship as well, a ship that had no existence in the world of ordinary events and laws and rules" ("Majic" 152). The sea was quiet, the boat moved smoothly, and the waves broke "in a thousand perfectly peaked wavelets like the waves in the background of a Botticelli" (*Tribute* 160). When she turned to search for Bryher, she saw a three-dimensional figure at the rail, a man who both was and was not Peter Van Eck. Taller, clearer, brighter than Van Eck, without his disfiguring scar and thick-rimmed glasses, this apparition summoned a band of leaping dolphins and gestured to a chain of hilly islands on the ship's seaward side. At the peak of the moment, H.D. reports, "his eyes, it seemed now, were my eyes. I was seeing his vision, what he (though I did not of course, realize it) was himself projecting. This was the promised land, the islands of the blest, the islands of Atlantis or of the Hesperides" ("Majic" 163).[14]

Was this a hallucination, a holographic illusion, an epiphany? Was it, as Freud would later frame the question, a symptom or a sign (*Tribute* 46)? If the former, what would be the diagnosis? If the latter, who was the being who directed or perhaps impersonated Peter Van Eck? In a strategy she would use again in *Helen in Egypt,* H.D. gives no consistent answer to her questions, a move that declines Freud's either/or gambit for the more capacious strategy DuPlessis identifies as H.D.'s both/and/*and* (*H.D.* 113). The writing on the wall may have been, H.D. tells us in *Tribute to Freud,* "a desire for union with my mother" (44), but her investment in such an explanation is perfunctory. What compels her is the mystery of the figure that appeared in the guise of Peter Van Eck: "Majic Ring" suggests he was "Anax Apollo, Helios, Lord of Magic and Prophecy and Music" (156); the letters to Silvia Dobson imply he was an astral double ("Friendship" 118); the story "Pontikonisi (Mouse Island)" compares him to Christ at Emmaus (7).

Whatever he was, all H.D.'s accounts position Van Eck as a projection from another dimension into this one, a phenomenon for which "Pontikonisi" gives the most extensive—and mechanical—explication. If every being is composed of two substances, "platinum sheet-metal over jelly-fish" or body over soul, Van Eck's appearance was a "galvanized projection": soul-stuff shocked into form, transmitted through the third-eye opening in his skull, perceived through the opening in hers. "The inside could get out that way," the story tells us, "only when the top was broken. It was the transcendentalist inside that had met [Van Eck] in the storm on deck, when [Peter Van Eck] was downstairs in the smoking room" ("Pontikonisi" 7, 8).

The terminology is awkward, the physics creak, but the experience haunted H.D. all her life. Van Eck's three-dimensionality was a kind of psychic phanopoeia—not at all what Pound meant but very much H.D.'s technique in her later poetry. The angels and messengers of *Trilogy,* the souls thronging through *Helen in Egypt,* the angelic forces of *Hermetic Definition* all are figures entering the imagination from another dimension and carrying with them the aura by which H.D. gratefully remapped a "dead, old, thousand-times explored old world."

Projection: The Display of Motion Pictures by Casting an Image on a Screen

When H.D. once again broached the Corfu material in the 1940s, she reported that "the story, in its new form, began unwinding itself, like a roll of film that had been neatly stored in my brain, waiting for a propitious moment to be re-set in the projector and cast on a screen" ("Majic" 127). This new twist to the term *projection* emerged from hands-on experience. With the help of a motor-driven, handle-fitted projector like the Agence Debrie Jacky, H.D. had taken an exhilarating step into cinematic technology.

In spring 1929, when asked by *The Little Review* what she most liked to do, H.D. had no trouble answering. "I myself have learned to use the small projector," she replied, "and spend literally hours alone here in my appartment [*sic*], making the mountains and village streets and my own acquaintances reel past me in light and light and light" ("Response" 38). Along with cameras, lights, and editing equipment, the projector belonged to POOL Productions. Between 1927 and 1930, H.D. acted in three of POOL's four films, did montage for one and publicity for two, and filled her contemporary poetry and fiction with images of light, focus, superimposition, and projection.[15]

Most of H.D.'s film theory is contained in a three-part series of essays composed for the initial issues of *Close Up* and titled "The Cinema and the Classics." By "classics" H.D. meant Greek culture and, more narrowly, the Greek amalgamation of the beautiful and the good ("Cinema and the Classics I" 107). Despite Hollywood's fixation on "longdrawn out embraces and the artificially enhanced thud-offs of galloping bronchoes" (105) and despite "our American Cyclops," the Hollywood censor, who prettifies beauty and has no apprehension of the good (107), cinema, H.D. argues, offers our best opportunity to recapture Greek wisdom. In the hands of the avant-garde, film repossesses the visionary consciousness of Athens, Delphi, and Eleusis. Here, at last, "Miracles and godhead are *not* out of place, are not awkward"; it is "[a] perfect medium . . . at last . . . granted us" ("Cinema and the Classics II" 112).

The word *medium* resonates through H.D.'s meditations on projection. Film is an artistic medium, one occupying a medial position between the filmmaker and the spectator, but for H.D. it also functions as a psychic medium externalizing and making perceptible inner intentions and coherencies. The announcement for *Wing Beat* promises "[t]elepathy and attraction, the reaching out, the very edge of dimensions in dimensions" (18). By reading and revealing the far reaches "[o]f minds and spirits" (18), avant-garde cinema serves the Delphic dictate "Know thyself" ("Cinema and the Classics III" 118), but it is also a way to know the gods: here, "Hermes, indicated in faint light, may step forward, outlined in semi-obscurity, or simply dazzling the whole picture in a blaze of splendour. Helios may stand simply and restrained with uplifted arm" ("Cinema and the Classics II" 112).

Because film calls together in a dark room witnesses of charged hieratic images, images that make manifest what was mysterious, because it brings light to darkness and conveys the will of beauty and goodness, cinema is to H.D.'s generation what the church was to H.D.'s ancestors and Eleusinian and Delphic rituals were to the Greeks. The long two-part poem H.D. entitled "Projector" and published alongside her essays in *Close Up* names the Delphian Apollo the god of cinema and envisions him reasserting his domain on a ray of image-bearing, world-creating light:

This is his gift;
light,
light
a wave
that sweeps
us
from old fears
and powers. (*Collected Poems* 354)

Just as Apollo claimed the power of prophecy at Delphi by slaying the monster Python, this projector-god destroys squalid commercialism and substitutes for Hollywood a "holy wood" where "souls upon the screen / live lives that might have been, / live lives that ever are" (358).

H.D.'s ecstatic poem greets Apollo as he begins his miracles. The poem's clipped, incantatory lines and detailed invocation of the Delphic paradigm, however, suggest something more than simple salutation. H.D.'s advocacy asserts a place and function for herself. Apollo at Delphi worked through his oracle, the Pythoness, who served as a medium between the god and the seeker. She has what *Notes on Thought and Vision* calls "womb vision," for it is she who receives, brings to form, and throws forth his knowledge. As the transmitter of the prophetic message, her position precedes and predicts H.D.'s. Who, then, is the poem's "Projector"? It is Apollo, light-bearer; it is his Delphic oracle; it is H.D. herself, the projector-poet; and it is also the machine in her apartment that rested, like the Pythoness herself, upon a tripod—symbol of prophecy, prophetic utterance, occult or hidden knowledge.

Projection: A Defense Mechanism in Which the Individual
   Attributes a Wish or Impulse of His or Her Own to
   Some Other Person or Object in the Outside World

Close Up contained reviews of German and Russian cinema, theoretical essays by the filmmakers Sergei Eisenstein and G. W. Pabst, vituperations against mainstream American and British film, accounts of avant-garde screenings, thoughts on "the Negro" and cinema, advice on the newest cameras and projectors, and editorials urging amateurs to seize the means of production, make "scraps of film that every commercial producer would refuse and project them on kitchen walls before small groups determined to tear them to pieces" (Bryher, "Hollywood" 281).

Throughout this range of positions and interests, the journal remained consistently and "substantially informed by psychoanalytic thought and theory" (Marcus 240). Macpherson bolsters his editorial pronouncements with psychoanalytic concepts; Bryher positions avant-garde film as a form of therapy capable of "freeing individuals and cultures from their stultifying histories and readying them for modernity" (Marcus 240); Dr. Hanns Sachs, Bryher's analyst and a member of Freud's inner circle, and the lay analysts Barbara Low and Mary Chadwick contribute essays; and many reviewers and commentators lace their arguments with Freudian terms and concepts. Psychoanalysis is also at the heart of POOL's most ambitious project, the feature-length film *Borderline,* directed by Macpherson, cut by Macpherson with the assistance of H.D. and Bryher,[16] featuring Robert Herring and Bryher and starring Paul Robeson and H.D. herself, thinly disguised in the film's credits as Helga Doorn. Completed in June 1930, the film takes a diagnostic concept as its title and builds its story on H.D.'s character, Astrid. A "white-cerebral [who] is and is not outcast, is and is not a social alien, is and is not a normal human being," H.D. comments, "[Astrid] is borderline" ("Borderline" 221). The film and the accompanying pamphlet provide a glimpse into the development of H.D.'s ideas about projection some three years prior to her analysis with Freud.

In an editorial from November 1930, Macpherson explains that he intends "to take [his] film into the minds of the people in it, making it not so much a film of 'mental processes' as to insist on a mental condition" ("As Is" 236). The plot is a tangle of desire, bigotry, and death. Astrid and her alcoholic husband Thorne come to a mountainous border town where Thorne engages in an affair with Adah, the mulatto wife of Pete, a black man played by Paul Robeson. When Astrid is stabbed to death by Thorne, the town persecutes Pete and Adah.[17] The frayed atmosphere is exacerbated by the movie's silence, by the camera's raking of symbolic landscapes and faces gouged with light, and, finally, by Astrid's staring into the camera—as if she were emptying her mind out onto the screen, or, even more uncomfortably, as if she were attempting a direct projection of her psychic content into the mind of the viewer.[18]

H.D.'s unsigned, thirty-nine page publicity pamphlet reminds us that the film's star, "Astrid, the woman, terribly incarnated . . . [is] 'astral' in [her] effect" ("Borderline" 236). The border between the earthly and the cosmic—the terrain of H.D.'s Van Eck vision and Corfu experiences—is only one of the film's many margins: geographical, social, political, racial, sexual, mental, and even professional, since Macpherson and his company were uncredentialed and the film was most definitely projected for "small groups determined to tear [it] to pieces." The film's terrain is the limbo that H.D.'s projection—imagist, clairvoyant, cinematic, or prophetic—always traversed.

If the stark, otherworldly sequences that punctuate *Borderline* have a hieroglyphic portentousness, it is because they in fact originated in Macpherson's picture-writing. Each of his 910 pen-and-ink sketches giving directions for the camera shots was a light sculpture, a dream scene, a hieroglyph designed for projection: "he is only satisfied," H.D. comments, "when abstraction coupled with related abstraction makes logical dramatic sequence" ("Borderline" 223). A telephone receiver, an in-blown curtain, a stuffed sea gull, a "woman-face": each image takes its place in "swift flashes of inevitable sequence" (223); each "weld[s] . . . the psychic or super-normal to the things of precise every-day existence" (235).[19] For H.D. this montage scripting places *Borderline* in the same psychic category as the Corfu pictures and the charged dreams that fill her accounts of analysis: "For myself," she writes in *Tribute to Freud*, "I consider this sort of dream or projected picture or vision as a sort of halfway state between ordinary dream and the vision of those who, for lack of a more definite term, we must call psychics or clairvoyants" (41).

"Borderline" is, of course, a psychoanalytic term designating a state between neurosis and psychosis. H.D. would know the term from Bryher, who in the late 1920s was both studying and undergoing analysis, from lectures she and Bryher attended in Berlin during these years, from the general theoretic climate of *Close Up*, and, finally, from Macpherson's intent in titling his film.[20] What is most interesting, however, is not H.D.'s attraction to the idea but her swerve away from it: while playing on all the term's other nuances, the pamphlet shuns its psychoanalytic denotation, resituating the borderline so that it lies not between the neurotic and the psychotic but between the neurotic and the psychic.

"*Borderline* is a dream," the pamphlet pronounces, entering its final summation, "and perhaps when we say that we have said everything. The film is the art of dream portrayal and perhaps when we say that we have achieved the definition, the synthesis toward which we have been striving" (232). For H.D., dream was always interior projection, a cinematic exhibition of the mind's submerged content. Like *Borderline* and the Corfu pictures, dreams display "the *hieroglyph of the unconscious*" (*Tribute* 93). It is for "open[ing] the field to the study of this vast, unexplored region" (93) that H.D. would be forever grateful to Freud.

Accounts of dreams are, as it were, projections of projections, and H.D. was justly proud of her command of this intricate transmutation. It was not simple. "The dream-picture focussed and projected by the mind, may perhaps achieve something of the character of a magic lantern slide and may 'come true' in the projection," H.D. explains in *The Gift* (*Complete* 83), but to make it do so demands all the strategies developed by Freud: free association, command of the parallels between individual, biological, and racial development, and mastery of concepts like condensation, displacement, dramatization by visual imagery, superimposition, distortion, and screen memory. An admonitory passage from *The Gift* conveys H.D.'s delight in her descriptive skill:

> The dream, the memory, the unexpected related memories must be allowed to sway backward and forward, as if the sheet or screen upon which they are projected, blows and is rippled in the wind or whatever emotion or idea is entering a door, left open. The wind blows through the door, from outside, through long, long corridors of personal memory, of biological and of race-memory. Shut the door and you have a neat flat picture. Leave all the doors open and you are almost out-of-doors, almost within the un-walled province of the fourth-dimensional. This is creation in the truer sense, in the *wind bloweth where it listeth* way. (84)[21]

Her delight was matched—perhaps even sparked—by Freud's delight in the haunting dreams of her two periods of analysis in 1933 and 1934. "[Freud] has embarrassed me," H.D. writes Bryher in April 1933, "by telling me I have a rare type of mind he seldom meets with, in which thought crystalizes out in dream in a very special way." In their sessions they pour over dream after enigmatic dream, Freud complimenting her on their "very 'beautiful' construction," their invention of symbols, their "almost perfect mythological state."[22] The fact that so much of H.D.'s postanalysis writing places her before a luminous dream that she both creates and analyzes, participates in and observes, brings the exhilaration of her experience with cinema forward into her experience with psychoanalysis.[23]

In their interpretations of her dreams, H.D. and Freud seem to be colleagues who heed, adjust, and validate each other's interpretations, but much of the analysis material indicates another kind of relationship. As she recounts their interaction in *Tribute to Freud*, H.D. is a small, confused seeker, and Freud is the old Hermit on the edge of "the great forest of the unknown" (13), Asklepios the blameless healer (50), "Hercules struggling with Death" (74), Jeremiah discovering the "well of living water" (83), St. Michael who will slay the Dragon of her fears (109), "the infinitely old symbol, weighing the soul, Psyche, in the Balance" (97), even "the Supreme Being" (16). These formulations, as Freud teaches, call on another sort of "projection": transference, or the process by which the patient directs toward the healer an intensity of feeling that is based on no real relation between them and can only be traced back to old fantasies rendered unconscious.

H.D. took the first step in analysis, the establishment of transference, easily, if somewhat ambiguously. To H.D., Freud became papa, the Professor, his study, like Professor Doolittle's, cluttered with erudite writings and "old, old sacred objects" (*Tribute* 25); to Freud, however, transference made him the gentle, intuitive mother. Both were right, for as Friedman points out, "in an ultimate sense, he became both mother and father to her as he fused her mother's art and her father's science in the mysteries of psychoanalysis" (*Psyche* 153). Her transference love for Freud enabled H.D. to affirm herself as poet and visionary, release her blocked creativity, and write with passion and continuity throughout the rest of her life.

There was another, murkier transference in the analysis, however, one subject not to resolution but to repetition. This rendered every figure in her life a stand-in for someone else, every love a deflection, every trauma a replay of earlier disaster. The records of analysis swarm with formulas as Freud and H.D. search for originary patterns beneath a palimpsest of repetition. Ellis as father, Freud as mother; Aldington as father, Bryher as mother; Rodeck as father, Bryher as mother; her "ideal" brothers Rodeck, Frances Gregg, and Bryher; her "real" brothers Pound, Aldington, and Macpherson—the list goes on and on.[24] A fevered letter to Bryher in March 1933 indicates both the exuberance and the suspicion of futility beneath all this activity:

> My triangle is mother-brother-self. That is, early phallic-mother, baby brother or smaller brother and self. I have worked in and around that, I have HAD the baby with my mother, and been the phallic-baby, hence Moses in the bulrushes, I have HAD the baby with the brother, hence Cuthbert [Aldington], Cecil Grey, Kenneth etc. I have HAD the "illumination" or the back to the womb WITH the brother, hence you and me in Corfu, island = mother. . . . Well, well, well, I could go on and on and on, demonstrating but once you get the first idea, all the other, later diverse-looking manifestations fit in somehow. Savvy?????? It's all too queer and at first, I felt life had been wasted in all this repetition etc. but somehow F. seems to find it amusing, sometimes. (H.D. to Bryher, 23 March 1933 [p. 2])

Until the end of her life, H.D. deluged near strangers with intensities of feeling belonging not to them but to their forerunners or even to the forerunners of their forerunners. In this dynamic, transference was a condition not of cure but of compulsion.[25]

Dreams and transference are projective in a general sense, but psychoanalytic theory, of course, defines the term *projection* more precisely as a defense mechanism that causes an individual to attribute an interior wish to a person or object in the exterior world. This charged term formed an exemplary site for the disagreement between Freud and H.D. about the nature of reality. Here H.D. took Freud on, if not directly, nonetheless deftly.

The word *projection* occurs frequently in *Tribute to Freud*, but, like the word "borderline" in the movie pamphlet, not once with its Freudian denotation. The "projected picture" (41), images "projected outward" from the subconscious mind (46), the strain of projection (49), the impact that "projected" a dream sequence (72): in each appearance, the term points to the Corfu vision. Of all the events that could have titled H.D.'s original account of analysis, her choice, "Writing on the Wall," privileges and gives biblical sanction to the vision at Corfu. The phrase draws our attention from the analytic to the mystical and prepares our confrontation with the main question raised by the Corfu pictures. Were they, as Freud maintained, a "dangerous . . . symptom" (41), or were they rather an upwelling of creativity, an inspiration, and a promise?

In Freud's use of the term, the "projected pictures" reduce to defensive exteriorizations of unconscious material. In this sense they would be desperate strategies of containment. By H.D.'s definition, however, the projected pictures are precisely the opposite: they open the boundaries of the self to another, higher reality, not in order to deny its operations but to claim and be claimed by them. The pictures predict—or project into the future—not a repetition of palimpsestic transferences but a transcendence, a breakthrough into a new dimension. In her final image, the angel Niké moving through a field of tents, H.D. recognizes the aftermath of the next world war: "When that war had completed itself," she writes, "rung by rung or year by year, I, personally (I felt), would be free, I myself would go on in another, a winged dimension" (*Tribute* 56). This vision of 1920, recalled and reaffirmed through analysis with Freud, predicts the transmutations wrought two decades later in the poem H.D. would call her "War Trilogy."

Projection: The Casting of Some Ingredient into a Crucible;
   Especially in Alchemy, the Casting of the Powder of the
   Philosopher's Stone (*Powder of Projection*) upon a
   Metal in Fusion to Effect Its Transmutation into Gold or Silver

H.D.'s "H.D. by Delia Alton," composed in 1949 for Norman Holmes Pearson, stresses *Trilogy*'s origins in the fires of World War II. Throughout the Nazi air assault, H.D. remained in her apartment in London, close to the Hyde Park anti-aircraft batteries and in the thick of incendiary raids. Bombs—buzz bombs, fly bombs, oil bombs, doodle-bugs, and low, close V-1 rockets—in often nightly bombardments tore open apartments, leveled buildings, lodged unexploded shells in areaways and under pavements, and threw survivors into new dimensions of panic and powerlessness.[26] "The actual fire has raged round the crystal," H.D. reported. "The crystalline poetry to be projected, must of necessity, have that fire in it. You will find fire in *The Walls Do Not Fall, Tribute to the Angels* and *The Flowering of the Rod*. . . . *Trilogy*, as we called the three volumes of poetry written during War II [*sic*], seemed to project itself in time and out-of-time together. And with no effort" ("H.D. by Delia Alton" 186).

After a decade of blockage, H.D. was writing with assurance and speed, her typewriter clacking across the noise of the raids. In the last eight months of 1944 alone, she composed three of her most powerful works: from 17 to 31 May, "Tribute to the Angels"; from 19 September to 2 November, "Writing on the Wall"; from 18 to 31 December, "The Flowering of the Rod." The Freud memoir slid easily between the last two parts of *Trilogy*, for *Trilogy* performs, in its way, a kind of analysis. If, as Robert Duncan suggests, "[i]n Freudian terms, the War is a manifestation of the latent content of the civilization and its discontents, a projection of the collective unconscious" ("From the *H.D. Book*" 41), *Trilogy* works to surface the terrors and redirect them to constructive ends.

As in analysis, dream is the agent of transmutation. *Trilogy*, however, builds on a disagreement with Freud about the source and value of dreams: in "Writing on the Wall" H.D. distinguishes between "trivial, confused dreams and . . . real dreams. The trivial dream bears the same relationship to the real as a column of gutter-press news-print to a folio page of a play of Shakespeare" (*Tribute* 35–36). Trivial dreams emerge from repressed desires, revelatory dreams from "the same source as the script or Scripture, the Holy Writ or Word" (36). Real dreams project material through the dreamer, casting it from one dimension into another. "Now it appears very clear," H.D. writes, "that the Holy Ghost, // childhood's mysterious enigma, / is the Dream":

> it merges the distant future
> with most distant antiquity,
>
> states economically
> in a simple dream-equation
>
> the most profound philosophy,
> discloses the alchemist's secret
>
> and follows the Mage
> in the desert. (*Trilogy* 29)

Each of the three parts of *Trilogy* generates a "real" dream, a vision that prompts the recovery of "the alchemist's secret," the process through which destruction precedes and permits new, more perfect life.

In war's reverse alchemy, as we have seen, rails are melted down and made into guns, books are pulped for cartridge cases, the Word is absorbed in the Sword, and people turn into "wolves, jackals, / mongrel curs" (3, 16, 17, 47). Casting back to "most distant antiquity" in order to project "the distant future," H.D. turns to the formulas of alchemy. Although Western culture cartoons alchemists as greedy bunglers who struggle to turn lead into gold, alchemists can also be understood as students of physical and spiritual transformation. Alchemy provides H.D. with yet another precise and complex turn on the trope of *projection.*

Until modern chemistry's quantitative postulates replaced alchemy's qualitative theory, scholars of physical transformation agreed on four basic principles.[27] At its base, for alchemists, the universe was everywhere alive, all matter possessing body, passion, and soul. Substances appear, grow, decay, diminish, and disappear, making transmutation the essence of life. All transmutation moves toward perfection: the seed becomes a tree, the worm turns into a butterfly, grains of sand round into pearls. And, finally, in this process, the seed splits, the worm bursts, and the sand dissolves, thereby demonstrating the fourth axiom: that all creation requires an initial act of destruction.

Projection is the technical term for the final stage in an alchemical transmutation: the precipitation of a new, more perfect form. The three parts of *Trilogy* move toward this moment as it is scripted in alchemical theory. Like Aristotle, alchemists believed that each substance consists of indeterminate prime matter and a specific form that has been impressed into it like a hot seal into wax. To change a substance, it was necessary to alter its form. In a process alchemists called "death" or "putrefaction," therefore, ingredients were cast into a crucible, heated, and reduced to prime matter; then, after many intricate maneuvers—calcination, distillation, sublimation, fermentation, separation, and more—the specific form of a finer substance was "projected" into the crucible, and a new shape sprang forth. However audacious or even preposterous such procedures now appear, to the alchemists they merely accelerated a process at work in nature and spirit alike.

The magical act—or the act of the Mage—was the making of the seed of perfection called the philosopher's stone or elixir of life. Formulas were inherited, debated, obfuscated, adulterated, encoded, translated, and mistranslated into and out of a dozen different languages, but the basic schema remained the same. To effect what was called "the alchemical marriage," sulphur, the male element, and mercury, the female element, were fused in the crucible and their union generated "the Royal Child," which redeemed all life to its highest form. H.D.'s spiritual challenge in *Trilogy* is no less than the reawakening of this generative power: "the alchemist's key, / . . . the elixir of life, the philosopher's stone / is yours if you surrender // sterile logic, trivial reason" (40).

Nearly every image in *Trilogy* enacts a transmutation designed to convince us of the validity of a process active across scales from the poem's smallest event to its largest. Each of these images is a cell that embodies the code of the whole. The alchemical transformation of lead to gold, for example, is embedded in a passing reference to "corn . . . enclosed in black-lead, / ploughed land." Washed by earth's waters, heated by sun's fire, and strewn with seed, black-lead land precipitates golden corn (56). "This is no rune nor riddle," H.D. reiterates; "it is happening everywhere" (84). Under pressure, through destruction, metamorphosis occurs: the mollusc shell, the eggshell, the cocoon, and the heart-shell are all crucibles for alchemical transformations (8, 9, 12, 35). Even the brain in its skull-case ferments and distills, dissolving sterile logic, generating new vision.

These images prepare our understanding of the poem's larger sweep. With traditionally cryptic encoding, the sections together retell the story of the making of the philosopher's stone. Each contains a crucible, a purifying fire, and a double movement of destruction and creation; each moves backward through time and inward across logic and custom, closer to the culminating moment of projection.

In "The Walls Do Not Fall," part 1 of *Trilogy*, the crucible is the city of London, flattened by ceaseless pounding, filled with the shards of civilization, flaming with "Apocryphal fire" (4). In its ruin, London becomes a matrix for a dream-vision in which "Ra, Osiris, *Amen*" appears to the poet:

> he is the world-father,
> father of past aeons,
>
> present and future equally;
> beardless, not at all like Jehovah. (25)

The luminous amber eyes of this slender figure shine like transforming fire. With his entry into the poem, H.D. has half the alchemical formula, traditionally represented as the sun, fire, sulphur, the fathering principle.

In "Tribute to the Angels," part 2 of *Trilogy*, the crucible becomes the poem-bowl and the shards the word fragments that survive as traces of the traditions of female divinity.[28] After proper invocations, the poet-alchemist begins a second transformative process:

Now polish the crucible
and in the bowl distill

a word most bitter, *marah,*
a word bitterer still, *mar,*

sea, brine, breaker, seducer,
giver of life, giver of tears;

Now polish the crucible
and set the jet of flame

under, till *marah-mar*
are melted, fuse and join

and change and alter,
mer, mere, mère, mater, Maia, Mary,

Star of the Sea,
Mother. (71)

This alchemical transaction creates a pulsing, green-white, opalescent jewel that gives off "a vibration that we can not name" (76). After distilling, purifying, and refining this force and meditating on "the moon-cycle . . . the moonshell" (92), the poet has a second dream-vision: an epiphany of the Lady, once Isis, Astarte, Aset, Aphrodite, the old Eve, the Virgin Mary, "Our Lady of the Goldfinch, / Our Lady of the Candelabra" (93), now without the bridegroom, without the child. She is not hieratic, H.D. explains, she is "no symbolic figure" (104), and the book she carries "is not / the tome of the ancient wisdom" but "the unwritten volume of the new" (103). This as yet unnamed essence is the renewed stuff of the other half of the alchemical formula, traditionally represented as the moon, mercury, the mothering principle.

In "The Flowering of the Rod," part 3 of *Trilogy,* the crucible is not a place or a poem but the legend of resurrection: "a tale of a Fisherman, / a tale of a jar or jars," an ancient story that in its Christian form is "the same—different—the same attributes, / different yet the same as before" (105). What the poet-alchemist breaks down here is the familiar reading of the scriptures that dismisses Kaspar as a dark heathen and Mary Magdalene as a devil-ridden harlot. In H.D.'s rewriting, Kaspar and Mary are not marginal but central. The first two parts of *Trilogy* had precipitated a new male and female principle; now, in part 3, they meet to effect the transformation. Kaspar is a forgetful and fallible philosopher, dream-interpreter, astrologer, and alchemist from a line of Arabs who knew "the secret of the sacred processes of distillation" (133). He carries a sealed jar of myrrh exuding a fragrance that is the essence "of all flowering things together" (172): the elixir of life, the seed of resurrection.

Kaspar was traveling to "a coronation and a funeral," like all alchemical transmutations "a double affair" (130), when found by Mary Magdalene, avatar of H.D.'s "mer, mere, mère, mater, Maia, Mary, // Star of the Sea, / Mother." When he momentarily abandons his patriarchal stiffness, assumes a posture of reverence, and stoops to pick up Mary's scarf, he has a vision that reaches back to "the islands of the Blest" and "the lost centre-island, Atlantis" (153) and forward to "the whole scope and plan // of our and his civilization on this, / his and our earth" (154). The spell he hears recovers a lost matriarchal genealogy, identifies Mary as heritor of "*Lilith born before Eve / and one born before Lilith, / and Eve*" (157), and convinces Kaspar to give Mary the jar of myrrh. This act—in H.D.'s rewriting—seeds the resurrection.[29] When she washes the feet of Christ, Mary Magdalene anoints him with the elixir of life, which insures that death will be followed by regeneration.

Mary Magdalene's washing of the feet of Christ is the act of the alchemist: the projecting of an elixir onto a substance prepared for transmutation. Behind the story of Kaspar and Mary is the tale of sulphur and mercury; ahead of it is the work of the poet-alchemist who wanted to transmute a damaged civilization. The ultimate, audacious hope of *Trilogy* is that it might itself carry and transmit a formula for regeneration.

The mechanical philosophy that superseded alchemy posited a world of matter without passion or soul. This world of objects is often experienced as a place of subjection, dejection, abjection, rejection—a place of energy thrown down, twisted, repressed, and subverted. The universe promised by the mana-word *projection* is, by contrast, kinetic and transformative. As the glow of radium with its puzzle of energy resident in matter led Marie Curie through her discoveries, this mana-word served as an instrument of verbal organization, a source of intellectual and spiritual inspiration, and an engine of generativity for H.D.'s developing inquiries.

PROJECTIVE   VERSE
           (PROJECTILE (PERCUSSIVE (PROSPECTIVE
                                   vs.
                       THE NON-PROJECTIVE
                                                          Charles Olson[30]

In his introduction to Charles Olson's *Collected Prose,* Robert Creeley laments the loss of Olson's "ranging, particularizing, intensely conjecturing mind" (xvi). Like H.D. and Pound, Olson was determined to put his knowledge to "*essential* use" ("Projective" 239). Although H.D. differs significantly from Olson in her commitments, she too understands poems to be projectile, percussive, and prospective. As we have seen, for H.D. words are cartridges, cartouches, cocoons, "high energy-construct[s]" designed to transfer "energy," as Olson put it, "from where the poet got it . . . by way of the poem itself to, all the way over to, the reader" (240). The half-parentheses that score Olson's title enact an idea active in imagist poetics forty years earlier: to do their work, poems must be open on their forward side. They must be transmissions.

What is the nature of H.D.'s projections or, to borrow Olson's ocular variant, her "prospective[s]"? Although it is easier to talk about projection as a variant of Freudian and Eisensteinian theory than as a variant of alchemical or prophetic paradigms, H.D.'s notions, like Olson's, are theoretical and mythological, historical and visionary, and she puts equal pressure on both dimensions of this mana-word. The poet's responsibility is to project material not available to ordinary apprehension: this, for her, is an *essential* use of art. "Absolute realism," for H.D. as for Eisenstein, is the domain of Hollywood: like her colleagues at *Close Up,* she is in pursuit of an art that is more strange and daring, awkward, assaultive, and ardent.[31]

Eisenstein's montage was an aesthetic technique designed to generate in its audience the mental and political conditions preliminary to a Russian Socialist Revolution. Although less attentive than Eisenstein to forms of state structure, Bryher, Macpherson, and H.D. despised the market economy that ruled Hollywood and labored to build an alternative amateur production and distribution network through their collective endeavors in POOL Productions. Of the three founders of POOL, Bryher was closest to Eisenstein in her determination to make cinema an instrument of education rather than indoctrination: "Eisenstein has probably one of the most complex minds in the world today," she writes, praising the "many sequences of his films . . . [which] require the spectator to think and not merely see" ("Hollywood" 281). Macpherson concludes his first editorial for *Close Up* with a commitment he never abandoned to "the film for the film's sake" ("As Is" [1927], 40). In the poems, essays, and reviews H.D. contributed to *Close Up,* she consistently aligns cinematic projection with a stance toward reality this mana-word also held for her in its imagist, clairvoyant, psychoanalytic, and alchemical implications. Like Olson, for whom "the projective act, which is the artist's act in the larger field of objects, leads to dimensions larger than the man" (247), H.D. desired to reach beyond the artist's ego, art for art's sake, or art on the market.

As a mana-word, *projection* lays out an aesthetics, a psychology, and, for H.D.

at least, a metaphysics, but, as we have seen in H.D.'s brief but energetic commitment to POOL Productions and in her antifascist pronouncements, her ideas about generativity can also take on a social and political edge. These commitments are suggested in the patterns that collect around the next mana-word, the word *gift*, which sets the artist's transmissive and prospective responsibilities within a vision of exchange and an ethics of connection.

Notes

1. A selection of essays, articles, editorials, illustrations, and advertisements from *Close Up*, edited by James Donald, Anne Friedberg, and Laura Marcus, gives an excellent sense of the ferment, idealism, and cross-genre experimentation conducted by modernist writers, filmmakers, and theorists between 1927 and 1933.

2. For stills from *Wing Beat*, see Donald, Friedberg, and Marcus 16–17. For a listing of work by Bryher, H.D., and Macpherson with "pool" in the title, see 324n.26.

3. As H.D. explains in her pamphlet on POOL's full-length feature film, *Borderline*, Macpherson used "metronome-cutting" in his work. "[*Borderline*] relates to set measures and beat," H.D. explains; "it moves rhythmically or unrhythmically to certain measures, one-two-three or one-two-three-four or one-one or two-two etc. etc." ("Borderline" 228).

4. For examples of this material, see Donald, Friedberg, and Marcus part 7, "Cinema Culture."

5. Examples of avant-garde fascination with hybrid human-machine blends in the 1920s include Hannah Höch's photomontages; George Antheil's *Ballet mécanique*, composed in 1924 for a percussion orchestra, two pianists, sixteen synchronized player pianos, seven electric doorbells, three airplane propellers, and an assortment of sirens; Fernand Léger's twelve-minute film entitled *Ballet mécanique*, also from 1924, which includes shots of swinging chrome balls, gears, dancing bottles, and rotating disks awaiting a female form trudging endlessly up and down the stairs; and Dziga Vertov's film *Man with a Movie Camera*, shot in 1929, with sequences fusing the two nouns of its title into a hybrid man-camera.

6. In this sense, H.D.'s vision at Corfu is a variant of a practice the poet Jack Spicer describes as dictation from outside. "The poet is a radio," Spicer declares, turning to acoustical technology to make his point (*Collected Books* 218). "[I]nstead of the poet being a beautiful machine which manufactured the current for itself, did everything for itself . . . until the poet's heart broke or it was burned on the beach like Shelley's," he explains, "instead there was something from the Outside coming in" ("Vancouver Lecture 1" 5). For more on this process, see Robin Blaser's essay on Spicer's poetics, "The Practice of Outside."

7. Herbert Read qtd. in Baker 118; Pound, *Literary Essays* 5, 6.

8. Another way to think of these poems is as performative speech acts, utterances that instantiate a relationship between addresser and addressee. In saying to the gods

"you *will* come" (my italics), H.D. in effect enacts her conviction that there are presences capable of answering. In this way, her poems place the speaker in a series of specific discourse situations that perform a reality the poems declare to be the case.

9. For an argument that identifies H.D. as the catalyst for imagist poetics, see Pondrom.

10. In his discussion of the modernist fascination with phantasmagoric phenomena, Michael Davidson cites Terry Castle's work on the history of nineteenth-century phantasmagoric exhibitions and "the gradual 'absorption of ghosts into the world of thought,' [as] a rationalization of unreal elements in modern life by regarding them as projections of the mind" (2).

11. "Majic Ring" and all previously unpublished material by H.D. is copyright © 2003 by the the the Schaffner Family Trust. Used by permission of New Directions Publishing Corporation.

12. See Gilbert and Gubar, *Madwoman in the Attic* 3–44, for an account of the phallic metaphors for creativity that H.D.'s "womb vision" radically revises. As Eileen Gregory points out, the dynamic of projection also plays a part in the anthropologist Jane Harrison's understanding of the Eleusinian mysteries: as "'the god of the ecstasy of the worshipper,'" Harrison writes, "'[Dionysos] *is* the ecstasy projected'" (qtd. in Gregory, *H.D. and Hellenism* 119). In this sense, projection is a reciprocal movement in which the worshippers are possessed by the god as they, in turn, enter into him.

13. This passage may be the origin of the code Bryher and H.D. use in their correspondence to talk about psychic manifestations (fish matters), psychic foresight (fish-eye), psychic mobility (fish-tail), the guide to the psychic realms (the always-capitalized Fish), and even the psychic era to come (the Fish-age, Pisces). See correspondence of Bryher and H.D., Beinecke Rare Book and Manuscript Library.

14. The structure of this episode repeats the transfer of sight from H.D. to Bryher at the end of the vision she calls the writing on the wall.

15. For accounts of H.D.'s film experience, see Friedberg, "Approaching *Borderline*" and Introduction. In addition to H.D.'s pamphlet on *Borderline,* she composed an essay on *Wing Beat* that was probably intended for *Close Up* but never published. For sustained analysis of H.D.'s work with cinema, see Collecott, "Images"; Friedberg, "'And I Myself'"; and Mandel, "Magical Lenses" and "Redirected Image." Edmunds's study, although not primarily focused on film, reads H.D.'s long poems through Eisenstein's theories of montage and notions of the "creating spectator" (115). In a chapter entitled "Autobiographical Fantasy: Cryptobiography, Cinematobiography, Otobiography," Chisholm argues that "[u]nderstanding H.D.'s adaptation and application of Freud's term *projection,* a concept metaphor that he himself derives from cinematography, is the key to reading the psychopoetic intertext of *The Gift*" (92).

16. In "Autobiographical Notes," H.D. reports that when Macpherson fell ill, she and Bryher "work[ed] over the strips, doing the montage as K[enneth] indicates" (20).

17. Because the film is highly disjunctive and elusive, POOL distributed a printed "libretto" at its screenings to help viewers grasp this plot. See Friedberg, Introduction 218.

18. See H.D.'s gaze reproduced in a still from *Borderline* (Donald, Friedberg, and Marcus 214).

19. H.D. refers the reader to "the best of the advanced German and Russian montage" exemplified by the meticulous cutting required to create the "lift, fire, pause, lift, fire, etcetera" sequence in Eisenstein's film *Ten Days That Shook the World* ("Borderline" 230).

20. For H.D.'s knowledge of psychoanalysis, see Friedman, *Psyche Reborn*, part 1 (17–154).

21. This passage, edited out of the New Directions abridgment of *The Gift,* has been restored in *The Gift: The Complete Text.*

22. Letters to Bryher: 22 April 1933 (p. 2); 28 April 1933 (The Dream, p. 2); 25 April 1933 (p. 1); 26 May 1933 (p. 2). For the correspondence between H.D. and Bryher during the course of H.D.'s analysis, see Friedman, *Analyzing Freud.*

23. H.D.'s grasp of Freud's techniques of dream interpretation may owe something to her familiarity with Macpherson's alignment of his project with Sachs's directive to "make perceptible . . . invisible inward events" and to her knowledge of Eisenstein's notions of the active spectator. In his December 1929 commentary, "As Is," Macpherson writes, "'We must go to psychoanalysis to understand that action is the modified outgiving of interacting conscious and unconscious adjustment. . . . We are not watching something happen to someone else, we are experiencing our own reaction to something which has been dissected and spread out for the precise purpose of our comprehension and unconscious participation'" (qtd. in Friedberg, Introduction 219).

24. Letters to Bryher: 10 March 1933 (p. 2); 19 November 1934 (pp. 2–3); 7 December 1934 (p. 1).

25. See DuPlessis, "Romantic Thralldom," for a summary of one of the repetitive patterns in H.D.'s intimate relationships.

26. For a detailed and moving account of the period, see Bryher's memoir *The Days of Mars.*

27. In this summary, I am indebted to Allison Coudert, *Alchemy.*

28. For an extended discussion of this section of the poem, see Gubar, "The Echoing Spell of H.D.'s *Trilogy.*"

29. H.D.'s novel *Pilate's Wife* also attributes Christ's resurrection to the intervention of a woman.

30. Both in Olson's *Collected Prose* and in *The New American Poetry, 1945–1960,* edited by Donald Allen, the title of Olson's manifesto is set like a concrete poem. In throwing the syllables across the line and marking his terms with open parentheses, Olson's title enacts the open field poetics his essay advocates.

31. "Absolute realism," Eisenstein writes, "is by no means the correct form of perception. It is simply the function of a certain form of social structure. Following a state monarchy, a state uniformity of thought is implanted. Ideological uniformity of a sort that can be developed pictorially in the ranks of colors and designs of the Guards regiments . . ." ("Cinematographic" 35).

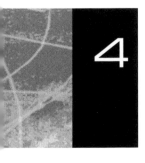

4

Giving in Turn: H.D. and the Spirit of the Gift

The debt creates an obligation to give in return, but to give in return does not mean to give back, to repay; it means to give in turn.
—Maurice Godelier, *The Enigma of the Gift*

Luxuriant and insurgent language, narratives that bring forth "always another and another and another" (*Helen in Egypt* 167), a preference for both/and/*and* profusions over either/or exclusions, and the insistence and outreach of projection endow H.D.'s writings with a forward momentum that seems both generous and generative. This amplitude, however, runs counter to what appears to be a withholding, even in some instances a stinginess, in H.D.'s actions. Three quirks in particular have puzzled H.D.'s readers and resisted the explanatory efforts of her biographers. Judged by conventional standards, her handling of money, her manipulation of her writing signature, and her management of motherhood appear at best odd, at worst suspicious or perhaps pernicious.

Unlike Pound, Eliot, and Williams, H.D. did not build a public career. This hesitation to come forward leaves her open to scriptings that resemble each other only in their vehemence: Is H.D., as Robert Duncan began to argue in the 1960s, a victim of New Critical aesthetics? Is she, as feminists began to argue in the 1970s, the target of a more diffuse modernist misogyny? Or was she, on the contrary, not a victim at all but, as Lawrence S. Rainey suggests, the darling of a coterie that circulated her writings "like bonbons at a dinner party" and the favorite of another that currently promotes her writings in pursuit of its own agendas (*Institutions* 148)? Although they represent an important disagreement about H.D.'s work, these assessments are alike in one respect: they measure her value within an economy of scarcity that canonizes the work of a few and relegates the rest to oblivion. In this chapter, I will argue that the practices of having, tending, and augmenting that build fortunes, reputations, and families had little hold on H.D.'s habits of life and thought. It is not the ethos of the market but the spirit of the gift that provides the structures of her writing.

The gift economy received its classic elaboration in the work of the anthropologist Marcel Mauss, who first discerned the extent to which tribal societies organize themselves through obligations to give, receive, and reciprocate.[1] For Mauss, the significance of gift exchange is the creation and affirmation of social bonds between gift partners. His most striking example of the ways in which giving, receiving, and reciprocating distribute wealth and reinforce community comes from Bronislaw Malinowski's work with inter- and intra-tribal trade among the peoples of the Trobriand Islands of the southwest Pacific. In a system that goes under the name of *kula*, Trobriand Islanders pass red shell necklaces clockwise and white shell bracelets counterclockwise through the archipelago. As the gifts travel from person to person, island to island, tribe to tribe, each donation is an act of social faith binding individuals into a larger collectivity. This kind of exchange collapses categories carefully held apart by economic theories focused on individual rights and responsibilities. Each gift in a kula ring is, as Mauss explains, "at the same time property and a possession, a pledge and a loan, an object sold and an object bought, a deposit, a mandate, a trust; for it is given only on condition that it will be used on behalf of, or transmitted to, a third person" (*Gift* 22). Instead of the "giving in return" characteristic of market exchange, the kula represents the "giving in turn" of gift economies. As a second mana-word that guided H.D.'s inquiries, the concept of the gift supports her intuitions of a projective universe and contributes to her effort to think her culture away from codes of war toward more generative notions of community and collectivity.

In the cultures Mauss describes, gift giving is a wide, enduring, fundamental social contract, a "'system of total prestations' . . . which is not only juridical and political but economical and religious as well" ("Gift" 28). This exchange of goods, wealth, property, "courtesies, entertainments, ritual, military assistance, women, children, dances, and feasts" (Mauss, *Gift* 3)[2] seems a far cry from the habits of the communities of H.D.'s youth in Pennsylvania and expatriate adulthood in London and Switzerland. As I will show, however,

H.D.'s eccentric handling of three common relay points of twentieth-century life—the circulation of money, a name, a child—opens into an ethics of the gift that animates her poems, novels, and autobiographical tributes.

*   *   *

Although H.D. came from a comfortably middle-class professional family, through her association with Bryher she was in touch with one of the largest fortunes in Europe. The riches amassed by Bryher's father, Sir John Ellerman, included control of one of England's greatest shipping fleets, vast holdings in British and continental real estate, the bulk of shares in the *Times* of London and Associated Newspapers, and major financial and editorial interests in several leading London magazines. In the 1950s, by Barbara Guest's reckoning, H.D. had several million dollars in the bank, the fruit of large settlements from Bryher and a family inheritance wisely invested by her brother Harold (264). In these years, however, H.D. resided in modest hotels, traveled sparingly, dressed modestly, and seemed to regard a daily cigarette and cup of coffee as something of an extravagance.[3]

Why did H.D. virtually ignore her money? The interpretation that has tempted H.D.'s biographers is that she thereby bound herself to Bryher in a reciprocal pathology. Janice S. Robinson suggests that Bryher used her fortune not only to buy Robert McAlmon and Kenneth Macpherson, her two husbands of convenience, but also to keep a tight rein on H.D. In Robinson's scripting, Bryher was an active, even tyrannical partner who demanded allegiance in return for support. This hypothesis flattens exchange into extortion, so that, to give only one example, the copious letters H.D. wrote Bryher during her analysis with Freud appear not to be a continuation of decades of correspondence, a stabilizing force during a period of spin, and a canny alternative to the journal Freud's analysands were forbidden to keep but merely the defrayal of a debt: "Bryher was paying for the analysis," Robinson explains, "and she demanded a firsthand account of the proceedings" (278). Like Rainey, who suggests that Bryher's "bounty may have had its price" in isolating and infantilizing H.D. (*Institutions* 148), Guest implies that Bryher's patronage gave H.D. "the mentality of one to whom things are given, but are not earned, nor even rightfully inherited" (*Herself Defined* 265).

These explanations use the terminology of market exchange—paying, accounting, earning, extorting—to describe an intimate relationship. Their scandal is the extension of market practices into a personal sphere. The not-quite-veiled implication, of course, is that H.D. was, in some sense, kept, a commodity like Irigaray's "women on the market" who "[relinquish] their right to speech and even to animality" (190).[4] Given a bank account that easily sustained H.D., her daughter Perdita, Kenneth Macpherson, Kenneth's troupe of douracoulis monkeys, and the multiple enterprises of POOL Productions throughout the early thirties in a Swiss villa designed for them by the Berlin architect Hermann Henselmann, such imputations were perhaps inevitable, but they don't stand up to scrutiny of the daily comings and goings of this earnest and awkward cast of characters.

The forty-two years of correspondence between H.D. and Bryher record a continuous exchange of news, gossip, and advice, mutual encouragements and recriminations, nicknames, standing jokes, memories, irritations, and affection. Over the years, H.D. pays scant attention to Bryher's financial arrangements. When Bryher sends her a check, she files it away; when she receives a settlement, she seems mute and discomfited.[5] Bryher's side of the correspondence, in turn, supports Robert Herring's sense that she had an "anonymous way [of giving], which makes it difficult to 'thank her,'"[6] and substantiates H.D.'s portrait of Bryher as a wary but dogged and discreet benefactor: "When I met her first—a little thing,—all tense, dressed like a princess, buns over her ears—," H.D. told Pearson, "she said to me 'you're the first person who treats me like a human being. Everyone else looks at me as though they saw just over my head a funnel out of which pours gold coins.' And I said, 'yes but you should meet my friends, they're not like that.' But they were like that" (Pearson, Notes 4–5).

Rainey's supposition that Bryher's patronage kept H.D. out of a literary fray that could have strengthened her writing runs counter to another anomaly in H.D.'s behavior: well before H.D. met Bryher, she took pains to avoid establishing and consolidating a public identity for herself. A writer's signature is a currency of accountability: it stands for her achievements in the same way paper money stands for commodities. As Susan Stanford Friedman points out, however, "With one early exception, H.D. never published anything under her legal names—Hilda Doolittle, Hilda Aldington" (*Penelope's Web* 35). Her early stories appeared under the signatures "J. Beran" and "Edith Gray," her poems under the rubric Pound designed, "H.D., Imagiste," and then simply "H.D."[7] She signed her autobiographical novels from the 1920s "Helga Dart" or "Helga Doorn," her fiction from the 1920s and 1930s "Rhoda Peter," "D. A. Hill," or "John Helforth," and her late prose—including the novel *The Sword Went Out to Sea*, the text she considered "the crown of all my effort"—"Delia Alton" ("H.D. by Delia Alton" 190).

A name is a stamp of property or ownership. Because the benefits of labor accrue to the signature that over time becomes one's record and reputation, to "make a name for oneself" is an author's equivalent to building capital. Several explanations for H.D.'s array of pseudonyms are possible, even plausible. Caution is one. In a homophobic culture, even before *The Well of Loneliness* trial in 1928, it seemed prudent to mask or suppress such homoerotic material as H.D.'s autobiographical novel of 1921, *Paint It Today,* signed in typescript "Helga Dart" and first published in full in the New York University Press Lesbian Life and Literature Series in 1992. Caution might also play a part in the pseudonymous publication of a story like "Pontikonisi (Mouse Island)" (1924), since its speculations about "galvanized projections," "platinum sheet-metal over jelly-fish," and spirit doubles were extravagant even in an era fascinated by the occult.[8] H.D. never shied away from scandalous stances, however, collaborating openly with Sappho in her early work[9] and throughout her life freely and frequently conjuring strange apparitions. The territory H.D. claimed as her own was from the first marginal and suspicious.

Although it might be argued that "H.D."—the carefully tended hieroglyph that she called her "writing signet or sign-manual" (*Tribute* 66)—is a simple or perhaps more dignified substitute for the given name "Hilda Doolittle," the abbreviated signature is more striking in its erasures than in its claims. Without gender, nationality, chronology, or biography, the sign "H.D." is as impersonal as the imagist lyrics reviewers called "crystalline." Many of the titles and signatures H.D. invented for her post-imagist writings—*Hedylus,* "Heliodora," Helga Dart, and Helga Doorn among them—follow out vectors of this signature as if to pry it "out of the 'niche' she and the critics had built in collaboratively constructing the 'early H.D. legend'" (Friedman, *Penelope's Web* 40). Among the other pseudonyms H.D. constructed with an inventiveness verging on glee are anagrams ("Rhoda Peter" reversing Peter Rodeck, "D. A. Hill" scrambling her first name, Hilda), rebuses (John Helforth, the scientistic editor of *Nights,* come forth, like Koré, from the nether regions), or puncepts ("Delia" expands into Cordelia, Delilah, or, as Friedman points out, "she of Delos, i.e., Artemis" [*Penelope's Web* 43], while "Alton" contracts Aldington into two syllables that chime with *altar, alter, alteration, alternate,* and *alter ego*).

Throughout her life, signatures like these functioned not to fix but to extend and disperse H.D.'s identity. Like the money she ignored, H.D. expended little effort to tend or augment the market value of her name. This failure to take care of, watch over, or look after also—and more damagingly—marks a third important aspect of her life: her relationship with the child she conceived with Cecil Gray after her separation from Richard Aldington and shared, first informally, then legally, with Bryher. As H.D. explained to her friend Brigit Patmore, Bryher's formal adoption of Perdita occurred during a period in which H.D. feared the recurrence of Aldington's earlier threats of a perjury suit and "five years penal servitude" for her false registry of the child as his legitimate offspring.[10] The alignment of this gesture with other distances in her mothering, however, suggests there was more at stake than prudence or caution. H.D.'s treatment of Perdita was neither abusive nor neglectful, but its departures from a prescribed or expected norm suggest that here as elsewhere H.D. was operating within a different system of values.

A child is a soul we bring into life, a financial, legal, and moral responsibility, and (like money and a name) a force that extends our identity, power, and reach into the future. That H.D. placed her child within a wider, more rarified economy is suggested from the first by the name she gave her: Frances Perdita. As Frances, she returns to H.D. her lost companion Frances Gregg; as Perdita, the lost one, child of Hermione in Shakespeare's *The Winter's Tale,* she evokes the baby lost in H.D.'s 1915 stillbirth, now found again.[11] The story that informs this circulation from absence back into presence or from death back into life is Koré's yearly return to Demeter, a myth that reinforces the sense that a child is a gift bestowed at the will of larger powers, a notion central to H.D.'s fictional recreations of her child's conception. In all her fictional renditions of the birth of her child, the apparent father is a veil or double for a "Father who art in Heaven," usually designated as the sun god Helios/Apollo.[12] This child was fathered by "some sun-daemon . . . God, her Lover," H.D. summarizes, and as such it stands as a visible token of an exchange that circulates between and ties together divine and material worlds (*Asphodel* 157).

A child is, of course, less ethereally, a being that bonds those who participate in its care. For H.D., the child was never primarily hers, much less Gray's or Aldington's, but rather the nexus of the group Rachel Blau DuPlessis has called her "sufficient family" (*Writing* 76). In naming her daughter for Frances Gregg and passing her on to Bryher, H.D. bound past and present together and firmed her new alliance with Bryher through shared responsibility for the child. When Bryher married Kenneth Macpherson, Macpherson took the place of the father in this unconventional but tenacious family of four.[13] In many groups outside Western twentieth-century white middle-class culture, child keeping was a shared responsibility, part of the flux and elasticity of kinship networks. The adults who cared for Perdita (including, variously, Bryher and her parents, H.D.'s mother and Aunt Laura, Kenneth Macpherson, and Silvia Dobson) constitute H.D.'s chosen kin.[14]

In one of Perdita Schaffner's superb essays on her childhood, she notes that H.D. "was intensely maternal—on an esoteric plane" ("Sketch" 143). The level on which H.D. consented to motherhood is, like that on which she conduct-

ed her financial and authorial affairs, abstracted from the drive that leads people to hold and hoard those things they mark as theirs. Although it's tempting to condemn H.D.'s choices as irresponsible or to pathologize them as neurotic, her treatment of her money, her name, and her child suggest that she
understood herself to be functioning within the aura of another economy.

*   *   *

Two parables from H.D.'s *Tribute to Freud* adumbrate features of this alternate
system of giving and taking. The first, from "Advent," is the story of a trick
exchange; the second, from "Writing on the Wall," a tale of a genuine one. In
juxtaposition, these two anecdotes suggest the persistence in twentieth-century Western economies of features associated with gift economies from other centuries, regions, or cultures.[15] These two ways of imagining an exchange
or transmission of goods resonate with a tension that runs throughout H.D.'s
thinking between social structures that privilege reason, competition, and the
individual ego and those that privilege emotion, social bonding, and an ethic
of generosity.[16]

In "Advent," following a trail of associations from the statue of Pallas Athené
on Freud's desk through the bust in Poe's "Raven" to the cryptic analyst hud-
dling like an old owl behind the couch, H.D. recalls "a special gift" from her
father. In his study was a large white snow owl under a bell jar. As if she were
in a fairy tale, the child asks her father to give her his owl, for, perhaps, she
reasons, if he is Zeus, the all-powerful one, she could be Pallas Athené, born
from his head with her sigil the owl. Yes, Professor Doolittle replies, the owl is
hers, hers forever. Announcing that he is not an Indian giver and won't ask for
it back, he adds a rider that reveals him instead to be a Yankee trader: he agrees
to give her the owl on the condition that it stay where it is (124–25).

Contrary to Professor Doolittle's use of the term, an "Indian giver" is, as Lewis
Hyde points out, the opposite of a "white man keeper" (*Gift* 3–4). Keepers re-
move property from circulation by bargaining shrewdly and laying up treasures.
Unlike H.D.'s father and his ancestors—"those Puritan fathers who wear high
peaked hats in the Thanksgiving numbers of magazines . . . fought with Indians and burned witches" (*Tribute* 34)—Indian givers pass gifts along, each receiver becoming in turn a donor. Unlike "giving in turn," which passes goods
along in the faith that having passed through a larger collectivity they will, like
the items in the kula ring, reappear, the deal Professor Doolittle proposes to his
daughter is giving without transmitting, a pseudo-donation that leaves the
boundary between exchange partners unbreached.[17] No one is richer or poorer,
no bonds are created, no change occurs: the gift that does not move is not a gift.

H.D.'s second parable is the story of a cluster of gardenias she sent "[t]o greet the return of the Gods," the arrival of Freud's collection of Greek and Egyptian antiquities, Chinese and Oriental treasures, shipped to London after his flight from Vienna in 1938. Although H.D.'s note is unsigned, Freud recognizes the giver and in his acknowledgment puts his finger on the key difference between the two economies: what H.D. calls Gods, he notes, "*other people read: Goods*" (*Tribute* 11).

The gift of gardenias emerged from a conversation H.D. and Freud had had in Vienna five years earlier. As they reminisced about Rome, "The shuttle of the years," as H.D. put it, "ran a thread that wove my pattern into the Professor's. 'Ah, the Spanish Steps,' said the Professor. 'It was those branches of almond,' I said; 'of all the flowers and the flower baskets, I remember those the best.' 'But,' said the Professor, 'the gardenias! In Rome, even *I* could afford to wear a gardenia'" (9). Hoping to re-evoke the memory he circulated to her, H.D. scoured Vienna for gardenias for Freud's birthday that year; not finding them, she gave him nothing. Another year, she sent money to a friend in Vienna to find gardenias for Freud's birthday, but her friend heard that Freud liked orchids—"people always ordered orchids" (9)—and sent orchids in H.D.'s name. This, too, for H.D., was nothing.

The gift of gardenias so deeply satisfies H.D. because it is a real gift. Unlike the owl, it comes unexpectedly rather than as part of a bargain, through generosity rather than calculation, and with an intimacy that reciprocates Freud's gift to H.D. of his recollections of Rome. His reminiscences allowed her to trade not in the conventional token of orchids but in the currency of his memory and desire, for in telling her of the gardenias, he gave her "a present that was in the past or a past that was in the future" (9). The crucial point, however, is Freud's perception that the gift entails gods, not goods. The spiritual dimension of the gift is suggested by two fissures characteristic of "giving in turn": the gap in time between H.D.'s impulse and its accomplishment and the gap in space opened by the third term of this exchange, the figure of the returning antiquities.

The story of the gardenias is the initial gesture of H.D.'s *Tribute to Freud*, and it stands in the position of the larger gift to follow: the composition of the tribute itself, completed ten years after the conclusion of H.D.'s second series of sessions with Freud in December 1934. The interval between the analysis and H.D.'s tribute is crucial because, unlike Professor Doolittle's owl, Freud's gift to H.D. was transformative. The story H.D. is telling fits the folktale paradigm of the apprentice who asks a master for wisdom and receives a threshold gift, a gift that opens a passage from one state into another. Unlike a stationary gift, the gift that passes from a master to a pupil creates an imbalance that requires a stretch of time to intervene before the gift can be passed along. In the interval between the moment a gift comes and the moment it is released and forwarded, the recipient suffers what Hyde calls "the labor of gratitude," the effort to rise to the level of the gift and make it his or her own so it can circulate back into the culture (*Gift* 47). H.D.'s struggle with Freud's fundamental presuppositions is a labor of incorporation and transformation, labor conducted in the period between her first impulse to send the gardenias and the gardenias that greeted the return of the gods.[18]

The second interval is the space opened in the exchange by the figure of Freud's antiquities. Giving-in-return involves reciprocal circuits of two: I give my friend x, he gives me y, and we each privately wonder whether our gifts are commensurate, whether x could be said to equal y. This calculation, characteristic of giving-in-return, aligns it more closely with trading or bartering than with gift giving, for such exchanges require not only precision but canniness. In exchanges characteristic of a gift culture, by contrast, not only are the bestowals not simultaneous or even predictably related in time but before a return donation the gift must leave the boundary of the ego and circle out into mystery.

Elaborating on an example from Mauss's essay, Hyde clarifies this transit through a detailed description of a Maori hunting ritual.[19] On return from a successful expedition, Maori hunters give a portion of their kill to priests who prepare the birds at a sacred fire, eat a few of them, and return the rest as a gift to the forest. In reciprocating the forest's gift to the tribe, the priests assure continued abundance, but, more importantly, their inclusion in the ritual opens the circle beyond a simple give-and-take between hunters and forest and moves the transaction from the realm of barter into the realm of the sacred. As Hyde points out, this Maori ritual has the same structure as the Old Testament ritual of first fruits, in which priests also consume a portion of the gift before making a sacrifice that returns the rest to the Lord in smoke (*Gift* 18–20). The inclusion of the priests in the cycle directs gratitude beyond the personal, temporal, and quantifiable and makes exactly the point Freud understood H.D. to make: the crux of the matter is gods, not goods.

As the middle term in the parable of the gardenias, Freud's collection of antiquities functions like the priests in the Maori and Hebrew rituals to route the exchange through the gods. This third term aligns the gift of gardenias, the most recent interchange with Freud recorded in *Tribute*, with the first, the moment when H.D. entered Freud's study and gazed not at him but at his statues—"'you,'" he grumbled, "'are the only person who has ever come into this room and looked at the things in the room before looking at me'" (98). Freud no doubt noted that the gardenias greeted not him but his antiquities, but

H.D.'s point remained: for her, the best of Freud's wisdom was contained in the treasures of which he was "part and parcel," treasures that represented "another region of cause and effect, another region of question and answer" (97, 99).

*   *   *

While there is no evidence that H.D. knew the work of Marcel Mauss, the listing of her library at the Beinecke shows her to have been a passionate student of religion, mythology, classical archeology, and ethnology. Where Mauss's research drew on fieldwork from places like Samoa, New Zealand, Melanesia, the Andaman Islands, and Northwest America, H.D.'s interests lay in the arc she drew from Egypt through Crete into classical Greece, in the history of the Unitas Fratrum or Moravian Church, founded in 1457 by followers of the Bohemian reformer Jan Hus, and in the interactions between eighteenth-century Moravian settlers in Pennsylvania, the nearby Lenape or "Delaware" Indians, and the members of the Six Nations of the Mohawks, Oneidas, Onondagas, Cayugas, Senecas, and Tuscaroras.[20] Although the cultures that interested Mauss and H.D. were different, both researchers regarded the social and ethical organizations of these cultures as valuable correctives to the excesses of the twentieth-century market economy.

As E. E. Evans-Pritchard points out in his introduction to *The Gift,* Mauss was Émile Durkheim's nephew and most distinguished pupil. Born in 1872, Mauss was fourteen years older than H.D., but like hers, his life was deeply afflicted by the two world wars. In World War I, as H.D.'s artistic circle dissolved and dispersed, Mauss lost most of his colleagues in Durkheim's younger cohort of scholars. During World War II, as H.D. suffered through the bombing of London, Mauss inhabited Nazi-occupied Paris, where he not only lost additional colleagues and friends but also, as a Jew, suffered terrors that contributed to his mental collapse, like H.D.'s, after the war (Evans-Pritchard v–vi).

Like H.D., who was a student of Greek and a passionate investigator of spiritual and mystical traditions, Mauss was not only a sociologist but a Sanskrit scholar and an historian of religions. These classical and historical interests inflect their theories of the gift with an archaic and spiritual cast antagonistic to the assumptions and procedures of modern materialist economics. Although H.D. lacked the academic training that undergirded Mauss's formulations, her Moravian upbringing provided her with a lived connection to the cultures his concepts illuminate. This overlap becomes apparent in the way a crucial feature of the gift economy, the Maori notion of the *hau,* passes through ceremonies like the Moravian love feast into H.D.'s own poetry and poetics.

Marshall Sahlins identifies Mauss's master concept as "the indigenous Maori idea *hau,* introduced . . . as 'the spirit of things and in particular of the forest and the game it contains'" (149). For Mauss, the hau is the god in the goods. It is alive and active, a part of the donor that travels along with the thing given and eventually draws the gift or its equivalent back toward its source. The birds the hunters take contain the forest's hau, just as, in another register, Freud's analysis of H.D. might be said to contain his. Failure to return the gift poisons the recipient and destroys the life-sustaining gift cycle (Mauss, *Gift* 10–11).

Returning to Mauss's Maori source-text, however, Sahlins makes a crucial observation. If the hau were simply a spirit that compels return, gift exchange would require just two stations; the Maori explanation involves three, the hau appearing first in the transition from the second to third. The introduction of the third station demonstrates what for Sahlins is the key fact of gift exchange: the yield, power of increase, or augmentation of the gift as it moves from station to station (160). The birds the priests return to the forest are more elaborate and complex than the initial gifts of the forest to the hunters and the hunters to the priests. The hau or increase given in turn to the forest is at once environmental (a nourishing of the ecosystem), spiritual (an affirmation of a mutually sustaining connection with nature and the gods), and social (a community bonding) (Hyde, *Gift* 37). For the Maori, these three aspects overlap and fuse, each implicating and enabling the others. The hau of the gift binds the material, spiritual, and social realms that market economies compartmentalize and set into opposition.

Modeled on the early Christian *agape,* the Moravian love feasts were a ritual of giving-in-turn used to celebrate not only religious and social occasions but the start or finish of economic enterprises: the laying of a cornerstone for an oil mill, for example, or the harvesting of a crop of wheat. These simple meals accompanied by hymn singing passed the yield of the gift back toward its source, enacting the hau as at once an economic, social, and spiritual increase. The food shared by the worshippers or workers nourished them, affirmed their connections to the land and the Lord, and situated their community within the mutual obligations of giving, receiving, and reciprocating.[21] The hau that circulates through a gift economy represents for Mauss, H.D., and Hyde the increase of the life force, a circulation of power and affirmation of peace dynamically opposed to the competitive ethos of the market economy.

The contrast between the two economies is severe, perhaps, as Mauss, Hyde, and H.D. draw it, too severe, since gift rituals like the kula contain competitive and conflictual elements, and even the most wholehearted capitalist economies sustain ceremonial gift exchanges.[22] All of these thinkers, however, were profoundly moved by war in their time—for Mauss and H.D., the two World Wars; for Hyde, the Vietnam War—to the conclusion that the bonds a gift economy sustains are the opposite of the calculation and competitiveness that leads to war. As they understood it, gift exchange moves from reverence toward abundance and alliance, while market exchange moves from exploitation toward scarcity and conflict. This sequence leads them into their summary oppositions: for Mauss, the will for peace against the will to war (*Gift* 80); for Hyde, the forces of *eros*, "the principle of attraction, union, involvement," against the forces of *logos*, "reason and logic in general, the principle of differentiation in particular" (*Gift* xiv); and for H.D., the animating impulses of *Eros* and *Eris*, love and strife (*Helen in Egypt* 115).

Binary oppositions tend to seem most clear and compelling at the borderlines where systems intersect or collide. The borderline is the place of maximum difference, tension, and potential for change, and it is here, at the flashpoint of opposition, that H.D. situated many of her poems and much of her life. Her choice to form an alliance with an heir to one of capitalism's great fortunes and yet ignore her own money and live as closely as possible by the dictates of a gift economy could not have seemed as odd to her as it does to her biographers, for this conjunction replicated the tensions and intersections of her childhood. The circumstances of H.D.'s birth placed her precisely at the juncture of the two economies: the coexistence in Bethlehem, Pennsylvania, of the Moravian religious community and the Bethlehem Steel Corporation.

Bethlehem was founded by Moravians in 1741. The church, schools, and community buildings that were the scene of H.D.'s early life constitute, according to one architectural historian, "the purest expression of Moravian thought" (Murtagh vii). Unlike more abstract theologies, Moravian doctrine can emerge so clearly in architecture because it is less a dogma than a design for living. At its center is the binding power of love, which Hyde identifies as the heart of the gift culture, an eros that determined not only Moravian rituals of connection like the love feast and kiss of peace but also the daily arrangements of their economy.[23]

The economy that formed the town was codified in the Brotherly Agreement of 1754, a pact whose name recalls the church's founding as the Jednota Bratrska or Unitas Fratrum. This contract obliged its members to give, receive, and reciprocate, made no distinction between the material and the spiritual, and, at least at first, ruled out the key institutions of bourgeois capitalism: private enterprise and the patriarchal nuclear family. The entire community was considered one family, headed by Christ and his bride the Church and embracing all church members. All Moravians worked for the community, which, in turn, housed, fed, clothed, and supported them.

Extending along Church Street, where H.D. grew up, were the Church, the Gemeinhaus, the First Single Brothers' House, the Sisters' House, and the Widows' House. The Gemeinhaus was the settlement's first permanent structure, containing the kitchens and communal dining hall, the chapel, and a dormitory divided into rooms for the groups the Moravians called Choirs (girls, boys, older girls, older boys, single sisters, single brothers, married women, married men, widows, and widowers). Although provisions were made for them to meet privately once a week, in the early years of the settlement couples lived apart (Gollin 85).[24] Children entered the Choirs at eighteen months, were separated by sex at five or six years, received their educations within their Choirs, and lived in separate structures like the Sisters' and Widows' Houses on H.D.'s street.

Among other early buildings were a water works, a slaughterhouse, oil and grist mills, a tannery, and a blacksmith, locksmith, and nailsmith (Murtagh 13), structures that indicate the town's function as a center into which the surrounding population funneled materials and from which they took finished articles. By 1760, Bethlehem was complex enough to sustain thirteen hundred inhabitants and a corps of missionaries that traveled among the Indians (Gollin 198). Although the Brotherly Agreement was abrogated in 1762,[25] the successful meshing of the material and the spiritual continued across the century. Only in 1844, forty-two years before H.D.'s birth, were the settlement and the church formally separated, their property reallocated, finances decentralized, and communal responsibility for missionary work redefined (Sessler 207).

Even after the 1840s, however, the Moravians struggled to preserve the semblance of a gift economy. Wanting to benefit from the rich manufacturing resources of the Lehigh Valley without destroying their village culture, they struck a compromise by organizing a new town across the river to house the blast furnaces, factories, railroads, and secular workers of the industrial economy.[26] In South Bethlehem was the Union Paper Bag Machine Company, which produced the paper bags invented by H.D.'s grandfather, the Reverend Francis Wolle, and the Bethlehem Rolling Mill and Iron Company, ancestor of Bethlehem Steel, established by Francis's brother Augustus (Bethlehem Book Committee 28–30).

The split between the religious and secular communities inscribed in the landscape that surrounded H.D. was written as well into each generation of her mother's family. The Wolles were direct descendants of members of the Unitas Fratrum and leaders of Bethlehem's Moravian community, but the family also included prominent members of the industrial sector. The contrasting pairs begin with H.D.'s pious and scholarly grandfather Francis and his brother Augustus, reduplicate in Francis's sons J. Fred Wolle, who established the famous Moravian Bach Choir and Festival, and Hartley, a businessman, and reappear in H.D. herself and her brothers Harold and Melvin, both of whom became wealthy and successful businessmen.[27]

*   *   *

The question of whether Freud's returning antiquities are "goods" or "gods" is a variant of the conflict between the market and gift economies in H.D.'s early poems "Calypso," "Cities," and "The Tribute." "Calypso" is an angry poem with a taut dialogic structure (*Collected Poems* 388–96). In this poem, Odysseus's point of view is not the whole tale but a version of the tale: here, as Friedman notes, "most probably for the first time in cultural history, 'Callypso Speaks' her own story" (*Psyche Reborn* 236).[28] The variance between the speeches of Odysseus and Calypso is a clash not only of personalities or genders but of orientations toward the world. In the disjunctive monologues that constitute this poem, Calypso speaks from a gift economy, Odysseus from a market economy.

In the usual recitation of the episode, Calypso is a nymph who welcomes Odysseus to her island, offers her love, then, after eight years, compelled by the gods, releases him to continue his journey. The two parts of H.D.'s poem elide the story's middle—their romantic enthrallment[29]—to focus the reader's attention instead on parallels between Odysseus's arrival and his departure. In the first, Odysseus hunts Calypso down and rapes her; in the second, he counts, stashes, and sails away with her gifts. Both parts focus on a disjunction that fails to be negotiated. On Odysseus's arrival, Calypso identifies herself as "priestess, occult, nymph and goddess," a station in the gift economy, but Odysseus sees her only as a commodity: "A nymph is a woman" and "All men are fathers, / kings and gods," he tells her, therefore, "You will do as I say" (389, 393).

The second disjunction provides the poem's conclusion. In rapt antithetical speeches—a litany and a curse—Odysseus enumerates Calypso's gifts and Calypso marshals the forces in her command to batter and blight his journey (394–96). The clash of refrains, his "she gave" against her "he took," drives home the incompatibility of the gift and the market.[30] He has treated her gifts as his capital, misused their hau, and broken the gift cycle, thus earning Calypso's summation: "man is a devil, / man will not understand" (395). In this rescripting of Odysseus's first appearance in Homer's epic, rapacity is the initial sin, cause of exile and source of suffering.

"Cities," the final poem of *Sea Garden,* and "The Tribute," the conclusion of the 1925 sequence H.D. called "The God," focus on the terrain of exile: the urban marketplace. These are uneasy productions that jut away from the preceding poems, poems which are, for the most part, celebrations of the acts of giving, receiving, and reciprocating. First published in 1914 and 1917, these poems describe squalid cities in which individuals swindle and blight each other, "ring false coin for silver, / offer refuse for meat" (*Collected Poems* 59). As the ties of community break, beauty is banished, the old gods flee, and profit taking replaces poem making, bringing what Mauss and H.D. understood to be the market's inevitable consequence: the worship of war. The god of these poems is Mars, whose "blackened light" (*Collected Poems* 62) is egotistical, hierarchical, and monotheistic.[31] Although "Cities" and "The Tribute" have a programmatic pitch that undermines their effectiveness as separate poems, their function in the series they conclude is important, for they tie the pastoral poems that precede them to an urban, industrial present and delineate what H.D. and Mauss experienced as the nightmarish alternative to the spirit of the gift.[32]

*   *   *

If the enemies of the gift are calculation, hoarding, and egotism, its champions are the patrons of circulation and connection, Eros and Hermes, who occasion H.D.'s more nuanced meditations on the hau that builds as gifts pass from station to station. Eros is the god who compels inclusion, affiliation, and community, and, as we have seen, violations of his imperatives are dire. "*[W]ho caused the [Trojan] war?*" H.D. asks. "*[Helen] has been blamed, Paris has been blamed but, fundamentally, it was the fault of Thetis*" (*Helen in Egypt* 111). Thetis's exclusion of Eris from her wedding feast breaks the gift community's tenet that "[e]veryone who can, will or does attend . . . must be invited. Neglect has fateful results" (Mauss, *Gift* 38). Wantonness is damaging, but as Eris demonstrates with the golden apple dedicated "To the Fairest," exclusion rends the communities of gods and mortals alike.

As if to include strife in his lineage, Eros's father is sometimes said to be Eris's brother, Ares, but in other writings he is Hermes, loosener of property from the hands of graspers, god of the crossroads, and protector of travelers. Hermes is a transmitter who, like Mauss's Maori hunters, passes on what he takes. In a pattern established as an infant when he stole the cattle of the sun and sacrificed them to the other gods, Hermes' passion for circulation makes him the messenger of Zeus. He and his inventions—the lyre and the alphabet—pass along divine or esoteric secrets, thus aligning him for H.D. with Thoth, Hermes Trismegistus, and Hermes Psychopompous. "[H]is metal is quicksilver," H.D. writes, with a nod at his Roman incarnation as Mercury, "his clients, orators, thieves and poets" (*Trilogy* 63). Hermes is the patron of the band of initiates that constitutes the most insistent of the gift communities in H.D.'s writings.[33]

H.D.'s lyrics have sometimes been read as cries out of "loneliness, a metaphysical estrangement that confronts her at every moment with the perilous condition of her own identity" (Riddell 447). The sustaining pronoun of H.D.'s poetry, however, is not "I" but "we." Most of her poems are social, creating an "I" that is one of a choros, rewriting shared mythologies, or enacting rituals designed to draw others into alliance. When H.D. translates Greek drama, what compels her is not the speech of the estranged but group commentary on displays of perilous individuality. The choros is, for H.D., "the play's collective conscience" (*Ion* 24) or "a manifestation of its inner mood" (7). The choroses she chose to translate from *Iphigeneia in Aulis, Hippolytus, Ion, The Bacchae,* and *Hecuba* are spoken by women who have a strong sense both of the group's wisdom and the individual's anguish. When single speakers step forward from the choros, they speak for the group in the same way soloists sing for the "religious choirs and choruses" H.D. considered the choros's "direct descendant" (9).

To a culture that exalts the individual, the choros may seem the least compelling part of the play, but to H.D. it presented a model for community. Poems like "The Mysteries: *Renaissance Choros*" or "Adonis" recreate this band directly; others, like "Huntress" or "Hymen," locate analogous instances in myth or ritual; still others, like "We Two," create a diminished but effective private community. Even the exemplary lyric "Oread" speaks for more than one: "hurl your green over us," the oread cries, "cover us" (*Collected Poems* 55). From the point of view of the poems, the fissure in H.D.'s work is not between "I" and others but between "us" and "them," between the members of a gift culture and the members of a market economy.

To the extent that such a poem's "we" constitutes a community it fails to entice its readers to entertain, H.D.'s use of this pronoun can seem not only smug and exclusive but coercive.[34] In a sense, this pronoun sets up a double bind for its readers: resisted at the risk of making "us" one of "them," it is accepted at the risk of jeopardizing an "I" that retains a capacity for critical distance. Gift transmission is dangerous to the ego, particularly when, as is often the case in H.D.'s writings, the donor is a figure of power or mystery. A recipient who cannot meet the obligation to receive the gift risks being consumed, overwhelmed, or driven mad; a recipient who cannot meet the obligation to pass it on risks violating its spirit. Successful negotiation of these dangers demands the labor of gratitude that feeds the gift's hau, but the form this process takes varies according to the nature of the donor, who is usually figured as a mentor, a lover, or a god.

The mentors H.D. called her "masters" were figures she experienced as having "blasted, dynamited, shattered" her world ("Compassionate" 22). In the case of Pound, D. H. Lawrence, and Freud, the three most important of these figures, the cycle involved a period of intense contact, an interval of incorporating and reworking their teachings, and the composition of a tribute that acknowledged and passed on their gifts.[35] H.D.'s struggles with Lawrence, recorded in *Bid Me to Live,* are released in "Compassionate Friendship"; her struggles with Pound, recorded in *HERmione,* are released in *End to Torment* and "Winter Love"; her struggles with Freud, recorded in "The Master," are released in *Tribute to Freud.* Each tribute is at once a payment levied and a gift rendered. One of H.D.'s favorite genres, the tribute follows the law she spelled out to Pearson when he suggested she change the title of her poem "Tribute to the Angels": "I must keep *Tribute,*" she writes, "as it is a *payment* that I owed them—and I hope [I] did pay!" The "homework" she assigns him is three biblical passages that spell out the injunctions to give, receive, and reciprocate.[36]

When H.D. tries to work out Lawrence's place in the sequence of her initiators, she lists him in the midst of seven: Ezra Pound, Richard Aldington, John Cournos, D. H. Lawrence, Cecil Gray, Kenneth Macpherson, and Walter Schmideberg ("Compassionate" 35). In another tally, she mentions Peter Rodeck, Dr. J. J. van der Leeuw, Freud, and Sir Hugh Dowding ("Sword Went Out to Sea" 1:83–86, 95); to this list, one might also add from her final years Erich Heydt and Lionel Durand. It is an odd assortment. Schmideberg and Heydt were analysts, van der Leeuw the analysand who preceded her in Freud's hours; Aldington, Gray, and Macpherson were lovers, Cournos a friend; Rodeck, Dowding, and Durand were at most acquaintances. In what way did these figures serve as initiators? What part do they play in the gift economy of H.D.'s work?

Viewed historically and biographically, H.D.'s erotic attachments do seem to enact the dismal drama of obsession, polarization, dominance, submission, and betrayal that DuPlessis identifies as "romantic thralldom" (*Writing* 66–83), but it was precisely from this point of view that "love-affairs" began to strike H.D. as "rather tiresome and not very important" ("Majic" 97). To comprehend the giving-in-turn she sought in erotic encounters, it is necessary to understand them as moments of gift exchange that Mauss identifies as "total": at once "religious, mythological and shamanistic" because those "taking part are incarnations of gods and ancestors, whose names they bear, whose dances they dance and whose spirits possess them" (*Gift* 36). As in Psyche's encounter with Eros or Gatsby's obsession with Daisy, the other in the drama is not primarily historical or even personal. It is when the lover reclaims his or her human particularity or human frailty that the bond begins to fray.

Like many of H.D.'s other ideas about the gift, this ritualization recasts elements of Moravian doctrine. Because Moravians believed Christ to be the Divine Bridegroom of all souls, male and female, a husband was considered a "Vice-husband" or "Proxy-husband" who stood in for Christ in the same way H.D. imagined Gray standing in for Helios or Macpherson for Hermes.[37] These imaginings transform the erotic from a giving-in-return or reciprocity of two into a giving-in-turn or circuit of many, so that, to give only one example, Gray comes to seem to H.D. to be both a "god-send" from Helios and a relay of erotic force from Lawrence.[38]

The heterosexual structure of these mythic paradigms leads to a final recurrent element in H.D.'s writings on the gift: the sudden appearance, often as if from nowhere, of a child who embodies the hau or increase of the gift.[39] In early work like *Asphodel*, *Hedylus*, and H.D.'s translation of Euripides' *Ion*, the child is the issue of sexual union with a lover who is (also) a god; later, in *Helen in Egypt*, *End to Torment*, "Hermetic Definition," and "Winter Love," the child is the issue of a less specific—but no less generative—moment of "inseminating beauty" (*End to Torment* 36). In "Winter Love," when all Helen's paramours—Menelaus, Paris, Odysseus, Achilles, and Theseus—vanish, a "grandam, great *Grande Dame*, // midwife and *Sage-Femme*" recalls her from the edge of death to bring forth and nurture a child named *Espérance* (115).[40] This figure of the grand-mother stands, as we will see, as the source of H.D.'s creativity in *The Gift*. The generativity she represents is H.D.'s answer to the destructiveness of the market economy.

If the increase from teachers is the tribute and the increase from lovers the child, the increase from the final partner in gift exchange, the gods, might be thought of more simply as a generalized or abstracted generativity. The gift rituals in the early poems—the rite of first fruits in "Orchard," the "love-offering" in "Holy Satyr," the marriage in "Hymen"—invoke the gods in order to repay the gods and contribute to their work; the rituals in later poems like *Trilogy* and "Hermetic Definition" invoke the gods to offer homage and receive, in turn, the dreams and visions that sustain her work. Here the gift as Mauss and Hyde describe it merges not only with the gift in its conventional meaning as talent but also with the gift in its Moravian inflection as prophecy or preaching.[41] The law of the gift culture dictates that what is received must be disseminated: "write," as the poem "Hermetic Definition" puts it, "write or die" (7).

*   *   *

H.D.'s primary text—her primer—of gift exchange is the autobiographical fantasy she called *The Gift*. In this manuscript, composed in London in the midst of World War II, H.D. returns to her Moravian childhood to describe "a Gift of Vision" and a vision of the gift (214).[42] In his notes toward a biography of H.D., Pearson sets her labors in percussive counterpoint to the Nazi air bombardments: "tap, tap, tap on the machine when the explosions come," Pearson reports, "& Mrs. Asche [*sic*] saying—'But Madame' + H saying—'Go away! go away; let me type!'"[43] Like Mauss, who used his post–World War I investigations of gift communities to point the way toward less catastrophic "procedures for our societies" (*Gift* 69), H.D. tapped out her research into the Moravian secret in order to counter—encounter, press back against, oppose—its militaristic antithesis. Like her counterpart across the channel, the poet René Char, who embedded Resistance radio code into his poems, H.D. used her writing as a way to wage peace.[44]

Preceding *The Gift* were the years during which H.D.'s writings clotted into the poems of *Red Roses for Bronze* and flared into the polemics of *Close Up*. Following the conclusion of her analysis with Freud, her first compositions were a translation of Euripides' *Ion* and a draft of *Bid Me to Live*. Robert Duncan sees *Ion* as "a turning point" in H.D.'s work, "the crowning achievement of her first phase [and] also the declaration of her later work" ("Nights and Days" 107), while Friedman marks *Bid Me to Live* as the end of blockage and beginning of maturity (*Psyche Reborn* 31), but *The Gift* is the first full writing of the "vision of power and of peace" (214) through which H.D. submits her personal, political, and spiritual life to the laws of the gift economy.

Although *Ion* and *Bid Me to Live* aspire to bring together the sacred and secular economies they evoke, these works falter in opposite directions. Euripides' play, set in Delphi during the Persian Wars, chronicles the return of Ion, born of the union of Kreousa and Helios, to his mother, now Queen of Athens. Although the juxtaposition of a moment in a sacred gift cycle with a moment of political conflict carries a kind of magic for H.D., her translation fails to connect the two economies in a meaningful way. The lengthy italicized comments dispersed throughout the text show H.D. laboring to return the play to circulation in a form that might "somehow . . . ameliorate the terror and destruction of the contemporary world" (Gregory, *H.D. and Hellenism* 207), but the aspirations toward material relevance in this commentary falter against her decisions to omit or curtail many of the play's "ethical, sophistical, or political" passages (209) and render the remainder in the broken apostrophes of *Red Roses for Bronze*.

The opposite emphasis unbalances *Bid Me to Live,* an autobiographical fiction set in London during the aerial bombardments of World War I. Rafe and Julia, this roman à clef's main characters, absorb and replay the war in their erotic and creative lives, "[v]ictims, victimised and victimising," locked in "not so much a losing as a lost-battle" (7, 49). Poetic incantations, mystical intuitions, and an auratic haze Julia calls the *gloire* (176–77) swirl around the novel's renditions of personal and political combat, but the novel is memorable not for the connections it makes between these realms but for its evocation of the paraphernalia of war: a service wristwatch with its disc encased in wire, a stack of letters from the front, "the desolation of the empty street" in a city under aerial attack (109).

The trick of *The Gift* is the interpenetration of the sacred and secular economies held apart in *Ion* and *Bid Me to Live.* The narrator, who experiences "the ingredients of the Gift" in "flashes of flash-backs" from her Moravian childhood (42) and the terror of the contemporary world in "the great fires and the terrible bombing" of World War II London (209), labors like a sapper to detect, defuse, and rewire these energy fields. "There was a time-bomb that had neatly nosed its way under the pavement edge, less than two minutes' walk from my door," H.D. writes in the vignette that opens the book's middle chapter. "At night, with carefully hooded flares, a party of the London demolition squad, prodded and poked; delicately, they inserted little wires or tubes or blades of steel and disemboweled the monster" (109). The book concludes with the coinciding of these two economies in an all-clear siren that signals, simultaneously, the retreat of the bombers and the retrieval of the vision of the gift (223).

Neither fiction nor memoir, *The Gift* is a kind of "autobiographical fantasy" ("H.D. by Delia Alton" 189) that conflates individual and cultural memory. In an effort to establish not only incidents but laws, each chapter of *The Gift* returns the narrator to a specific moment—a summer evening, a parade, a nightmare—that can be used to access the experience of "all the children of all the world" (47). Although it sets off alarms for a reader schooled in postcolonial theory, this swift transit from the personal to the universal was a familiar habit in early twentieth-century archaeology, anthropology, ethnology, and psychology. The work of Sir James Frazer, Jane Harrison and the Cambridge Ritualists, Mauss, Durkheim, Freud, and Jung relied on the assumption of correspondences across cultures that enabled H.D. and others to imagine autobiography as a kind of research into culture.[45] The emotional saturation inherent in this kind of research, a saturation that gives *The Gift* its hypnotic rhythms and eerie clarity of recall, should not obscure the larger argumentative aims of her project.

For H.D. the move from personal to global was not metaphoric—a sense that her childhood was somehow *like* an Egyptian or Greek girl's childhood—but biological: the theory of memory operative in the text suggests that the mind "contains cells . . . which can be affiliated to the selves of people, living or long dead" (51).[46] In chapter 1, "Dark Room," therefore, the children's witnessing of a parade meant to drum up business for a traveling production of *Uncle Tom's Cabin* is not a local but a universal event—"It was Alexandria, it was a Roman Triumph, it was a Medieval miracle-play procession with a Devil who was Simon Legree and the poor dark shades of Purgatory, who were the negroes chained together, and . . . Pallas Athene in her chariot with the winged Victory . . . who was coming to save us all" (47–48): this event "comes true" in her memory not because she finds factual confirmation for it but because it aligns itself with parallel moments in myth and sacred history.

The intertwining of selves and cells makes it possible for the narrator to retrieve her mother's and her maternal grandmother's experiences as if they were—as in a sense they are—her own. In chapter 2, she relives her mother's visit to a fortune teller who predicts her own birth; in chapter 7, she relives her grandmother's recovery of a moment of suppressed Moravian history. This memory-at-one-remove is not a narrative strategy but, we are to believe, a somatic event that occurs when "the curious chemical constituents of biological or psychic thought-processes" (49) are loosed and events are restaged in the consciousness of those who inherit them.[47]

The secret unearthed in H.D.'s text as at once a spiritual truth and a secular strategy is the obligation to give, receive, and reciprocate, to suffer the labor of gratitude and feed the hau of the gift. The opening chapters prepare for the relay of the gift, first from the grandmother to the child, then from the narrator to the reader, by instantiating a mode of thinking that is less rational or analytic than communal, associative, and symbolic. Although the "I" of the text is its child-narrator, its dominant pronouns are the first-person "we" of the gift community and a second-person "you" designed to pull the reader toward this community: "you may wonder," "you may glance," "you may know," the narrator insists, "I want you to know" (84–85). The secret the reader is to learn depends on his or her consent to move beyond the circle of the ego into more elastic and affiliative subject positions.

Linearity, logic, and distance have little purchase in this text. Quirks of style that at first seem atmospheric gain force as means to restructure consciousness: constantly shifting verb tenses pleat past, present, and future into a four-dimensional "now"; sentences cluster, aggregate, or repeat rather than analyze; paragraphs beginning with formulas like "There was," "What he did, was," or

"What it was, was" proceed into lush participatory descriptions; metaphors prevail over similes;[48] words accrue meanings through echoic repetitions. Like the oral recitations described by Havelock and Ong, the phonotexts analyzed by Stewart, and the puncepts described by Ulmer, *The Gift* operates as "a game . . . a way of making words out of words . . . a way of spelling words, in fact . . . a *spell*" (42). The child's fascination with words and proper names—*aisle, virgin, sister, Wunden Eiland, Gnadenhuetten,* to name only a few—leads her to another word whose "ardent, complex, ineffable, and somehow sacred signification gives the illusion that by this word one might answer for everything" (Barthes, *Roland Barthes* 129): the text's title and mana-word, *gift*.

To try to grasp the meaning of this word, the child prods and pokes her way through a tangled set of connections: at first the gift seems to belong to men—her father, the brilliant astronomer; her uncle, the musician—*but* if artists are people with gifts, then ladies too can be gifted (43), *yet* her mother seems to have lost her gift by allowing her own father to frighten her into the role of a dutiful daughter[49] or by giving it away to her brother, *but* then perhaps not, because the fortune teller promised her she would bear a child who would have a gift, *so* is Hilda, then, the child "marked with that strange thing they called a Gift" (42)? These ruminations tell the child that the gift is alive and mobile, that it binds those through whom it passes, demands a labor of gratitude, and entails the obligations to receive and reciprocate, but it is not until chapter 5, "The Secret," that it is understood to be a wisdom that could make "a united brotherhood, a *Unitas Fratrum* of the whole world" (214).

It is a hot summer night streaked with falling stars: Papa is at his telescope mapping stars; Mama and the aunts and uncles are outside counting and wishing on them; and Hilda and her maternal grandmother, Mamalie, are in an upstairs bedroom where Mamalie, in a trance initiated by the phrase "shooting star," relives the event at the heart of the text. This event is a ceremony that took place on Wunden Eiland in 1741, which Mamalie, deciphering encoded records, relived in 1841 and which the narrator, in her turn, will reenact in 1941. The chapter, heavily scored and much reworked in manuscript, is tangled with the complexities of establishing an erased Moravian history through an old woman's ecstatic murmurings to an enthralled young girl. The device by which H.D. maintains control of the incident, however, also functions to turn it into a collaboration: as Mamalie works back into her vision, she projects onto Hilda the identities of those who surrounded her in the past, identities Hilda in turn takes up and plays out to keep Mamalie in her trance.

Mamalie's story is a tale of encounter, mutual recognition, and gift exchange between the Moravians and the Indians. Mamalie emphasizes that the Moravians were not interested in exploitative exchange: they "had not asked for furs, they had not traded with the Indians, this in itself seemed strange," but, in addition, "they had not taken land," purchasing it from John Penn and then purchasing it again from the Indians (164).[50] When they first meet, the Indians and Moravians, like the initiates in *Trilogy*, recognize each other by secret symbols: the Indians perceive their Great Spirit in the Moravians' music, and the Moravians recognize their iconography in the hieroglyphs on the Indians' ceremonial belt. When the Indians pass the belt to the Moravians, Mamalie explains, it was, like all gift transmissions, "more than an exchange of outer civilities, it was an inner greeting and it seemed a pact had been made" (165).

The pact was a plan to enact an ancient ritual of connection: a symbolic exchange through which the Moravian Anna von Pahlen would be initiated into the Indian mysteries and the Native American Morning Star would be baptized Moravian, each taking a name from the other, bonding the groups into kinship.[51] The first draft of this chapter indicates that for H.D. this giving-in-turn marked the confluence of two streams, one bearing the gift eastward from Asia, China, and Tibet to the Indians, the other westward from the Knights Templar and Cathars to the Moravians ("Gift" typescript, first typed draft, "The Secret," 34). The connection at Wunden Eiland completed a kind of global kula ring, "linking up all the mysteries through time, in all lands and for all peoples" ("Gift" typescript, first typed draft, "Morning Star," 27). The secret exchanged in this moment, the narrator comments, "properly directed, might have changed the course of history, might have lifted the dark wings of evil from the whole world" ("Gift" typescript, first typed draft, "The Secret," 29–30).

The hau of the gift stopped at Wunden Eiland, however, its promise broken by both parties when Moravian officials condemned the ceremony and repressed the records and renegade Indians burned the Moravian settlement at Gnadenhuetten. One hundred years later, after Mamalie and her first husband decipher the buried scroll, he dies, and she burns in the fever that recurs on the night of the falling stars and ceases only when she transmits the gift to Hilda, who, in turn, one hundred years after Mamalie's vision, suffers in the *now* of the text the agonies of "the great fires and the terrible bombing of London" (*Gift* 209) and "passionately regret[s] only this. That the message that had been conveyed to me, that the message that my grandmother had received, would again be lost" (213).

Mamalie's terror at the words "shooting star" is her fear that "the papers would be burnt or she would be burnt" before she could pass the gift on, and "now," the narrator in the final chapter fears, "I would be burnt" by another form of shooting star (209). As the book closes, the all clear sounds, and the two scenes coalesce "in one voice" (223). At this moment, the gift passes on, and the reader is left, like Mamalie, then Hilda, holding the burden of the future.

"[W]hile one's own walls still shake with the reverberation," the narrator writes, "there is that solemn pause; time is wiped away. In three minutes or in three seconds, we gain what no amount of critical research or analytical probing could give us" (109). In the flash of this moment, the linear falls away and it seems possible to move beyond factions toward fraternity. "I do not think in journalistic truisms," the narrator continues, "in terms of nation against nation. . . . [W]e must never forget how each one of us (through inertia, through indifference, through ignorance) is, in part, responsible for the world-calamity" (109–10). The autobiographical fantasy that grounds the gift in the circumstances of H.D.'s life establishes the circuit connecting the personal, political, and spiritual that failed in *Ion* and *Bid Me to Live,* passes the gift forward enriched and elaborated by its connections to war in our time, and holds the reader responsible for continuing the relay of power and of peace that constitutes the secret of the gift.

Notes

1. Translated as *The Gift: Forms and Functions of Exchange in Archaic Societies,* Mauss's *Essai sur le don* (1924) initiated a rich literature on the structuration of cultures through gifts and gift giving. For Claude Lévi-Strauss, Mauss's contribution was to shift the study of social behavior from observations of customs toward an understanding of the rules that organize them, thus anticipating Lévi-Strauss's own structural anthropology. Important commentators on the gift include Jacques Derrida, Hélène Cixous, Luce Irigaray, Georges Bataille, and Pierre Bourdieu. For a summary of readings and reappraisals of Mauss's theories, see Alan D. Schrift's introduction to his collection of essays, *The Logic of the Gift.* My understanding of the spirit of the gift is indebted to the commentary of Lewis Hyde in *The Gift,* Marshall Sahlins in *Stone Age Economics,* and Maurice Godelier in *The Enigma of the Gift.*

2. The term in Mauss's series that became central to Lévi-Strauss's structural anthropology is, of course, "women." For analyses of the place of women in social exchange, see Rubin, "The Traffic in Women," and Irigaray, "Women on the Market."

3. See Guest, *Herself Defined* 112–13, 295–97. For additional details about the Ellerman fortune, see Robinson 262.

4. H.D.'s sensitivity to such imputations may play a part in her allusion to an anniversary gift from Bryher—a fur coat, no less—as "the wages of sin" ("Compassionate" 9), but the caricature is too broad to conclude, as Guest seems to do, that H.D. took such a charge to heart (265).

5. See, for example, H.D. to Bryher, 1 February 1919, 26 December 1932 (letter 1, p. 3), 23 September 1945.

6. In a letter to H.D. from April 1933, Herring writes, "Bryher has been being marvellous to me lately in that kind of anonymous way of hers, which makes it difficult to 'thank' her. She is like a kind note fluttering in through the window . . . [;] the sender has gone [and] there's just a sentence in one's mind, a white miracle, left" (Herring, Letters p. 2).

7. For the pseudonyms H.D. devised for her earliest magazine publications, see Boughn, "Bibliographic Record."

8. As Timothy Materer points out, "a modern poet who lacks a sense of irony when exploring this world may seem hopelessly naïve" (4), not to mention intellectually disrespectable and/or emotionally unbalanced. On modernism and the occult, see also Sword, "Necrobibliography" and "H.D.'s *Majic Ring*."

9. As Louis L. Martz points out in his introduction to H.D.'s *Collected Poems*, perhaps the most interesting twist in H.D.'s early "translations" of Sappho is the care she took to veil her references to Richard Aldington. "In all the revisions of these poems," Martz comments, "the evidence that the faithless lover is male has been removed" (xviii). For more on H.D.'s collaborations with Sappho, see Gubar, "Sapphistries," and, especially, Gregory's discussion of H.D.'s masque, "Hymen," in *H.D. and Hellenism* 156–61.

10. See H.D.'s letter to Brigit Patmore, dated 18 February 1925 (Letters). In the concluding scene of H.D.'s autobiographical novel *Asphodel,* the characters who stand in for H.D. and Bryher exchange a child as part of a mutual pact to live: "'I make a bargain with you,'" Hermione says. "'If you promise never more to say that you will kill yourself, I'm going to give you something. . . . I want you to promise me to grow up and take care of the little girl'" (205–6). Guest mentions the adoption in *Herself Defined* 155, 203.

11. Guest makes this suggestion in *Herself Defined* 111.

12. *Hedgehog* 27. The god Helios is the father of Phoebe Fayne in *Asphodel,* of Hedylus in *Hedylus,* and of Ion in H.D.'s recreation of Euripides' *Ion.*

13. Long after the dissolution of this ménage à quatre, Macpherson continued to father his adopted daughter. On a trip in 1947, in fact, Kenneth and Perdita encountered Gray and, as Perdita summarizes this tangled moment, "my legal father introduced me to my father. 'Cecil, my daughter Perdita'" (Schaffner, "Profound" 191–92).

14. For alternate family arrangements, see especially Carol B. Stack's description of the community she calls "The Flats" in *All Our Kin,* particularly chap. 5, "Child-Keeping" 62–89. For a description of Perdita's many family groupings, see Guest, *Herself Defined* 243. My intent here is not to justify or condone H.D.'s style of parenting—she was, by all accounts, a mother who had little time for her child—but, more simply, to suggest another context within which this behavior can be understood.

15. The imbrication of the gift and market economies is as complex and vexed as the cultural overlap among orality, literacy, and secondary orality. The argument that follows is not meant to suggest that H.D. conceived of herself as living outside a market economy but rather that she also—and importantly—saw herself as living within an economy of gift exchange.

16. See, for example, the contrasts in *Helen in Egypt* between Agamemnon's chain of command and Clytemnestra's domestic network or in *The Gift* and *Tribute to Freud* between her father's Puritan ancestry and her mother's Moravian lineage. In these texts, H.D.'s juxtapositions of two differently organized systems of value anticipate Carol Gilligan's gendered comparison between an ethic of rights based on abstract principles of reciprocity and an ethic of care based on interpersonal needs and responsibilities.

17. In *The Gift*, Mauss discusses an "evolved" form of gift exchange exemplified by the potlatches of the Kwakiutl Indians and their neighbors on the northwest coast of North America. "The rules of potlatch," Godelier explains, "seem to oppose term for term the principles animating the gift-exchanges [among the Maori and the Trobriand Islanders]. In potlatch, one gives in order to 'flatten' the other" (56). This agonistic use of the obligations to give, receive, and reciprocate is a form of warfare that differs significantly from the giving-in-turn that is the focus of this chapter.

18. It must be emphasized that the work H.D. did in these years both assimilated *and* countered Freud's insights. See DuPlessis and Friedman, "'Woman is Perfect'" and, especially, Friedman, *Psyche Reborn,* part 1 (17–154).

19. Mauss's account draws on an explanation gathered from Tamati Ranaipiri by the anthropologist Elsdon Best. Following the initial publication of *Essai sur le don,* Mauss's interpretation of Ranaipiri's account was contested, first by Raymond Firth, then by Marshall Sahlins. For a description of the controversy and a valuable reinterpretation of the Maori ritual, see Godelier 49–56.

20. For H.D.'s research into the history of Northeastern American Indians, see especially her "Notes" to *The Gift,* reprinted and annotated in Jane Augustine's edition of *The Gift: The Complete Text.*

21. These obligations are detailed in Mauss, *Gift* 10–11. For a description of the Moravian love feasts, see Gollin 20–21.

22. For an argument that "the two worlds, the world of gifts and that of commodities," not only coexist but "are in fact comparable," see Godelier 70–71.

23. The best explications of Moravian theology are Gollin's *Moravians in Two Worlds* and Sessler's *Communal Pietism among Early American Moravians.* See also two books by Adelaide L. Fries, *The Moravian Church: Yesterday and Today,* a book H.D. seems to have consulted, and *The Road to Salem,* a text she owned, annotated, and cited in her "Notes" to *The Gift.*

24. For further information about the Choir system, see Gollin's chapter "The Development of the Choir System" (67–89) and Sessler's chapter "A Holy Brotherhood" (93–105). Pictures of the Gemeinhaus and other Moravian buildings can be found on the Web page of the Moravian Museum of Bethlehem at <http://www.moravianmuseum.org/museum/sites.jsp>.

25. For a discussion of the complex causes for the dissolution of this agreement, see Gollin 198–203 and Sessler 182–212.

26. For more details, see *Bethlehem of Pennsylvania: The Golden Years, 1841–1920,* a publication of the Bethlehem Book Committee.

27. In *The Gift,* H.D. records this split by tracing lines of inheritance forward from their childhood: while she will inherit her mother's family's visionary capacities, H.D. tells us, her brother "Harold will inherit the mills and the steel and numbers too and become a successful business-man like Uncle Hartley" (121).

28. "Callypso Speaks" is the title Pearson gave to the second part of H.D.'s poem in *H.D.: Selected Poems* 59. For H.D.'s stratagem of displacing narrative by giving voice to the "other side," see DuPlessis's discussion of H.D.'s "Eurydice" in *Writing beyond the Ending* 70–71, 109–10.

29. See DuPlessis, *Writing beyond the Ending,* chap. 5 (66–83).

30. In Friedman's summary, "she gave and gave and gave; he took and took and left" (*Psyche Reborn* 239).

31. James Hillman's elaboration of the differences between polytheism and monotheism are useful in understanding this dimension of H.D.'s narration of the shift from a gift to a market economy.

32. H.D.'s review of a collection of Marianne Moore's poems identifies the impulse behind poems like "Cities" and "The Tribute": "[Moore] is fighting in her country a battle against squalor and commercialism," H.D. writes. "We are all fighting the same battle" ("Marianne Moore" 119).

33. For more on Hermes, see Hyde, *Trickster Makes This World.*

34. Lawrence Rainey's response to what he perceives as the exclusive first-person plural of *Trilogy* is to return insult for insult: the poem's "we," he comments, "flatters its audience," "gratifies its readers' wish to believe that knowledge comes without pain," and "embraces only the initiates who already share the poet's belief in a heady brew of astrology, Tarot cards, and séances" (*Institutions* 162).

35. In this sense, each tribute was, as H.D. called her memoir of Pound, an "end to torment," a release from the grip of an "[i]mmensely sophisticated, immensely superior, immensely rough-and-ready" initiator (*End to Torment* 3).

36. H.D.'s communication to Pearson, dated 24 October 1944, is transcribed in his folder of notes labeled "*Trilogy* (annotated)." The biblical passages to which she refers him are Numbers 31:28, Deuteronomy 16:10, and Romans 13:7.

37. For Moravian ritualizations of marriage, see Sessler 151–52. For the rewritings of Gray as a god, see especially *Asphodel* 156–58; for Macpherson as Hermes, see "Narthex" and *The Usual Star.* H.D.'s most lush and extended descriptions of hierogamy occur in *Nights.* With H.D.'s habit of conflating figures in her life, the superimpositions in her erotic entanglements are dizzying: thus, for example, H.D. confesses to her friend George Plank that she had an erotic relationship with Bryher in Greece, "a sort of 'marriage by prozy' [*sic*]," in which Bryher stood in for Rodeck, while other texts show Rodeck standing in for Helios and thereby redoubling the figure of Cecil Gray (letter to Plank, 1 May 1935, p. 2; "Majic Ring" 156).

38. See especially *Bid Me to Live* 110; "Majic Ring" 150.

39. In "Narthex" H.D. speaks of the lover's seed as "soul-sperm" (236). Hyde finds a similar formulation in the writings of the fourteenth-century Christian mystic Meis-

ter Eckhart, who believed that "[w]hen God pours himself into the soul, the Child is born, and this birth is the fruit of gratitude for the gift" (*Gift* 55).

40. For more on maternal paradigms in H.D.'s work, see Friedman, *Psyche Reborn* 229–72; Kloepfer, "Flesh Made Word" and *Unspeakable Mother;* DuPlessis, *Writing beyond the Ending* 66–83; and Hollenberg, *H.D.: The Poetics of Childbirth and Creativity.*

41. A telling definition of the Gift in its Moravian sense comes from the polemics of the eighteenth-century pamphleteer John Roche: when the Moravians found potential converts, Roche fulminates, "then would they tell them they were sure, by many Signs and Reasons they knew, that that Person would soon receive the Gift, and that so soon as they would, they should preach and instruct the people" (72).

42. The New Directions edition of *The Gift,* published in 1982, omits one of H.D.'s seven chapters and cuts or elides significant portions of others. As many scholars have pointed out, this edition is in effect an abridgment of H.D.'s text. Fortunately, however, the complete text of *The Gift,* based on H.D.'s third and final typescript and including her extensive historical and biographical notes, has been edited and annotated by Jane Augustine and published by the University Press of Florida. All citations refer to Augustine's edition, although, occasionally, as noted, I have included material from earlier typescripts of *The Gift* at the Beinecke. For a synopsis of the publishing history of *The Gift,* see DuPlessis, "A Note on the State of H.D.'s *The Gift,*" and Augustine, "A Note on the Text and Its Arrangement."

43. Pearson's notes toward a life of H.D. are filed at the Beinecke Library in a folder labeled "H.D. Biog." Mrs. Ashe was the charwoman who worked for Bryher and H.D. in their flat in Lowndes Square.

44. For a description of Char's World War II poetry as a kind of military operation, see Noland, chap. 6.

45. Eileen Gregory points to "an uncanny parallelism between Harrison and H.D. in terms of their intellectual affinities and imaginative emphases," which testifies not to direct influence but to "a broad and diffused intertextuality" (*H.D. and Hellenism* 110). See especially chap. 4 of *H.D. and Hellenism.*

46. This idea recalls Freud's notion that experiences of the ego "when they have been repeated often enough and with sufficient strength in many individuals in successive generations" can "transform themselves . . . into experiences of the id, the impressions of which are preserved by heredity." For this citation and discussion of other Lamarckian traces in Freud's thought, see Clark, *Freud* 437.

47. Access to memories that are not one's own is a familiar trope in contemporary science fiction films like *Total Recall* and *Conceiving Ada.*

48. "[T]his is not only like that town," the narrator has Count Zinzendorf proclaim, "this is indeed that town, Bethlehem" (67).

49. Adrienne Rich's contention that "the dutiful daughter of the fathers in us is only a hack" links a "primary intensity" between women to the ability to say "no" to the fathers (201–2). The contrast between Helen Doolittle's tie to her father and Hilda's tie to her grandmother seems to make a similar point.

50. "The Death of Martin Presser," a short story H.D. considered appending to *The Gift,* makes the same point.

51. In a dizzying twist of conflationary zeal, in an earlier draft of chap. 7 H.D. had Hilda, who is at this point in the story playing Mamalie's daughter Aggie, reason that since Anna von Pahlen's inner name was, like Aggie's middle name, Angelica, "I would be part of Anna von Pahlen, too, and I would be part of the ceremony at *Wunden Eiland* and I would be Morning Star along with Anna" (32). For the exchange of women from the perspective of a market economy, see Rubin; for the exchange of women in the history of gift rituals, see Hyde, chap. 6 (93–108).

5 Strange Attractors:
Science and the
Mythopoeic Mind

[W]hen I say that a word is beautiful, when I use it because I like it, it is never by virtue of its sonorous charm or of the originality of its meaning, or of a "poetic" combination of the two. The word transports me because of the notion that *I am going to do something with it:* it is the thrill of a future praxis, something like an *appetite.* This desire makes the entire motionless chart of language vibrate.
—Roland Barthes, *Roland Barthes*

"Somehow the wondrous promise of the earth is that there are things beautiful in it, things wondrous and alluring, and by virtue of your trade you want to understand them."
—Mitchell Feigenbaum, quoted in James Gleick, *Chaos: Making a New Science*

The modern poet not only by the example of tradition but by the very compulsion of a desire to know things has amplified the way of the scientist.
—Norman Holmes Pearson, "The American Poet in Relation to Science"

The terms *projection, gift,* and *science* have neither sonorous charm nor originality of meaning. Like *projection,* they crop up in multiple and competing belief systems; like *gift,* they are sometimes central, sometimes peripheral to these systems; like *science,* their meanings within these systems are contextual rather than absolute, palimpsestic rather than precise. Although it would be possible to use these terms in a paradoxical or counterintuitive fashion—"the science of magic," "the gift of death"—it is not particularly rewarding to do so since they are more absorptive than resistant. As a cluster, these terms don't constitute a paradigm or closed set: one could add to the list nouns like *hieroglyph* or phrases like *come true* without significantly expanding or contracting the work they do. Because H.D.'s mana-words are less a terminus of thought than its relay, their power lies in their mobility and generativity.

For Barthes, the lure of mana-words is their application: "the thrill of a future praxis" (*Roland Barthes* 129). "The word's work," Barthes explains, "is to give to one and the same phrase inflections which will be forever new, thereby creating an unheard-of speech in which the sign's form is repeated but never is signified" (114). The mana-words in Barthes's lexicon—he lists "'body,' 'difference,' 'Orpheus,' 'Argo,' etc." (127)—are, like H.D.'s *projection, gift,* and *science,* at once everywhere and nowhere, full and empty, recurrent and available. Both writers avoid abstractions like *truth* or *nature,* which lay claim to a single origin, privileged denotation, or a fixed or transcendent answer. The word *projection* patterns H.D.'s ideas about imagism, cinema, psychoanalysis, and alchemy, the word *gift* structures her notions of how to live and what to do, the word *science* tracks her thoughts about ways of knowing, but none of her texts gives these words a final or definitive formulation.

The differences between Barthes's and H.D.'s mana-words could be mapped onto received notions about the differences between poststructuralism and high modernism by arguing that whereas Barthes's goal is an endless process of signification, H.D.'s goal might be seen to be a unitary or sacred signified—a vision, perhaps, a mythopoetics, a transcendence. While it is true that mana-words seem to function for H.D. as clues, traces, or tracks that lead toward something out-of-time, in her work *projections* vanish before they can be seized, *gifts* perish if they do not continue to circulate, and *science* is a process rather than a product, a way of knowing rather than a thing that's known. Like the chaologist Mitchell Feigenbaum, Barthes and H.D. both conceive of their trade as an effort to understand something that will always elude them. "*[T]here is meaning,*" as Barthes puts it, "but this meaning does not permit itself to be 'caught'; it remains fluid" (*Roland Barthes* 97–98).

Barthes's term for writing that forgets or occludes its own provisionality is "triumphant discourse" or, more simply, borrowing a term from Georges Bataille, "*arrogance.*" There are, Barthes continues, "three arrogances: that of Science, that of the *Doxa,* that of the Militant" (47). The Doxa is "Public Opinion, the mind of the majority, petit bourgeois Consensus, the Voice of Nature, the Violence of Prejudice" (47); the Militant is the Doxa armed in the service of its assumptions; Science is the Doxa "erected into a Law by the scientists who [have] constituted themselves its procurators" (160). H.D.'s name for the procurators of triumphant discourse is "them," and they are everywhere in her work. "[A] Juggernaught crushing out mind and perception" ("Cinema and the Classics I" 105), they are cast as Roman legionnaires and English matrons in her novels, Anglo-Saxon officers on leave in London or "Anglo-saccharine" Bryn Mawr graduates at tea in Philadelphia in her autobiographical fiction (*HERmione* 129), one-eyed enforcers of the Hollywood code in her film criticism. In *HERmione,* the novel at the center of this chapter, "they" is the alliance of Carl Gart, guardian of Science, and his wife Eugenia, guardian of the Doxa—the first with his "biological-mathematical definition of the universe" (6), the second with "a dart in her hair" and a "dress cut mathematically square" (31).

If in their polemics against the arrogance of invariance H.D. and Barthes tend toward caricature, their depictions of science as a day-to-day praxis are more tempered. "He suspected Science," Barthes writes of himself in the third person, "reproaching it for what Nietzsche calls its *adiaphoria,* its in-difference, erected into a Law by the scientists who constituted themselves its procurators. Yet his condemnation dissolved each time it was possible to *dramatize* Science (to restore to it a power of difference, a textual effect); he liked the scientists in whom he could discern a disturbance, a vacillation, a mania, a delirium, an inflection" (160). What interests Barthes and H.D. alike is a challenge that also fascinates scientists like Feigenbaum and his colleagues in the investigation of chaos: a thinking about pattern that does not drop out disturbance, difference, wonder, and generativity.

In February 1949, Norman Holmes Pearson wrote H.D. about a lecture he was planning to entitle "The American Poet and Science" (H.D., *Between History* 87).[1] "Will you be surprised," he asks, "to find yourself in it? Well, you are, and whether or not you know it, you have been influenced by science, though you proceed on a conceptual basis of intuition rather than inductive reason" (115n.69). In addition to H.D., Pearson cites Pound, Eliot, Williams, Hart Crane, Marianne Moore, Wallace Stevens, and Muriel Rukeyser in support of his claim that "[t]he basic influence of science on the modern American poet has not been merely a matter of bringing over into verse the terminology or the artifacts of science" ("American Poet" 118). Although Pearson sticks to generalities about the new science of "time, space, curvature" and "the mystery of the fourth dimension" (120), he is vehement in his contention that poets must replace a "language of esthetics . . . based on outmoded propositions" (119) with "a new vocabulary and syntax for giving extension to [their] conclusions" (117).

In April 1949, having read Pearson's lecture, H.D. wrote back in praise of his ability to "steer a middle-course between very dangerous shoals" (*Between History* 115n.69). The shoals H.D. has in mind are the familiar Scylla and Charybdis of Western thought: subjectivity and objectivity, imagination and reason, intuition and induction, qualitative values and "quantitative, measurable things" (Pearson, "American Poet" 122), "the fog of abstract words," as Pearson puts it, quoting Hermann Weyl, and "'the concrete rock of reality'" (117). Scientists would do well to listen to poets, Pearson argues, quoting Wallace Stevens, for "who is to say of [imagination's] deliberate fictions . . . that they are not forerunners of some . . . science" (123); poets, in their turn, would do well not to "walk out on the language of the pure mathematician" (121) but to incorporate the lexicon of the new physics into the vocabulary of the imagination.

Although Pearson is correct to include H.D. in the roster of poets who heed the claims of new science, H.D.'s intuitions about poetry and science were more radical than she or Pearson could describe in the decade after World War II. During the half-century since Pearson's essay, the divide between subjectivity and objectivity, which he took for granted, has crumbled, and, in Bruno Latour's summary, "'The active locus of science . . . has shifted to the middle, to the humble instruments, tools, visualization skills, writing practices, focusing techniques, and what has been called "re-representation." Through all these efforts, the mediation has eaten up the two extremities: the representing Mind and the represented World'" (qtd. in Tiffany 4). As Daniel Tiffany has shown, such a shift has significant consequences for an understanding of poetry's participation in cultural discourse: "To historicize and aestheticize science . . . is to grant reciprocally to art and literature a deterministic role in the construction of the real. In this light, the forms of mediation and imagination proper to lyric poetry begin to resemble the tools and practices of science—especially, as in physics, when it is a question of depicting unobservable phenomena" (5). In including *science* as one of H.D.'s mana-words, my argument is not that H.D. anticipated these changes, much less that she influenced or stimulated them, but rather that her writing takes part in a cultural ferment that has reconfigured the categories through which we think the world.

In H.D.'s best work, as Pearson surmised, poetry and science are mutually supportive discourses. The axis of opposition in her thinking lies not between poetry and science, fog and rock, but between kinds of knowledge that could be styled "Science" and "science": on the one hand, Newtonian Science backed by the Doxa and the Militant; on the other hand, post-Newtonian science as it has been elaborated by scientists like Einstein, Bohr, and Feigenbaum, artists like Picasso, Joyce, and Stravinsky, psychoanalysts like Freud and Lacan, and thinkers like Barthes and Derrida. As a third and final mana-word, the term *science* allows us not only to investigate affinities between projects that valorize fluidity, variance, and provisionality but also to perceive the overlap in the generative construction of the real in the mana-words *projection, gift,* and *science.*

*   *   *

"[M]ythopoeic mind (mine) will disprove science and biological-mathematical definition," H.D. proclaimed in her autobiographical novel about a girl who fails Conic Sections, flunks out of college, and takes on the task of undermining the science of her biological-mathematical father (*HERmione* 76). Throughout her long career, in the questions she asked and in the answers she attempted, H.D. aspired to recalibrate science and poetry by becoming what one of her characters calls "a sort of scientific lyrist" (*Nights* 24). Her poems bristle with terms from biology, chemistry, physics, and astronomy, with geometrical angles and shapes, with mathematical signs and equations, all of which she uses to align small details with larger patterns and formulate ever more inclusive and elastic laws. Although her work does not disprove her father's science, it has much to tell us about the interrelations between science, poetry, and the "mythopoeic mind" of the culture that contains them.

H.D. grew up in a household of patriarchs who spent their days or nights peering through powerful magnifying lenses: her maternal grandfather, the Reverend Francis Wolle, an internationally known microbiologist, examined algae; her father, Professor Charles Leander Doolittle, charted the orbit of the earth around the sun; and her much older half-brother, Eric Doolittle, catalogued double and multiple star systems. Throughout the first decade of H.D.'s life, her grandfather worked in the sitting room of the house next door and her father in a small transit house behind their home; after 1896, when her father became the director of the University of Pennsylvania's Flower Observatory, her family lived on the grounds of the observatory where her father and half-brother conducted their research and H.D. helped to introduce large companies of visitors to the wonders of the night sky.[2] Throughout her early life, scientific activities were as much a part of H.D.'s environment as the bustle in the kitchen or the garden. Conducted around-the-clock and debated over dinner, these enterprises not only widened her familiarity with observational science but encouraged her to stay current with and appropriate for her own work some of twentieth-century science's most complex and consequential advances.[3]

In these ways, science was a direct influence and source of inspiration for H.D., "a new Muse," as one of her characters puts it, "one not to be treated lightly" (*Hedylus* 25). For many of the most interesting intersections between science and H.D.'s mythopoeic mind, however, direct influence is unlikely or even impossible. In contrast to the one-way, causal, science-to-poetry model Daniel Albright has recently used to argue that "the methods of physicists helped to inspire poets to search for the elementary particles of which poems were constructed" (1), this chapter is based on a model of intellectual history as a conversation conducted simultaneously on many disparate fronts.[4] Here the challenge is not to specify a new muse but to comprehend a shared musing. That H.D.'s poetry plays out patterns formalized by chaos theorists more than a decade after her death is, in this sense, not a matter of cause and effect but a manifestation of a culture's broad and faceted attempt to imagine its way out of the dilemmas it creates for itself.[5]

*   *   *

H.D.'s life spanned the most important revolutions in science since Copernicus's contention that the earth is not the center of the universe. When H.D. was born in the late nineteenth century, physics was widely considered "a closing book." Newton had explained gravitation, James Clerk Maxwell and Ludwig Boltzmann had explained heat, Maxwell and Michael Faraday had explained electromagnetism, and scientists had begun to advise their students to abandon hope of further breakthroughs and devote themselves to the labor of refining existing laws. By the time H.D. reached mid-career, however, almost every existing scientific law had been disputed, diminished, or discarded. "Nothing," Alfred North Whitehead exclaimed in the 1930s, "absolutely nothing was left that had not been challenged, if not shaken; not a single major concept. This I consider to have been one of the supreme facts of my experience."[6]

The breakthroughs that created the new physics coincided with H.D.'s formative years. In 1900, while she was listening to her father and half-brother discuss astronomy at the dinner table, Max Planck took the first crucial step toward quantum theory by noting that energy is absorbed and emitted not smoothly or continuously, as classical physicists had assumed, but in chunks, packets, or "quanta." Einstein published his theory of special relativity in 1905, while H.D. was pursuing her studies at Bryn Mawr, and his theory of general relativity in 1916, the year she published her first volume of poetry. In 1927, the year H.D. completed the bildungsroman in which her heroine pits her mythopoeic mind against her father's Newtonian certitudes, Niels Bohr and Werner Heisenberg formulated the principles of complementarity and uncertainty, which together convinced most physicists of the coherence and correctness of quantum theory. And finally, in the early 1970s, some ten years after H.D.'s death, isolated mathematicians, physicists, chemists, biologists, and meteorologists began the investigations into the nature of irregular phenomena that resulted in chaos theory, the third major scientific revolution of the twentieth century.

The heroes of H.D.'s meditations on creativity are thinkers like Leonardo da Vinci and Sigmund Freud who unsettle any easy opposition between induction and intuition, science and art. In a self-reflexive crisscross executed throughout her career, H.D. liked to define exemplary artists as those who push toward truth and exemplary scientists as those who devote themselves to beauty. As she describes them, investigators like Sappho, da Vinci, Einstein, and Freud combine "scientific precision" and "artistic wisdom" to embody the Greek definition of the physicist as the student of the nature of things. These artistic scientists and scientific artists ask the kinds of questions that compel children—What is the universe made of? What are dreams? How does love work?—and come to their answers not only through sophisticated reasoning but also in hunches, flashes, and imaginative flights.[7]

In most of H.D.'s writings, artistic labor is described in terms that also fit the investigations she witnessed in the households organized around her grandfather, father, and half-brother. With rare exceptions, artists in H.D.'s poetry and fiction are workers in a collective enterprise, members of a team, a troupe, or a group addressing a shared problem. When William Carlos Williams reported that the Doolittle household was dominated by the spirit of "a life of scientific research" ("Letter" 2), he meant the day-by-day, year-by-year, slow, sustained, exact, and exacting observation of a multitude of similar instances. This, the life of the "research worker," was the vocation H.D. claimed for herself, a vocation she played out not as a microbiologist or an astronomer but as a poet.[8]

The activity that drove the men in H.D.'s family to spend long hours at the eyepieces of powerful lenses was the collection and classification of data characteristic of late Victorian science.[9] The lenses they looked through took them toward the edges of Newton's three-dimensional, linear, deterministic model of the universe. Beyond the reach of her grandfather's microscope lay the subatomic units of matter whose behavior provoked the theories of quantum mechanics. Within the range of her father's and half-brother's telescopes but beyond their understanding lay the phenomena that verified Einstein's theories: the deflection of starlight near the sun, which supports the hypothesis of curved space, the furious stellar burning that demonstrates the formula $E = mc^2$, and the double stars that illustrate a key postulate of special relativity, the notion that light, whether it comes from the side of the star rotating toward us or the side of the star rotating away, always moves with a constant speed.

Despite their approach toward the very small and the very large, the researchers in H.D.'s household stayed within Newtonian parameters, and it was within these parameters that H.D.'s "scientific lyrism" began. Before examining her drive to disprove Newtonian science, it is useful to look briefly at her opposite and earlier desire to align herself with it. Although traces of this desire linger throughout H.D.'s life, it is dominant in the initial phases of her career during which she developed three strategies to harmonize her poetry with her grandfather's and father's science. Each of these strategies is linked with a figure from her youth: the two simplest, imitation and supplementation, are associated with her grandfather and father; the third and most ambitious, assimilation, is associated with her early companion and suitor, Ezra Pound.

*   *   *

H.D.'s grandfather, the Reverend Francis Wolle, was a passionate amateur. An inventor, schoolteacher, educational administrator, and Moravian minister, he retired in 1881 at the age of sixty-four to devote himself to his longstanding hobby: the collection, microscopic observation, and classification of cryptogamous plants. For at least four hours each day he peered through a J. Zentmayer "Army Hospital" microscope at slides smeared with pond scum and recorded his observations in a series of notebooks that provided the basis for his internationally recognized publications: *Desmids of the United States* (1884), the two-volume *Fresh-Water Algae of the United States* (1887), and *Diatomaceae of North America* (1890).[10] These catalogues not only name, classify, and describe thousands of varieties of algae, desmids, and diatoms but contain, in addition, some six thousand precisely scaled and meticulously rendered front, lateral, and vertical views of cryptogamous plants, two-thirds of them handtinted to reproduce the colors he described in meticulous detail.[11]

At a time when aspiring poets wandered the twilight landscapes of the symbolistes, compendia of precisely rendered pond scum seem an unlikely model, but Charlotte Mandel is surely correct in contending that the Reverend Wolle's botanical passion, eye for structure, and attentiveness to detail helped to shape H.D.'s first volume of verse ("Magical Lenses" 307–8). The terrain of *Sea Garden* is the coastland, salt marsh, and stream banks where earth and water sustain small and resourceful life-forms. Carefully spaced through the volume are poems that identify and describe small watery plants most poets overlook. H.D.'s "Sea Rose," "Sea Lily," "Sea Poppies," "Sea Violet," and "Sea Iris" reproduce not only the singular beauty Wolle found in small plants but also his delicate descriptions, transfixed interrogating gaze, and taxonomic precision (see, for example, *Diatomaceae* ix).

Wolle's descriptions of the varieties of algae are succinct and sensuous. Prefaced by a name created from Greek or Latin components, each entry is situated in a particular locale—"Attached to rocks," a typical example runs, "in rapids below water-fall, Pike Country, Pennsylvania"—then catalogued in precise, rhythmic prose. "Oscillaria Froelichii," Wolle writes: "Stratum dark steel blue, or dark olive green, often elongated, radiating, opaque, shining." "Floridiae": "Plants rosy red or purple, dark reddish brown or blackish; multicellular, various in form; crustaceous, filamentous, fasciculate, verticillately branched" (*Fresh-Water* 1:77, 315, 51). There is no cackle here, nothing overblown, vague, or sentimental.

The entries in *Sea Garden* are similarly taut and exact. Like Wolle's Greek and Latin nomenclature, their classical settings and mythological references give them an air of inscribing universal truths and enduring laws. Each poem is carefully situated in a specific landscape where, like a microscopist, H.D. isolates, suspends, and magnifies one or another aspect of the organism she examines. In the clarity of this gaze, each fleck, each streak and leaf spine of the plant becomes visible. Many of the poems move with mesmerized precision toward a definitive description or name: "Amber husk," "Sea Poppies" begins, "fluted with gold, / fruit on the sand / marked with a rich grain" (20); "Weed, moss-weed, / root tangled in sand," a second poem starts, "sea-iris" (40). These poems describe the processes through which wind, water, sand, and sun fling, lift, slash, stain, or shatter the plants and release the specimens only after their vitality has been caught and recorded.

H.D.'s imitation of the Reverend Wolle's botany was facilitated by the fact that in his catalogues her grandfather felt equally comfortable classifying his life-forms, exclaiming over their beauty, admiring their resourcefulness, and comparing them to mythological beings.[12] Professor Charles L. Doolittle's *Treatise on Practical Astronomy as Applied to Geodesy and Navigation* (1885) is another matter altogether. Doolittle's dryness is partly attributable to disciplinary differences between astronomy and botany, but it is also an effect of a professionalization that the historian of science Margaret W. Rossiter identifies as beginning in the 1880s and 1890s with "women's almost total ouster from major or even visible positions in science" (xvii).[13] Attacking a precisely formulated problem within his discipline, Doolittle hews a line that separates the professional from the amateur, the scientist from the poet, the gentlemen from the ladies. "[W]arm hearts," in Stephen Toulmin's summary of this ethos, "rarely go with cool heads" (230). It would be almost a century before scien-

tists like Feigenbaum once more felt free to exclaim over the wonder and al-
lure of their discoveries.

Although H.D. tells us that the professor wanted his daughter to become a
"scientist like (he even said so) Madame Curie,"[14] she chose not to imitate what
she understood to be the masculine, intellectual, critical cast of his science but
rather to supplement it by positioning her work as its feminine, emotional, and
creative complement. Such a configuration repeated the mix of science and
art in her parents' marriage, but with a crucial difference: unlike that marriage,
this was to be an alliance of equals and collaborators.[15] Its most succinct figuration is encoded in the name she selected for her fictional counterpart in a
story set in classical Rome portraying a writer whose poems are to be inset in
and thereby complete a rare scientific manuscript. Her name—and the story's title—is "Hipparchia," female counterpart of Hipparchus, the classical
astronomer who made his fame by calculating the positions of the stars in their
nightly transit across the skies (*Palimpsest* 71).

H.D.'s strategy of supplementing her father's science is at once conservative and critical, for it leaves conventional notions of gender intact while attempting to correct the privileging of the masculine. Professor Doolittle's clarity of mind, coolness, and rigor of approach made him an almost parodic
conflation of the "scientific," "objective," and "masculine." Leading the ardu-
ous life of an academic astronomer, Doolittle conducted regular classes in
astronomy and mathematics, directed an observatory, and made observations
by night that he turned into calculations by day. Acclaimed for its exactitude,
his work was to mark, again and again, the instant of time stars crossed the
threads in the eyepiece of his zenith telescope and to use those observations
to formulate mathematical laws for variations in latitude.[16] "My father studied or observed the variable orbit of the track of the earth around the sun,"
H.D. explained. "He spent thirty years on this problem, adding a graph on a
map started by Ptolemy in Egypt" (*Tribute to Freud* 142).

H.D.'s reference is accurate but not innocent, for in the end she prefers Ptolemy's map to her father's diagram. Ptolemy formulated laws for determining
variation in latitude, struggled, like Doolittle, with the problem of atmospheric
refraction, and developed a predictive model to understand planetary motions,
but he also codified the ancient Babylonian astrological tradition and became
the founder of modern popular astrology (Sagan 50–53). For Ptolemy there
was no clear line between Mars the astronomical notion and Mars the astrological presence. It is this amalgam of science, poetry, and religion that H.D.
wills back into being in *Tribute to Freud* when she chooses to describe her father's work from the point of view of the child for whom the "hieroglyph" at

the top of his "columns and columns of numbers . . . may stand for one of the Houses or Signs of the Zodiac, or it may be a planet simply: Jupiter or Mars or Venus" (25).

As if to correct the formalized and instrumental cast of her father's science and thereby remedy its diminished enterprise, throughout her life H.D. sought out astrological star-maps, star-lore, and star-catalogues. In her thinking, astrology seems to stand as a kind of synecdoche for the hermetic traditions left behind at the birth of modern science, traditions that assumed matter to be everywhere suffused with spirit.[17] As the twentieth century progressed through two world wars toward the atomic and hydrogen bombs, H.D.'s desire to temper modern materialistic science with ancient hermetic wisdom became more and more urgent. In 1957, long after she had found more effective means of displacing her father's science, she recorded a dream that revived and reenacted her old strategy of supplementation, a dream in which she escorted her distinguished father up the steps of a cathedral to meet "the Queen, the Mother" and "reconcile [his] purely formal, rational, scientific mathematics + astronomy with the inner mystery of the letters and numbers + the astrology + star lore + 'myth' of the *Kabballe*."[18]

Each time H.D. scanned, recorded, and dreamed about the great drift of stars overhead, wore her zodiac ring, signed her letters with the sigil of a star, or conducted the reading, chart deciphering, and meditation she called her "star research," she was engaged in the strategy of supplementation. For the most part, however, this strategy fails to nourish her art. When astrology enters H.D.'s poetry and novels, it most often results in a forced and elaborate rhetoric of starry puns, allusions, and parallelisms.[19] Although this rhetoric can be interpreted as a hermetic metaphysics, it cannot function as a counterpart or corrective to modern science. However yoked through their common ancestry in Ptolemy, astrology and astronomy have diverged too radically to be effectively reconciled: as modern practices they inhabit separate spheres, speak different languages, and satisfy disparate human needs. Although it persisted in the rituals of H.D.'s life, in her writing the strategy of supplementation gave way to a third, more ambitious and dynamic approach toward science.

Where supplementation makes science and poetry into adjacent and complementary disciplines, assimilation, H.D.'s third strategy, like imitation, her first, overlaps the two enterprises. Instead of turning poets into apprentices, however, assimilation gives them status in their own right. In imitation the poet follows a scientific pattern, model, or example, as H.D. did in copying her grandfather's botany; in assimilation, the poet takes up a position as a practitioner who contributes to knowledge in his or her own right. The claim of this strategy is not that poetry is *like* science but that in some fashion it *is* science. Here poets aspire to bring into focus regions hitherto invisible, record what they see accurately, and turn this data into verifiable laws or formulations.

The man who most vigorously formulated this aspiration was a poet who wooed the astronomer's daughter with such panache that he induced her, she tells us, to choose, "because my life depends upon it, between the artist and the scientist."[20] H.D.'s fable, however, has a deconstructive twist: having compelled her to choose between two apparently opposite vocations, her suitor goes on to elaborate a program that collapses these vocations into one. Between 1910 and 1920, the years during which he most had H.D.'s ear, Ezra Pound constructed his aesthetics on the conviction that the proper method of poetry is the method of science, a conviction he defended in a discourse that drew heavily from the terminology of chemistry, biology, mathematics, electromagnetism, radiology, and telecommunications.[21] Although, as we will see, H.D. eventually abandoned the Newtonian premises of Pound's argument, she never rejected its gist: the insistence that poets, like scientists, can discover and report on fundamental and enduring laws.

"Consider the way of the scientists rather than the way of an advertising agent for a new soap," Pound advised aspiring imagists. "The scientist does not expect to be acclaimed as a great scientist until he has *discovered* something. He begins by learning what has been discovered already. He goes from that point onward. He does not bank on being a charming fellow personally" ("Retrospect" 6). Soap salesmen, charming fellows, and conventional poets persuade through force of personality; scientists and imagists persuade through their ability to generate new data, which, in turn, produces new equations, formulas, or laws. For Pound, art has the two-phase rhythm of Doolittle's nightly observations and daily calculations: artists observe, collate, and record occurrences, then formulate laws to explain them, laws that have the precision and authority of mathematics. "We learn that the equation $(x - a)^2 + (y - b)^2 = r^2$ governs the circle," Pound explains. "It is the circle. It is not a particular circle, it is any circle and all circles. It is nothing that is not a circle. It is the circle free of space and time limits. It is the universal, existing in perfection. . . . It is in this way that art handles life" (*Gaudier-Brzeska* 91).[22]

Like the botany and astronomy practiced in H.D.'s family, imagism relied on the Newtonian assumption that there is a real world separate from the observer, a world it is possible to assess without in any way altering. When Einstein demonstrated that measurements depend on the observer's particular clock or ruler, he pegged relativity to the observer's location and in this way maintained his belief in an objective world that exists apart from the observer, but when Heisenberg demonstrated that our choice of what to observe makes an irretrievable difference in what we find, the foundations of Newtonian science began to erode. When she turned from imitating, supplementing, or assimilating classical science and moved instead to disprove it, H.D. did so by formulating in her own way insights that also animated the sciences of relativity, quantum mechanics, and chaos theory. Her first sustained explorations of this cultural matrix occur in *HERmione,* a comic bildungsroman in which she blasts free of all her mentors—the Reverend Wolle, Professor Doolittle, and Ezra Pound alike—in order to commit herself to the "mythopoeic mind (mine)."

*   *   *

"Her Gart went round in circles," H.D.'s novel begins. "'I am Her,' she said to herself; she repeated, 'Her, Her, Her'" (3). Her is in a hurry; Her has been hurt; Her is hurtling home through the woods carrying letters written to her (Her). The name of this heroine is a mass-energy that manifests now as object, now as subject, now as possessive pronoun, now in some indeterminate form that seems to contain all the others. Always in a flurry of self-referentiality and usually with a grammatical wrench, Her doesn't fit. Friedman and DuPlessis have explored the way in which this "object case, used in subject place, exactly locates the thematics of the self-as-woman" (DuPlessis, *H.D.* 61).[23] I am interested in the way Her's challenge to the Doxa of gender and grammar also challenges the assumptions of Science. Her refusals put into question the foundations of the Order of Gart, among them the distinction between subjectivity and objectivity, the notion of absolute space and absolute time, and the feasibility of precise linear statements.

At the opening of the book, our heroine, having flunked Conic Sections, returns home from college in disgrace. "Science . . . failed her" (6), the narrator explains in a formula that at first seems clear but quickly shimmers into opacity. What does it mean to "fail"? Who has failed whom? Science in the guise of the academy has defined Her as lacking, which means Her has disappointed Science in the guise of her father and brother, the brilliant Carl and Bertrand Gart, formulators of "the Gart theorum of mathematical biological intention" (4).[24] Her has been declared inadequate; she has not passed. During the course of the novel, however, Her turns the tables: stimulated by the poet George Lowndes and the visionary Fayne Rabb, her mythopoeic mind finds science wanting. "Words may be my heritage," she declares, "and with words I will prove conic sections a falsity" (76). When words undermine Euclid's lucid schema, Her dismisses Science. Because Science has failed Her, that is, Her now fails Science.

The purposeful, even perverse slipperiness of a phrase like "science failed her" draws the reader's attention to language. Its oscillation between opposing meanings and refusal to endorse an absolute or proper interpretation mark the divide between Newtonian physics and the physics of relativity and quantum mechanics. Like the Reverend Wolle and Professor Doolittle, classical scientists strove to make true statements about a world they assumed to exist independently of its observers; Einstein's relativity theory and the quantum mechanics of Heisenberg and Bohr make statements about a world they assume to be intimately entangled with its observers. Although relativity and quantum mechanics both start in a critical evaluation of the process by which scientists observe the world they inhabit, however, there is a key difference between them: while theorists of relativity aim to extend the possibility of making true statements about the world, quantum theorists argue that all the mind can ponder is its own cognitive constructions. Written in 1927, H.D.'s novel is situated at a crossroads of these three visions of science. The science of the Gart theorum looks back toward Newton; the mythopoetics of Hermione Gart looks forward toward Einstein and Heisenberg.

The Garts are the Doolittles squared. Charles Doolittle becomes the rigid and Germanic Carl, Hilda becomes the elusive Her, and the Doolittle house, which was merely adjacent to an observatory, becomes Gart Grange, where every outbuilding has been converted into a lab and every closet, cupboard, and pantry has been crammed with bottles, zinc tanks, aquariums, and little dishes of sizzling acids. In the center of it all, in the midst of the family living room, perched under a screw of bright light at a desk stacked high with professional journals, is the unmoved mover of this enterprise: Carl Gart, with his eye affixed to a microscope. Last and also—in this context—least, Hermione's mother, Eugenia, knits in an obscure corner: "'He can work better,'" she explains, "'if I'm sitting in the dark'" (79).

Gart is a comic composite. Part Wolle (his microscope slide is smeared with algae), part Doolittle (he explains the variations in planetary orbits), he is a microbiologist, biologist, chemist, meteorologist, and astronomer. Like Newton's law of gravity, which joins the fall of an apple with the motions of the moon, the Gart theorum applies across all scales and explains everything from molecules in solution to earthquakes in Peru. Like Newton's, its theater is absolute time and absolute space, its geometry is Euclidean, and its claims are universal. With his tall skinny frame and piercing abstract eyes, Gart is the naive imperialist, master of Barthes's triumphant discourse, "some sort of Uncle Sam, Carl-Bertrand-Gart God" (96) with hegemony over everything that moves. "There is only one solution," Her explains (96), and we know she means "Gart, Gart, Gart and the Gart theorum of mathematical biological intention" (4).

The only science Gart shuns is psychology (4), a lapse H.D. accentuates by making his primary preoccupation not physical science but the study of living organisms. For him vital processes are explicable in terms of matter alone; there is no need to posit a psyche. The materialism of his theory clashes merrily with the "art" in "Gart," the learning (*mathema*) in "mathematics," and, most specifically, the resolve or intent of "intention." A subject who believes his work is objective, Gart is so detached that when his daughter appears before him to announce *her* intention, her plan to marry the poet George Lowndes, he cannot bring his eyes into focus to look at her (99–100). The Gart theorum, which kept Mrs. Gart in the dark, has also "dropped out Hermione" (4).

H.D.'s depiction of Gart family dynamics exposes the gendered substructure of a science that rests on the hypothesis that objectivity is male, subjectivity female. In the mythic merger of the Gart marriage, Gart is Athenian, his wife Eleusinian; he inhabits light, she dwells in darkness; he reasons, she emotes; he acts, she reacts. When fifteen years of his experimental findings wash away in a flood, Gart's wife is heartbroken but Gart remains impassive. "'Your mother takes these things too seriously,'" he explains to Hermione (92).[25] Understanding biology as the study of groups of organisms and mathematics as a study of interrelations and combinations, Hermione too has a "mathematical biological intention": her intention is to disprove her parents' triumphant discourse.

The problem is set in H.D.'s description of Gart Grange. "The house is columns of figures," she writes, "double column and the path at right angles to the porch steps is the line beneath numbers and the lawn step is the tentative beginning of a number and the little toolshed and the springhouse at the far corner of the opposite side is bits of jotted-down calculations that will be rubbed out presently" (83). As the novel begins, Bertrand's new wife, the whiny Minnie Hurloe, must be factored into the family "like some fraction to which everything had to be reduced," a common denominator by which the Garts are all minnie-mized, hurled low (15). The addition of Minnie divides the family into heterosexual couples so that at dinner "Gart and Gart sat facing Gart and Gart" (35), and, once again, Hermione is dropped out, rendered an odd number until she is normalized by her engagement to George, an equation that unravels when Hermione attaches herself to Fayne Rabb, attenuates her commitment to George, is dropped out (again) by the coupling of Fayne and George, and suffers a total nervous collapse, flunking Normal Life as definitively as she failed Conic Sections.

"'Normal . . . ,'" muses Hermione toward the end of the novel, "their vocabulary gets more meagre" (177). The upside of being thrust out of an institution is a glimpse of the limits of the norm. Hermione's "subtle form of courage" (4)—and, we surmise, her potential as a writer—is her ability to use this perspective to work her way toward a more flexible and generative understanding of the world. Surrounding the cleared space of Gart Grange, outside the "numbers fencing [Her] in" (97), is a "wild zone" where norms no longer apply.[26] This forest is Her's laboratory, the place where she conducts her own investigation into conic sections and discovers—or experiences—configurations of time-space and mass-energy coincident with the formulations of relativity and quantum mechanics.

To "prove conic sections a falsity" pulls the linchpin in Newton's celestial mechanics. Like the family dynamics that dropped Her from Gart Grange, the geometry that ejected Her from college is coextensive with Western common sense. In Euclid's formulations, material particles move through absolute space, which is empty, at rest, and unchangeable, and absolute time, which flows smoothly from past to present to future. Newton's equations for gravitational force demonstrate that on this stage the only possible orbit for a particle moving under the influence of another particle is a conic section: an ellipse, parabola, or hyperbola made by passing a two-dimensional plane through a three-dimensional cone (see fig. 6). These equations can be used to prove that a preordained universal order drives everything from atoms to solar systems: because orbits are fixed, the argument runs, if a particle's initial conditions are known in sufficient detail, it is possible to calculate its motion into the indefinite future. The course of the universe is, by these equations, both determined and, at least in principle, knowable.[27]

Newton's observations about orbits still have enough validity to get a voyager to the moon and back. What, then, would it mean to "prove conic sections a falsity"? Like Einstein, who displaced Newton by pondering the reaches of outer space, and the quantum physicists, who displaced him by pondering the realm of the subatomic, Her dislodges Newton by examining a region beyond the scope of his calculations. In the forest that surrounds the cleared space of Gart Grange, conic sections dissolve in a riot of vortices: here, in "cones of green set within green cones" (71), "[t]rees swung and fell and rose" (64), birds whirled up and whirred down, and "[h]eat seeped up, swept down, swirled about . . . with the green of branches that was torrid tropic water" (70; see fig. 7). In the absolute space of Newton's world, particles in orbit are as hard, massy, and discrete as billiard balls, but here in the forest surrounding Gart Grange what goes round is a dynamic, oscillating mass-energy, a matter-wave

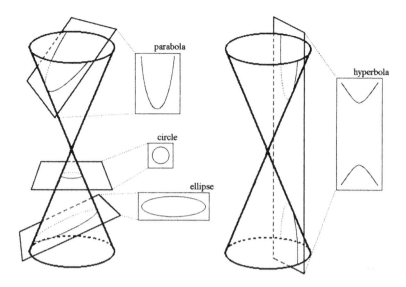

Figure 6. Conic sections. (Courtesy of José F. Candelaria)

manifesting now as color, now as heat, now as the whirl of bird wings, now as the swirl of leaves. In the forest there is no position apart from or above this turmoil, no universal clock or ruler to provide a "true" or "objective" or "enduring" measurement of time and space: any observer's angle is only one among many, each partial, contingent, and relativistic.

Once these Einsteinian postulates are in play, the Gart theorum tumbles. "Her Gart peered far," the narrator tells us, "adjusting, so to speak, some psychic lens" (5). Like an exuberant lab notebook, the novel registers Her's relativistic measurements: a mosquito near the ear on a hot night is as huge as a chicken hawk (85), a peony petal near the eye covers the whole house (71), a bee buzzing close "almost blot[s] out the sun itself with its magnified magnificent underbelly and the roar of its sort of booming" (13). Given the hegemony of "Gart, Gart, Gart, and the Gart theorum," it takes grit to affirm these perceptions as valid statements about the world, but to do so confirms two key postulates of relativity theory: the contention that measurements of size, distance, and duration vary from one frame of reference to another, and the insistence that no one frame is inherently superior to any other.

When the poet George Lowndes dances into the novel wearing a conical hat, he seems at first to be the one who can free Her from the reductive formulas

Figure 7. "Consecutive side views of the short-wavelength breakdown, visualized by a light sheet in the plane initially separating two vortices." (From T. Leweke and C. H. K. Williamson, "Cooperative Elliptic Instability of a Vortex Pair," *Journal of Fluid Mechanics* 360 [1998]: 112. © 1998 by Cambridge University Press. Reprinted with the permission of the authors and Cambridge University Press.)

of Gart Grange. Like Pound, however, Lowndes is a classical scientist in poet's clothes. For him the observer retains objectivity and mastery because he possesses a universally valid system of measurement. When Hermione enters the forest, she lets its dynamic swirl dissolve her preconceptions; when Lowndes enters the forest, he makes it align with his angle of vision. His literary-critical measurements make Gart Grange's oak trees first into "*the forest primeval, the murmuring pines and the hemlocks*" (65), then into "*the forest of Arden*" (66). Together these tags transform the forest into a backdrop for his parody of Longfellow and a stage for his play of amorous "intentions." Far from liberating Hermione, Lowndes's presence renders the forest yet another cleared space for "the heated scrape of slate pencil across slate surface," so that, once again, "Numbers jogged and danced and long division made a stop in [Hermione's] brain" (66).

At the end of the novel Hermione dismisses both the Gart and the Lowndes formulas for the mode of visualization she calls "mythopoeic mind (mine)." Mythopoeic mind is the intuition that draws H.D. to figures like "cones of green set within green cones," to mana-words like *gift* or *projection,* and to the echoic and metamorphic soundplay—the sound-splay—that gives her language its flex and multiplicity. "Mythopoeic mind (mine)" is a standpoint—the particular clock or ruler by which Hermione measures the world—but it is also, and simultaneously, a "mind (mine)," a repository of materials with more than personal or subjective provenance as well as an entry into "the mysterious," which is for Einstein—as it was for da Vinci and Freud—"the fundamental emotion which stands at the cradle of true art and true science" (Einstein 22).[28] Once committed to the workings of the mythopoeic mind, H.D. did not again aspire to imitate, supplement, or assimilate the science of her father and grandfather.

*   *   *

Relativity theory and the theory of quantum mechanics, both of which emerged in the first third of the twentieth century, diverge on the issue of certainty. Because he believed it was possible to attain certainty in scientific measurements, Einstein initially considered calling his theory the "Theory of Invariance" (Hayles, *Cosmic Web* 45). Although relativity shows that no single frame of reference can be privileged, it does not show that everything is relative: to the contrary, Einstein's accomplishment was to develop equations that allow for translation from one frame of reference to another. This means that even when observers measure phenomena from divergent points of view and thereby come up with divergent readings, it is possible for them to agree on the parameters of a fundamentally law-abiding universe.

Quantum mechanics, as formalized in Werner Heisenberg's uncertainty principle and Niels Bohr's principle of complementarity, replaces invariance with indeterminacy. Drawing on experiments that show that in some circumstances electrons behave as particles while in others they behave as waves, Heisenberg concluded that indeterminacy is not a result of limitations in observers and their instruments but is inherent to the process of measurement itself. In N. Katherine Hayles's summary, for Heisenberg, "there is no way to measure a system without interacting with it, and no way to interact with it without disturbing it" (*Cosmic Web* 51). For Heisenberg's colleague Niels Bohr, indeterminacy is not only a result of disturbance but also an inevitable consequence of limitations in language: since the phenomenon that sometimes appears as a wave, sometimes as a particle, is in fact neither one nor the other, every description we give it will be incomplete. The upshot of the "Copenhagen intrepretation" of quantum theory—the name given to the combination of Heisenberg's uncertainty relation and Bohr's principle of complementarity— is the conclusion that it is not possible for observers to agree on the parameters of a fundamentally law-abiding universe.

Although his discoveries were foundational to its development, Einstein found quantum theory insufficient because he could not believe in the universe it described. "'Quantum mechanics demands serious attention,'" he wrote the physicist Max Born in 1926. "'But an inner voice tells me that this is not the true Jacob. The theory accomplishes a lot, but it does not bring us close to the secrets of the Old One. . . . I am convinced that He does not play dice'" (qtd. in Bernstein, *Einstein* 192). Some thirty years after Einstein's declaration to Born, H.D. echoes his syntax and sentiment—"'*God does not weave a loose web,*'" she writes in a headnote for *Helen in Egypt*, "*no*" (82). The universe described in *Helen in Egypt*, however, is closer to Heisenberg's and Bohr's hypotheses than it is to Einstein's, for it relies on probabilistic claims, mutually exclusive formulations, and insubstantial eidolons. To make sense of the disparity in H.D.'s articulations—her sense of a universe that is determinate but also uncertain, law-abiding but also unpredictable—it is necessary to leave behind the either/ or debate between relativity and quantum physics and read her work against one last movement in twentieth-century science: the theory developed to represent the determined-but-unpredictable phenomena of chaos.

The Gart theorum drew back at the edge of chaos. The green swirl of the forest, the clouds over Gart Grange, and the storm that ruined Carl Gart's experiments were exceptions to the rule of ordered systems, and, as Gart cautioned his daughter, only women took them seriously. Like Eugenia Gart knitting in the dark, turbulence was classical science's unrepresented, unarticulated, unthought other.[29] Just as Euclidean geometry represents mountains as cones and coastlines as curves, the conventional names for turbulence—"ir-regularity," "dis-order"—take regularity and order to be the norm. Precise scientific formulations of complexity and turbulence awaited the intuition that chaos is, in fact, not disorder at all but richly organized and essentially unpredictable pattern.

The chaos theorists who began their work in the late 1960s and early 1970s were mathematicians, meteorologists, astronomers, biologists, chemists, and physicists, many of them mavericks who worked on eccentric problems with improvised equipment and considered their results idiosyncratic because they had no systematic way to describe them.[30] What links their work is the hunch that the phenomena they study display a regular irregularity, a patterned looseness. In pursuit of this hunch, working at first independently and then in alliance, these scientists developed a sophisticated terminology, a set of mathematical procedures, and an array of astonishingly beautiful computer graphics to represent the patterns of chaos.[31] In their studies of phenomena like shifts in weather, formations in clouds, fluctuations in cotton prices, and fibrillations of the heart, these chaologists have been able to demonstrate that apparently random and accidental events have a structure that is in fact complex, flexible, and dense with information.

If relativity eliminated the illusion of absolute space and time and quantum theory put an end to the dream of precise measurement, chaos theory brings a full stop to the idea that the course of the universe is both determined and predictable. Including in its gaze not only the very large and very small but the everyday dynamics of "flapping, shaking, beating, swaying phenomena" (Gleick 262), this science is closer to the practice of Carl Gart and the Reverend Wolle than it is to Charles Doolittle's professionalized disciplinary discourse. Like Gart, for example, the chaologist Benoit Mandelbrot sought to formulate patterns at work "not at one scale or another, but across every scale" (Gleick 86), patterns that repeat in the ups and downs of personal income as well as the ups and downs of cotton prices, or, as Gart might put it, patterns that join earthquakes in Peru to populations of fish in tanks. The fractal geometry Mandelbrot used to visualize his findings gave scientists a way to represent the repetition of structure across scales from crystals to coastlines, from "snowflakes to the discontinuous dusts of galaxies" (Gleick 114). Mandelbrot's illustrations are as vital to his work as Wolle's were to his, and both men are unabashed in their admiration of the beauty of their findings.

H.D.'s mythopoeic mind also works across a broad range of phenomena to bring apparently random occurrences into relation by identifying patterns that repeat across scales or recur in nested series within structures. Chaologists call these patterns "scaling" and "recursion," locate them in price charts, coastlines, and weather maps, and give them a mathematical formulation; H.D. locates these patterns in cultural mythologies, history, and autobiography and gives them mythopoeic formulation. For her, it is, in fact, not empirical verification or logical deduction but symmetry across scales and within interlocking levels of a system that verifies events and makes them "come true."[32] Examples of scaling in H.D.'s writings range from the reiterations of mythological patterns in national, local, and personal events to the repetitions of forms in a seashell's whorl, the swirl of sparks from a bonfire, and the whirling of stars in a galaxy; examples of recursion include the dizzying links between the sounds in poems like "Sea Rose," *Trilogy,* or *Helen in Egypt* and the events or laws the poems attempt to describe.[33] For H.D., these patterns are neither metaphors that substitute for something similar nor metonymies associated with something analogous but mythopoeic equivalents of the laws of chaos theory.[34]

Scientists have developed several ways to visualize the intricate patterns of chaotic phenomena. The most haunting of these—and for our purposes the most revealing—is the strange attractor, a new variant of a familiar concept in physics. An attractor is any point in an orbit that pulls the system toward it. Classical physics recognizes two types of attractors—fixed points and limit cycles—both of which are usually demonstrated by pointing to the behavior of pendulums. Like a free-swinging pendulum, which eventually comes to a stop at the midpoint of its arc, fixed-point attractors are characteristic of systems whose behavior reaches a stasis or steady state; like a motor-driven pendulum that oscillates from one side of an arc to the other without stopping, "limit cycle" attractors characterize systems that stay in motion and repeat themselves continuously. Both fixed-point and limit-cycle attractors are simple and predictable; neither, therefore, is strange.

Strange attractors occur in the orderly disorder of chaos and are more complicated and difficult to comprehend. A pendulum's swing depends on only two variables, velocity and momentum, and can therefore be represented on a two-dimensional graph, but chaotic data like weather patterns, stock market prices, or shifts in animal populations depend on a vast array of variables and must therefore be charted in what physicists call "phase space." As a means of tracing the full complexity of a dynamic system on a computer screen, phase space can have as many dimensions as a system has variables. In this space, the state of the system at any moment in time is represented as a point that moves as the system shifts, tracing a continuous trajectory across a screen. "Phase space," Gleick explains, "gives a way of turning numbers into pictures, abstracting every bit of essential information from a system of moving parts, mechanical or fluid, and making a flexible road map to all its possibilities" (134).

Neither observer nor observed, neither mind nor world, phase space is one of "'the humble instruments, tools, visualization skills, writing practices, focusing techniques, and . . . "re-representation[s]"'" that Bruno Latour identifies as the terrain of contemporary science (qtd. in Tiffany 4). When data from chaotic events were fed into a computer, the patterns that appeared in phase space showed—much to the scientists' surprise—that chaos too has an attractor. Neither a fixed point nor a limit cycle, this strange attractor was first charted by Edward Lorenz, who used a set of nonlinear equations for the chaotic rotation of heated fluid to generate a figure in phase space that resembles an owl's mask or a butterfly's wings. This figure, composed of loops and spirals that never join, intersect, or overlap within the finite space they occupy, has become the exemplary strange attractor of chaos theory (see fig. 8).[35]

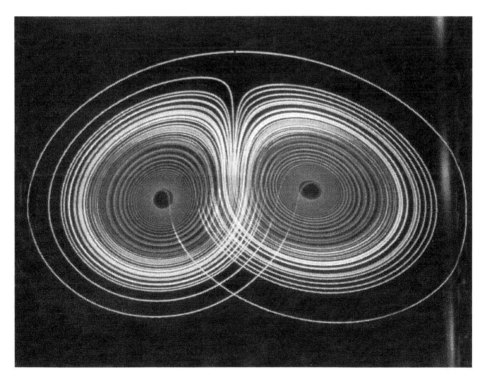

Figure 8. "The Lorenz Attractor"

Strange attractors are the forest that surrounds the Gart Grange of fixed points and limit cycles: they are everywhere and everything else. Whether the data charted in phase space comes from measles epidemics or lynx trapping, whether it spans a week or a month or a millennium, whether it is local or global, the same trajectory appears again and again in the diagrams that form on chaologists' computer screens: a line that never doubles over itself loops round and round the screen in an infinitely deep demonstration of the fine structure that constrains what has been thought to be disorder. Its trajectory is a path of infinite complexity that unfolds within a finite space.

The dependence of chaos theory on visualizations like the Lorenz attractor is an excellent example of the ways in which contemporary science relies on representations. "Although it may be the case that matter is nothing more than a constellation of events, intelligible only to mathematicians," Daniel Tiffany writes, "we cannot yet be absolved of the phenomenology of pictures dwelling about us and dwelling in matter" (33). For Tiffany, it is this phenomenology that brings science and lyric poetry into fruitful dialogue. In a coincidence that seems to witness yet another a strange attraction, then, it is interesting to note that the shape of the Lorenz attractor—a double spiral in three dimensions that resembles a butterfly with two large wings or an owl's mask with two deeply set ringed eyes—is a talismanic icon H.D. returns to again and again in moments of cultural tension in her poetry and prose (see fig. 9).[36]

The coincidence between H.D.'s mythopoeic mind and the science of chaos offers access to aspects of her work that have proven difficult to capture through conventional literary analysis. The cascade of images that structures *Trilogy* provides perhaps the best glimpse of H.D.'s approach to the formulation of pattern within apparent randomness. Composed in the midst of turbulence, *Trilogy* is a poem about forms in motion: in it, air thickens, wind tears, rain falls, bombs descend, and roofs tumble. Like Lorenz feeding his equations into the computer, H.D. scans these movements for patterns that prevail across scales, through time and over space, patterns that recur with "the same—different—the same attributes, / different yet the same as before" (105). The three sections of *Trilogy*, each presented as a result of research, are constructed hypotactically using connectives like "so," "yet," "but," "as when," and "for example" (19, 22, 51, 78, 54). In search of the "true-rune[s]" she believes to be "indelibly stamped / on the atmosphere somewhere, // forever" (5, 17), she locates them, like Lorenz's strange attractors, not in fixed forms or limit cycles but in mutating patterns that repeat without reiteration.

The shape that appears again and again in *Trilogy* is a looping spiral that is bounded and therefore finite but unending and therefore also "[i]n the mind's

Figure 9. The white-faced Scops owl that inspired H.D.'s poem "Sagesse" appeared on the same page with demonstrators dressed as hydrogen warheads. (From *The Listener*, 9 May 1957, 752)

eye . . . a way of seeing infinity" (Gleick 98).[37] The pattern, recurring across scales, works outward from the model of a seed, a cocoon, a heart-husk, a mummy, to increasingly larger instances of binding, destruction, and regeneration. The mollusc generates a pearl, the worm a butterfly, the heart "a Tree / whose roots bind the heart-husk // to earth" (8, 11–13, 53, 35). A tree in a bombed courtyard, "burnt and stricken to the heart" (82), blooms again; a city, scarred by "Apocryphal fire," waits to rise again (3–4); a world shattered searches for a "healing-of-the-nations" (36). The germ of new life comes in each case from outside the system to throw it into turbulence. Sand cast into the mollusc shell, a grain cast into the heart, a bomb cast into the city, the philosopher's stone cast into a crucible, a seed cast into the womb: each disturbance propels the system through turbulence into richly reorganized life. As in a strange attractor, so in this poem there is no end to the loop: the mummified pharaoh in the ruined tomb of the opening predicts the swaddled infant from the womb at the close. The beginning, which had seemed to be an end, turns into an end that is also a beginning (172).

From its largest structures through its smallest details, every level of *Trilogy* repeats the cycle of disturbance, disintegration, and reintegration. The patterns in the poem do not replicate each other exactly, but neither are they jumbled. They have a disorderly order that emerges slowly but surely, so slowly but so surely that in reading the poem it is possible to experience the same eerie effect observers describe in watching a strange attractor form on a screen: the pattern "appears," Gleick reports, "like a ghost out of the mist. New points scatter so randomly across the screen that it seems incredible that any structure is there, let alone a structure so intricate and fine. . . . The points wander so randomly, the pattern appears so ethereally, that it is hard to remember that the shape is an *attractor*. It is not just any trajectory of a dynamical system. It is the trajectory toward which all other trajectories converge" (150). What is crucial to remember is also a factor in the eeriness: for the scientist and the poet alike, these patterns are not decorations but visualizations of order at work in the world.

Numerous writers have explored the implications of the patterns in classical science's two attractors: the fixed-point downslide into entropy, the endless push-pull of limit cycles. The strange attractor, which provides a third way to conceptualize the interplay between stability and instability, determinism and unpredictability, suggests why, despite the second law of thermodynamics, nature continues to generate patterns of immense complexity and why, despite the repetitiousness of limit cycles, phenomena remain richly unpredictable. The forced repetitions of Science and the Doxa do not explain the

dynamic forces that build forests, snowflakes, arterial paths, or intricate poems: "my mind (yours)," H.D. insists,

> . . . differs from every other
> in minute particulars,
>
> as the vein-paths on any leaf
> differ from those of every other leaf
>
> in the forest, as every snow-flake
> has its particular star, coral or prism shape. (*Trilogy* 51–52)

In the dynamics of chaos, small scales interlock with large in such a way that
minute changes in initial conditions generate large changes overall as pertur-
bations cascade upward through a system in a manner that is determined but
not predictable. Lorenz called this effect "sensitive dependence on initial conditions" and provided its canonical example by suggesting that "a butterfly
stirring the air today in Peking can transform storm systems next month in
New York." For historians of science, this perception of interlocking dynamic
patterns at work across scales—a phenomenon, Gleick tells us, "only half-jok-
ingly known as the Butterfly Effect"—was the starting point for theorizations
of chaos (8). In attending so closely to patterns of sound and meaning in H.D.'s
writing—aural effects in ink and in air, mana-words in dynamical movement
throughout her career—I want to suggest a kind of "sensitive dependence on
initial conditions" at work in an interlocking series of transmutations that
cascade upward in her work from the microlinguistic to the metaphysical level.
In this sense, and coincidentally, H.D. has her own version of the Butterfly
Effect, a dependence that begins in

> the meaning that words hide;
>
> they are anagrams, cryptograms,
> little boxes, conditioned
>
> to hatch butterflies . . . (*Trilogy* 53)

and moves outward—or so she hopes—to make a difference in the world.

As Daniel Tiffany acknowledges in *Toy Medium: Materialism and the Modern Lyric,* "Poetry, for the most part, plays no role in the mechanism of institutional power or in the great public debates that determine what's real and
what's not" (21–22). This does not mean, however, that there is little at stake
for a culture in its poetry. The urgency behind H.D.'s aural transformations
and mana-words comes from an intuition that apprehensions and visualiza-

tions of the world provided by the mythopoeic mind also instigate change. Poetry, in this sense, is not only aesthetic and philosophical but also, at least in theory, instrumental.

When poems take their place on the air, in print, or on the screen of a computer, they enter a cultural matrix in which sensitive dependence on initial conditions is at work. Without words, H.D. writes, the world remains

> unmanifest in the dim dimension
> where thought dwells,
>
> and beyond thought and idea,
> their begetter,
>
> Dream,
> Vision. (*Trilogy* 18)

In 1927, when H.D. cut loose from her father and grandfather and committed herself to "mythopoeic mind (mine)," her turn away from imitating, complementing, or assimilating science paradoxically allowed her to keep up with it: she made good on her claim of disproving classical science, that is, by following intuitions that share their matrix with the insights that generated relativity, quantum mechanics, and chaos theory. When Mitchell Feigenbaum tells Gleick that "'[artists] can do some of my research for me'" (186), he makes from the perspective of a scientist the same hopeful point H.D. makes from the perspective of the poet: as researchers, that is, "[w]e are each one of us a Galileo, a Newton. We may make discoveries that the human mind has not yet, so far, been in a position to make, about the human mind" (*Within the Walls* 14).

Notes

1. This lecture appeared in *American Quarterly* in summer 1949 under the title "The American Poet in Relation to Science."

2. H.D.'s participation in observatory tours is noted by Pearson in his foreword to *Hermetic Definition*. Although I have been unable to locate them, Pearson reports that H.D. also at this time published articles on astronomy for children in a Presbyterian paper ("Norman Holmes Pearson on H.D." 437). For the Doolittle family's move to the grounds of the Flower Observatory, see Guest, *Herself Defined* 15–16.

3. "Einstein was right," H.D. repeats at crucial points in "Murex: War and Postwar London," part 2 of *Palimpsest* (see, for example, 165, 166). H.D.'s knowledge of Einstein's theories comes at least in part from such respected mathematicians, theoretical physicists, and astronomers as Sir Arthur Stanley Eddington and Sir James Jeans. For references to Eddington, see her correspondence with Clifford Howard and Viola Jordan at the Beinecke. Jeans's lucid and intelligent summaries of contemporary sci-

ence—*The Stars in Their Courses* and *The Mysterious Universe*—are among the books in H.D.'s library catalogued at the Beinecke.

4. See Richard Rorty's argument that "*conversation* [is] the ultimate context within which knowledge is to be understood. [Given such a definition] [o]ur focus shifts from the relation between human beings and the objects of their inquiry to the relation between alternative standards of justification, and from there to the actual changes in those standards which make up intellectual history" (389–90).

5. As Gérard Mermoz has emphasized in his investigation of modernist thought between 1900 and 1930, "to further our understanding of the epistemological status of the arts and sciences in a general theory of discourse, the search for influences . . . must be replaced by a study of structural correlations" (135). "In a field model [of culture]," N. Katherine Hayles argues in a similar vein in *The Cosmic Web*, "the interactions are always mutual: the cultural matrix guides individual inquiry at the same time that the inquiry helps to form, or transform, the matrix" (23). For a discussion of these and related arguments concerning the interrelation of science and the arts, see Vargish and Mook, chap. 1.

6. The summary statements and quotation from Whitehead come from Timothy Ferris's survey of twentieth-century astrophysics, *The Red Limit* (219–22). I am also indebted to March's formulations in *Physics for Poets*.

7. For H.D.'s meditations on creativity, see *Notes on Thought and Vision & The Wise Sappho* (esp. 64); for her account of Freud's "flash of inspiration," see *Tribute to Freud* 77; for a summary of one of the imaginative flights that generated Einstein's theories of relativity, see March 110–12. A persistent thread in *The Gift* is the child's fascination with a book called *Simple Science*, which gives nightmares equal status with such "real things" as the crystalline structure of snowflakes and the vaporization of water into steam (103, 104, 115).

8. To take seriously H.D.'s statement that her father "did make a research worker of me but in another dimension" readjusts the usual reading of repetition in her work. In light of this self-definition, reiterated plots, incidents, and characters cannot be regarded simply as a mark of obsession or blockage, for it is through reiteration that researchers confirm a pattern or establish a law. H.D.'s statement appears in "Hirslanden Notebooks" and is quoted in Pearson's foreword to *Tribute to Freud* (x).

9. For a helpful summary of the activities of her father and grandfather, see Mandel, "Magical Lenses."

10. H.D.'s first cousin, also named Francis Wolle, gives a detailed account of the Reverend Wolle's career in his memoir, *A Moravian Heritage* (see esp. chap. 4, 21–27). For more information about the Reverend Wolle, see H.D.'s "Notes" to *The Gift* 228–29 and an essay by Francis Drouet, the curator of Cryptogamic Botany at the Field Museum, entitled "Francis Wolle's Filamentous Myxophyceae."

11. "[G]reen," Wolle writes in a typical botanical entry, "then pink grading off into all the shades of purple, and finally olive, from golden green and bright tawny to black" (*Desmids* xii). H.D.'s cousin tells us that as a child H.D. earned pennies by carrying

the loosely rolled bundles of black-and-white key sheets to the "needy female relatives" whose task it was to tint them (Wolle, *Moravian Heritage* 25).

12. See, for example, his description of *Chlamydococcus pluvialis* in *Fresh-Water Algae of the United States* 1:164.

13. On the masculinization of science in the late nineteenth century, see also Harding and Keller.

14. From "Hirslanden Notebooks," qtd. in Pearson, foreword to *Tribute to Freud* x. In her essay "The tradition of marginality . . . and the emergence of *HOW(ever),*" Kathleen Fraser connects her own early fascination with the figure of Madame Curie with her career as an experimental poet (26–27).

15. For one of H.D.'s many figurations of the imbalance in her parents' marriage, see "The Sword Went Out to Sea" 144.

16. For Doolittle's professional standing, see the obituaries in *Publications of the Astronomical Society of the Pacific* 103–4 and *The Observatory* 219–20. For a description of the mathematical calculations involved in his work, see his *Treatise on Practical Astronomy* 283–339.

17. See Keller's description of the advent of modern science in *Reflections on Gender and Science* 43–65. For a full discussion of H.D.'s occult studies, see Friedman, *Psyche Reborn,* part 2 (157–296).

18. This dream, recorded in "Hirslanden Notebooks," is discussed in Friedman, *Psyche Reborn* 188.

19. For a typical stellar dream, see *Within the Walls,* "The Last Day," 24–25; for the zodiac ring that she considered a token of her "marriage to the 'STARS,'" see her letter to Bryher dated "Halloween 1930"; for her "star research," mentioned in a letter to Viola Jordan, 2 July 1941, see her letters to Silvia Dobson, Robert Herring, and Elizabeth Ashby, many of them signed with her star glyph. Finally, for a sustained example of H.D.'s rhetoric of starry puns and parallels, see her letter to Bryher, 28 May 1933.

20. The two most sustained versions of this courtship occur in *HERmione* and *End to Torment.* H.D.'s words here are from "Hirslanden Notebooks" 2:27.

21. For studies of the scientific strain in Pound's aesthetics, see Bell, *Critic as Scientist,* and Nänny. Although Albright allows that Pound "aspired to a genuinely quantum-mechanical view of the poetic act, as if poetry and physics were the same thing," his focus is exclusively on Pound's appropriation of scientific concepts as "an exercise in metaphor, and deceptive metaphor at that" (2).

22. See also Pound's statement that "[p]oetry is a sort of inspired mathematics, which gives us equations, not for abstract figures, triangles, spheres, and the like, but equations for the human emotions" (*Spirit of Romance* 14). For a few of the many examples of this mathematical vocabulary in H.D.'s work, see *Palimpsest* 155; "Pontikonisi" 1; and *Tribute to Freud* 146.

23. For a full elaboration of this argument, see Friedman and DuPlessis, "'I Had Two Loves Separate.'"

24. "Theorum" is H.D.'s spelling of the proper (and sleeker) term "theorem." Because it reproduces Gart's rough-cut mumbling, I have retained H.D.'s spelling throughout the chapter. For an account of H.D.'s failure in a Bryn Mawr course focusing on "Analytical Conics and Theory of Equations," see Wallace 116. I am indebted to Suzanne Araas-Vesely, who first pointed out to me the ambiguities in the refrain "Science failed her."

25. The configuration of this scene replays the dynamics in the advertisement for General Electric's "Golden Tone" speakers: caught between a mother's tears and a father's impassivity, the daughter has to console one without disturbing the concentration of the other.

26. The term "wild zone" is borrowed from the anthropologists Shirley Ardener and Edwin Ardener and applied to women's experience by Showalter in "Feminist Criticism in the Wilderness" 262.

27. For a succinct summary of Newton's equations and the Marquis Pierre Laplace's formulation of their deterministic consequences, see Bernstein, *Einstein* 29–31.

28. For a compelling reading of the resonance of the word "mythopoeic," see Duncan, *The Truth and Life of Myth.*

29. For an elaboration of this argument in the context of contemporary literary theory and the science of chaos, see Hayles, "Turbulence in Literature and Science."

30. In my understanding of the science of chaos, I am indebted to the work of James Gleick and N. Katherine Hayles, especially to Gleick's *Chaos* and Hayles's *Chaos Bound.*

31. For three of the most compelling of these graphics—the Lorenz attractor, Koch curve, and Mandelbrot set—see the illustrations in Gleick, inset after 114. For more extended treatment of the patterns of chaos, see Briggs.

32. For examples of H.D.'s use of the phrase "come true," see *The Gift* 47, 83, 101, 126.

33. For examples of the coincidence between global mythology and local events, see *Tribute to Freud* and *The Gift;* for the overlapping patterns of shells, sparks, and stars, see *Trilogy* and *Helen in Egypt.* For recursive patterns in H.D.'s poems, see chapter 1 and the analysis of *Trilogy* below.

34. For "scaling" and "recursion" in chaos theory, see Gleick 115–16, 179. The return of scaling to science in the 1960s and 1970s happened simultaneously in many disciplines, but for Gleick, it is clearest in the field of evolutionary biology, where "it became clear that a full theory would have to recognize patterns of development in genes, in individual organisms, in species, and in families of species, all at once" (116).

35. For more detailed descriptions of the Lorenz attractor, see Shaw, "Strange Attractors, Chaotic Behavior, and Information Flow"; Gleick 132–37; and Hayles, *Chaos Bound,* chap. 6.

36. For the butterfly, see especially "The Walls Do Not Fall," the first poem of *Trilogy;* for the owl, see especially "Sagesse."

37. Gleick elaborates his description of representations of infinity within finite forms

in his discussion of Mandelbrot's fractal geometry. The example he uses to illustrate his point is a Koch curve, a geometrical form constructed through the reiteration of a simple set of rules: take a triangle, attach to the middle one-third of each side a new triangle identical in shape but one-third the size, and repeat the process again and again and again. The pattern can be endlessly reiterated, but the area of the diagram as a whole remains constant. In this way, Gleick concludes, "an infinitely long line surrounds a finite area" (99).

Radical / Part 3
Modernisms

6 Angles of Incidence/Angels of Dust: Operatic Tilt in the Poetics of H.D. and Nathaniel Mackey

I tend to pursue resonance rather than resolution, so I glimpsed a stubborn, albeit improbable world whose arrested glimmer elicited slippages of hieratic drift.
—Nathaniel Mackey, *Bedouin Hornbook*

[Y]es—I drifted here.
—H.D., *Helen in Egypt*

Nathaniel Mackey opens "Palimpsestic Stagger," an essay on his affinities with H.D., with this call and response between N., the letter writer of *Bedouin Hornbook,* and H.D., the poet of *Helen in Egypt.* "I didn't consciously have H.D. in mind," Mackey writes, "but the fact that her initials are there in the last two words, 'hieratic drift,' seems appropriate" (225). While part 1 of this book is about drifts of sound that exert interpretive leverage and part 2 concerns hieratic patterns brought to bear on a culture in crisis, the two chapters that constitute part 3 take up relays or ricochets of thought between poets. As Mackey emphasizes, such relays may or may not be conscious, but H.D. imagines them as a sort of transmission: the passage of a signal, picture, or pattern of information from one mind to another across time or space.[1]

Like projections, gift exchanges, or scientific formulations, transmissions move unhurriedly between people who do not know each other: the gap in time between the act of sending and the act of receiving parallels a gap in space marked by the screen or tape or printed page. Although such transmissions take their time, they are not slack or random but formal, stylized, and spiritually resonant, or, as Mackey puts it, "hieratic." As H.D. explains in *Notes on Thought and Vision,* such transmissions consist of a "figure . . . created by a formula arrived at consciously or unconsciously." Turning to the technology of the telegraph to illustrate her theory, H.D. continues, "If we had the right sort of brains, we would receive a definite message from that figure, like dots and lines ticked off by one receiving station, received and translated into definite thought by another telegraphic centre" (26).

Mackey's essay on H.D. is contained in a collection entitled *H.D. and Poets After,* edited by Donna Krolik Hollenberg. Hollenberg's title posits a chronological movement—first H.D., then "poets after"—which she corroborates through a long list of writers who have testified to H.D.'s generativity in their creative lives.[2] Many of the poets in the volume speak of H.D. in a language of discovery and intimacy "as though," in Frances Jaffer's words, "H.D. had been waiting" (95) for them to find her. For most of these poets, H.D.'s impact is immediate, forceful, almost physical: for Alicia Ostriker, "[a] quality of aura or energy . . . transmitted" through language (2), for Kathleen Fraser the sensation of "a kind of female enspiriting guide that I'd been lacking" (171), for Robert Kelly, most vividly, "a presence, a sense of life . . . who stood there in the room beside and above me, just like (it of course only now occurs to me) the nurse, the muse" (33). Like many others in the volume, the poet Sharon Doubiago identifies H.D. as one of the "persons and real events I experienced as starters, as seeds, as 'transmitters' that enabled me to overcome internal and external hostilities to my writing" (54).

What is most compelling about the transmissions recorded in Hollenberg's collection is their generativity. The relays these essays record are reverberative: like sound, that is, they move in many directions at once. Most of the poets who write for the collection came to H.D.'s work through or with other poets, poet-critics, or readers: Mackey read H.D. through Robert Duncan, Kathleen Fraser read H.D. with other experimental women poets in San Francisco, Carolyn Forché read H.D. first as an Anglo-American modernist in a seminar taught by Professor Linda Wagner, then as a witness to global suffering whose poems she collected with the work of 144 other poets from thirty countries in her anthology, *Against Forgetting: Twentieth-Century Poetry of Witness.* Because Hollenberg pairs each poet's essay with an essay by a scholar who reads that poet side by side with H.D., the critics in the collection form yet another ripple in this pattern by rereading H.D. in juxtaposition with another poet who read her in the company of yet other poets.

The process of transmission Hollenberg's volume records is like a serial poem, "open-ended, unfinished and unfinishable" (Hatlen 135). In the wash back and forth across time between poets-as-readers and readers-of-poets, what is at stake is not, to return to Mackey's terminology, "resolution" but "resonance."[3] Because one of my aims in this book is to tune H.D.'s work to the work of contemporary innovative poets, the transmissions recorded in this chapter and the next are intended to restore to H.D. a strangeness that is lost when she is read with the intention of admitting her to the canon of Anglo-American modernists or aligning her career with those of other women who have struggled to publish and not to perish. To backread H.D. through her alliances with and differences from the experimentalism of Nathaniel Mackey, Jack Spicer, and Leslie Scalapino opens a new angle into her creativity, one that yields fresh access to the strengths and limitations of her work, puts into question conventional divisions between modernism and postmodernism, and reaches across the boundaries built up by the identity politics within which H.D. has been most recently read.

*   *   *

This is a chapter about alignments. Its aim is to make a tangent between two complicated poetics articulated through a mix of mathematics and mythology. H.D.'s "Tribute to the Angels," book two of *Trilogy*, and Nathaniel Mackey's *Djbot Baghostus's Run*, book two of his serial work *From a Broken Bottle Traces of Perfume Still Emanate*, are tangential in a geometric sense: they touch, that is, without intersection or overlap. Mackey does not cite H.D.; *From a Broken Bottle* is prose, not poetry; its angel is more Afro-Caribbean than Judeo-Christian, its angle more Riemannian than Euclidian. The event this chapter graphs is a reading—an "angle," as H.D. puts it, "of incidence"—that is also, inevitably, an "angle of reflection" (45). The extravagant, self-reflexive, mythopoetic word-work that aligns these poets is crucial to a poetics that exceeds not only the gendered and racialized vocabularies deployed to analyze it but also the modernist and postmodernist paradigms used to position it. The metathetic wobble between *angle* and *angel* is, for both poets, much more than a trick. It is a habit of thought, a method of reasoning, an improvisatory, self-reflexive, over-the-top poetics: "operatic extremity," in Mackey's phrasing, "operatic tilt" (*Djbot* 186).

Like much of H.D.'s and Mackey's writing, "Tribute to the Angels" and *Djbot Baghostus's Run* are constructed stereoscopically. They work, that is, like an optical instrument that creates three-dimensional illusions by bringing into a single focus photographs of the same scene taken from slightly different angles. The flash of depth—the stereoscopic moment—occurs in the instant the viewer's eye makes one picture out of two or more angles of access. H.D.'s evocation of this phenomenon comes in her description of the book carried by the Lady in the vision at the heart of "Tribute to the Angels." The pages of this book, H.D. suggests, will reveal a tale told from at least two distinct angles:

> a tale of a Fisherman,
> a tale of a jar or jars,
>
> the same—different—the same attributes,
> different yet the same as before. (105)

The wavering, perspectival energy of the writing in H.D.'s poem, like the narrative—"written / or unwritten" (105)—in the dream of the book within the poem, is a flicker, a glimmer of angles, a stereoscopic waver.

Mackey's evocation of the stereoscopic in *Djbot Baghostus's Run* is equally elaborate. As in "Tribute to the Angels," it emerges from the narrator's struggle to account for a series of dreams of a woman. In Mackey's book, the Lady is the drummer sought by the narrator's band, the Mystic Horn Society. In one night, all five band members dream of a genius, a genie, a djinn, variously called Jeannie, Djeannine, Penny, or, when she finally appears in the flesh, Drennette. "I saw it all," the trumpet-player Aunt Nancy says, giving her slant on the collective vision, "as though from a distance, as if thru an eye made of opera glass" (47). Aunt Nancy's odd locution—one eye made out of a double-tubed opera glass—generates the first paragraph of the extravagant opera starring Djbot Baghostus, a.k.a. Jarred Bottle: "I sat down and began a new after-the-fact lecture/libretto," Mackey's narrator N. explains in a letter to his interlocutor, the mysterious Angel of Dust. "[T]he first paragraph . . . came so effortlessly it seemed to be writing itself: 'Jarred Bottle's I made of opera glass dropped out'" (50).[4]

Like H.D.'s tale of "the same—different—the same," Mackey's lecture/libretto is multiple in plot and in construction. Layering sound as a stereopticon layers sight, its first sentence—"Jarred Bottle's I made of opera glass dropped out"—functions as an overture that the opera proceeds to develop in exuberant detail. "Jarred Bottle" is a bottle shocked, a bottle unbottled, a signifier warped to release multiple signifieds.[5] In the aural torque of N.'s phrasing, Aunt Nancy's "eye made of opera glass" twists into Jarred Bottle's "I made of opera glass"; the lingering phrase "Bottle's I" reaches outward toward its wind-instrument mutation, "Bottle's sigh"; and the drift of a final consonant across the divide between segments turns the verb "dropped out" into the directive "drop doubt." These sound effects—the lush transformations, the phonemic overlaps Garrett Stewart terms "transegmental drifts"—register for the ear the multiplicity that stereoscopy registers for the eye. What the ear hears in the sentence's operatic tilt is the convergence of two or more angles of sound: "an aural," in Stewart's words, "rather than scriptive palimpsest" (*Reading Voices* 246).

To enter the both/and/*and* world of the pun, it is necessary, as Mackey's transegmental waver suggests, both to drop out and to drop doubt. In the momentum of polyphony, the "eye" that becomes an "I" also evokes, in its unfolding, an operatic "aye": an assent, in this case, to the pluralization and destabilization of signifiers crucial to serious wordplay. If the conventions of reasoning that govern law and logic depend on discrimination, the poetics of operatic tilt puts its bet on assimilation: the wager of the pun is that words that sound alike are also—overtly or covertly—alike in meaning. Simplicity, earnestness, and stability are not foundational to the poetics of "Tribute to the Angels" and *Djbot Baghostus's Run*.[6] The logic of these texts rides on surprise and surmise: the surprise of aural overlap, the surmise of polyphonic thinking.

In operatic tilt, sound leads thought. Puns, for H.D. and Mackey, are wit in two mutually imbricated senses: they are not only ingenious engagements between discrepancies but also, more importantly, a kind of intelligence, perception, or understanding, a manner or method of thought. In his essay "The Puncept in Grammatology," Gregory Ulmer creates the neologism "puncept" to make this point: for Ulmer, as for Derrida, the pun is "the philosopheme of a new cognition" (165), a way of knowing that marks the postmodern. Like a concept, a puncept is a thought or notion that joins elements that have specific common properties, but unlike concepts, which establish sets on the assumption of similar signifieds, puncepts establish "sets formed on the basis of similar signifiers." "If it seems intuitively possible (if not obvious) that puncepts work as well for organizing thought as concepts," Ulmer writes, "then you are likely to possess a post-modernist sensibility" (164).

Ulmer aligns the difference between concepts and puncepts with the difference between the logic of mathematics and the logic of semiotics. "[U]nlike physics, in which two bodies may not occupy the same space," he explains, "language is a material in which the same names are capable of supporting several mutually exclusive meanings simultaneously" (165). One example of punceptual cognition would be the set formed by "eye," "I," and "aye," the triplet that generates the extravagant initial sentence of Mackey's "antithetical opera" (*Djbot* 7); another would be the set formed by the metathetical waver of "angels" and "angles," a puncept Mackey and H.D. share with a much earlier Gregory—Pope Gregory the Great—who rejoiced in the connection between the name of the tribe of two pagan English boys and their beauty: "'They are called Angles,' he was told. 'That is appropriate,' he [replied], 'for they have angelic faces.'"[7]

In carrying us back toward the punceptual blend of mathematics and my-thology in "Tribute to the Angels" and *Djbot Baghostus's Run,* Pope Gregory's wordplay points to a limitation in Ulmer's argument, for the puncept is not only a philosopheme of the postmodern but also a structural unit of premodern and/or non-Western modes of thought. For the classical philosophers H.D. admired and the Dogon philosophers Mackey invokes, puns are not so much quirks of language as its quick, its essence, its vital core.[8] Against the high modernist search for stable definitions and unified, monological meaning, Mackey poses his "slippages of hieratic drift" (*Bedouin* 23). His examples in this context are the eroding colors of a canvas in pastels and the smudged notes of a jazz im-provisation, but his phrase also fits the verbal play that again and again in these texts moves from similarities in sound toward similarities in signification.

In contrast to wisecracks, which close in a flash, hieratic drift is an open-ended and ongoing process in which meanings slip one from another in a swift generative series. The locus classicus of this process in H.D.'s work is the semi-otic alchemy of "Tribute to the Angels": "Now polish the crucible," H.D. be-gins, speaking to herself as well to her readers,

> and in the bowl distill
>
> a word most bitter, *marah,*
> a word bitterer still, *mar,*
>
> [...]
>
> ...till *marah-mar*
> are melted, fuse and join
>
> and change and alter,
> mer, mère, mère, mater, Maia, Mary,
>
> Star of the Sea,
> Mother. (71)

Gender-based readings of this passage tend to anchor its hieratic drift in one or another stable meaning—the re-vision of patriarchal tradition or restora-tion of female divinity in Susan Stanford Friedman's inaugural reading (*Psyche Reborn* 228, 254), the claim of "gender authority" in Rachel Blau DuPlessis's summary of the struggle of H.D.'s career (*H.D.* 86–100)—but Mackey's no-tion of slippage suggests a more radical reading practice, a practice that uses the generativity of language to undermine the way of knowing whose con-straints it brings to light. Instead of progressing along H.D.'s series of charged words—*marah-mar, mer, mere, mère, mater, Maia, Mary*—as if they were steps toward the right answer, "Mother," readings that start from the idea of slip-page "get the drift" by privileging process over outcome. Instead of a right answer—a logic of mathematics, in Ulmer's terms—we enter instead into the generative logic of semiotics.[9]

The *opus* of operatic tilt is a practice of extravagant, ongoing meaning mak-ing, which is for H.D. and Mackey at once a poetics, an ethics, and a politics. For H.D. in "Tribute to the Angels," as we saw in chapter 3, the vehicle of this insistence is alchemical; for Mackey, in *Djbot Baghostus's Run,* it is "operatic"; for both, more importantly and in the term's many meanings, it is an "opera-tion." Improvisatory and transformative, operatic tilt distinguishes "radical modernism" as a way of reading such writers as Stein, Williams, Pound, H.D., Duncan, and Mackey from its two better-known alternatives, high modernism, on the one hand, and poststructuralist postmodernism, on the other hand.[10]

*   *   *

Of necessity, in the following analysis, I employ these three terms—the bina-ry pair "modernism" and "postmodernism" and their interrupter, "radical modernism"—in a shorthand fashion, for they are useful not as truth claims but as speculative formations, heuristics that distinguish the poetics of H.D. and Mackey from the practice of high modernists like T. S. Eliot, on the one hand, and postmodernists like John Ashbery, on the other hand. All three terms are vexed, complex, and variously deployed. As a rough guide to their differ-ences, it is helpful to recall Brian McHale's distinction between modernism as an epistemological practice whose logic is that of the detective story and postmodernism as an ontological practice whose logic is that of a science fiction tale. Like the questor in *The Waste Land,* on the one hand, high mod-ernism looks to locate an answer, solve a problem, or lay out a structure of truth; like a speculator in an Ashbery poem, on the other hand, postmodern-ism looks to project or construct a world—or a world-within-a-world—a zone of imaginative constructions that supports, for a moment, a play of supposi-tions. The term "radical modernism" provides a third alternative. Its roots lie in the operations—the "operatic extremity, operatic tilt"—of language. Rad-ical modernism challenges "natural," "realistic," or scientist epistemologies by situating language as an entity with properties of its own rather than as an instrument to be used neutrally or transparently to transmit a pregiven com-munication. At the same time, however, radical modernism challenges post-modern notions of epistemic randomness by insisting on a fit—albeit, in Mackey's words, a "rickety, imperfect fit," a "discrepant engagement"—be-tween word and world (*Discrepant* 19).

To understand the semiotic logic of "Tribute to the Angels" and *Djbot Ba-ghostus's Run*, it helps to turn for a moment to a seminal document of radical modernism: Ernest Fenollosa's *The Chinese Written Character as a Medium for Poetry*, written prior to Fenollosa's death in 1908, edited by Pound between 1913 and 1916, first published in 1919 in *The Little Review*, put out in book form by Stanley Nott in 1936, and reprinted as a pamphlet by City Lights Books. "[T]he roots of poetry," Fenollosa declares, "are in language" (6). By "roots," Fenollosa means not only poetry's origin, source, base, support, or core but also, in a linguistic sense, its radical: the element that carries its main freight of meaning. The basis from which words are derived by adding affixes or inflectional endings or through phonetic changes, a radical is flexible, generative, "alive and plastic" (17). Because in Fenollosa's view Chinese written characters are an ideographic lexicon of radicals, they allow us to discern a join of word and world: they offer, that is, "a vivid shorthand picture of the *operations* of nature" (8, my italics).

The ideograph was crucial to Fenollosa and to Pound because they believed it to be capable of evading or exceeding the logic of scholasticism. Scholastic philosophy, for Fenollosa, is a language of nouns, "little hard units or concepts" (26); poetry, by contrast, is a language of radicals or roots. Like Ulmer's pairing of "concept" and "puncept," Fenollosa's argument pits monological and rigid signifieds against polyvalent and flexible signifiers, but the difference between Ulmer and Fenollosa is that for Fenollosa ideographs are "always vibrant with fold on fold of overtones *and* with natural affinities" (25, my italics). As an example of the Chinese written character in operation, Fenollosa points to the ideograph *ming* or *mei*, constructed from the sign of the sun together with the sign of the moon. The ideograph sun-and-moon is genetic code for the operation of light, verbal DNA for a core meaning "to shine," "luminosity," "bright." Appearing with the ideograph for *cup*, it can mean, all at once or by turns, "the cup sun-and-moons," "the sun and moon of the cup," "cup sun-and-moon," "[s]un-and-moon cup" (17–18). In apprehending *ming*, Fenollosa concludes, returning us to H.D.'s alchemy and Mackey's opera, "we attain for a moment the inner heat of thought, a heat which melts down the parts of speech to recast them at will" (17).

When, for H.D., the words in the poem-bowl melt, fuse, change, and alter, the poet's alchemy at once distills them—separates or extracts their essential elements—and de-stills them, setting them into motion by restoring to them a vitality beyond parts of speech. The parallel operation in Mackey's *From a Broken Bottle Traces of Perfume Still Emanate* is the Mystic Horn Society's practice of jazz improvisation. In an enlightenment culture that privileges prediction, precision, and reproducibility, alchemy and improvisation become the abjected others of science and notated composition: expedients, in the popular view, tricks, even flat-out quackery. Just as *Trilogy* supposes that the alchemical operations of medieval Arabs involved sophisticated and advanced science, however, Mackey describes the improvisations of the musicians in *Djbot Baghostus's Run* as highly structured assertions, counterassertions, and argumentative advances characterized by intense preparation, design, and method.[11] As Mackey explains in an interview with Ed Foster, the jazz improvisations of avant-garde musicians like Cecil Taylor are not free play but "a language of reflection" (Foster 77). Post-bebop black music makes "a significant break . . . with the tradition of the black musician as an embodiment of instantaneity, instinct, pure feeling, in some unmediated way uncomplicated by reflection and intellect" (77). Its conversations require disciplined, sustained, and rigorous listening from players and audience alike.

The Mystic Horn Society's tribute to Thelonious Monk, Bob Marley, Charles Mingus, and Lightnin' Hopkins performs what Mackey means in telling Foster that post-bebop's "key ethic is improvisational" (77). The tribute occurs at a specific time and place—"a three-night stint at a club called Earl's up north in Albany"—and is motivated by "the news that Monk had suffered a cerebral hemorrhage and was in a coma" (*Djbot* 172). "'[T]hree years ago Mingus, Marley last May, now Monk,'" one band member says, to which N. adds, "'Lightnin', you may know, died week before last'" (172). The band's response to the erosion of this generation is not to imitate their music but to regenerate it: like alchemists, that is, they break down and reconstitute—melt, fuse, change, and alter—the elements of compositions by Mingus, Marley, Monk, and Hopkins in a performance they call, formulaically, "Three M's and an H" (173).

To borrow Paul Zumthor's distinction between knowledge transmission in predominantly literate and predominantly oral cultures, the Mystic Horn Society's tribute to Mingus, Marley, Monk, and Hopkins is not a display of "memorization" but an act of "remembrance." Characteristic of cultures that depend on writing, memorization abstracts knowledge from its context so it can be precisely replicated in any place, at any time, by any agent; characteristic of cultures that depend on oral—or, in this case, aural—transmission of knowledge, remembrance regenerates knowledge through a process of integrating it into new contexts. "Three M's and an H" is the Mystic Horn Society's reflection on incidents from the past and, consciously or unconsciously, Mackey's riff on the trigonometry of "Tribute to the Angels," in which H.D. applies Euclid's classical formula to the now of aerial bombardment and finds that, once again but differently, "the angle of incidence / equals the angle of reflection" (45).

The terms "angularity" and "incidence" anchor N.'s description of the final segment of "Three M's and an H," in which the Mystic Horn Society improvises on Charles Mingus's composition "Free Cell Block F, 'tis Nazi USA." As Mackey explains in his essay "The Changing Same: Black Music in the Poetry of Amiri Baraka," to call the music of a composer like Thelonious Monk, Andrew Hill, or Eric Dolphy "angular" or "oblique" is to stress its "spirit of interrogation and discontent" (43). Less a mood than an argumentative tack, angularity undermines any knowledge that claims to be straightforward, complete, or sufficient. Because by definition it bends away from a previous assertion, improvisation underscores "the partial, provisional character of any proposition or predication . . . advancing a vigilant sense of any reign or regime of truth as susceptible to qualification. It thus calls into question the order by which it is otherwise conditioned on the basis of conditionality itself" (43). The sign of angularity in Mingus's piece, however, is less the music itself, which has, N. tells the Angel of Dust, "uptown flair and good feeling" (Djbot 177), than its title, which Mingus added after reading an Ebony article on southern prisons. The title is, therefore, in Mackey's summary, "a time-lapse equation linking before-the-fact tune with after-the-fact . . . intent" (177). In testing and qualifying the tune, the title makes the music only the beginning of the story.[12]

The performance of this part of "Three M's and an H" pays tribute to Mingus's improvisatory expertise. The members of the band open by reading in unison the first paragraph of Ralph Ellison's Invisible Man, jamming Mingus's "Nazi" into Ellison's not see.[13] In a solo that takes off from this misalignment, Penguin, the Horn Society's alto saxophonist, elaborates the phrase "not see" along the line of Mingus's indictment. "The Greensboro killings came up," N. tells the Angel. "The Atlanta child murders came up. The lynching last March in Alabama came up, as did a number of other such 'incidents' people choose not . . . to see for what they are" (178). Following Penguin on the tenor sax, N. torques Nazi and not see into the punceptual note C, which he plays over and over again, jumping octaves, varying placement and duration, insisting, until the audience gets the drift and yells, " 'Yeah, I hear you,' " " 'Yeah, break it down' " (179). In the improvisational alchemy of this moment, the listeners—who themselves now enter the equation—remember, witness, and take a stand by pushing the hieratic slip, the drift, from Nazi through not see to see.

In a pun that neatly superimposes the mathematics and mythology of Djbot Baghostus's Run, N. refers the Angel of Dust to "the doo-wop hyperbolics" of The Penguins' "Earth Angel," describing it as an "exponential aria" that "offers a clue to the sort of opera I'm working toward" (186–87). Foregrounding the generativity of operatic tilt, the radical of "exponential"—*exponent*—means both advocate or interpreter and the number or symbol placed to the right of and above another number, symbol, or expression to mark the power to which it is to be raised. In the Mystic Horn Society's improvisations, the interpretations of the five members of the band raise the power of the music of Monk, Marley, Mingus, and Hopkins. The equation for their performance might be written $(3m + h)^5$, but the audience's response suggests it could just as well be written $(3m + h)^n$. Just as *Trilogy* is a response to the Nazi bombs falling on London—"An incident," as the newspapers liked to put it, "here" and "there" (3)—"Free Cell Block F" is an ongoing, open-ended speaking back to the totalitarianism of Nazi politics, southern prisons, and the incidents in Greensboro, Atlanta, and Alabama, an angle of political, historical, and ethical reflection, an "antithethical opera" (7).

   *   *   *

There is, however, an important difference between the mathematical formulations in H.D.'s "Tribute to the Angels" and those in Mackey's *From a Broken Bottle Traces of Perfume Still Emanate,* a difference that helps to clarify these two writers' variant deployments of radical modernism. The equation H.D. embeds in *Trilogy*—the law that the angle of incidence equals the angle of reflection—depends on a match or adequation between two angles, visible in the diagram mathematicians use to represent it (see fig. 10).

Although many elements fall and rise again in *Trilogy*—among others, lightning, rain, flaming stones, bombs, cities, and angelic messengers—it's easiest to imagine this diagram as a depiction of a ray of light approaching and reflecting off a flat mirrored surface. The approaching ray of light is the incident ray (labeled I in the diagram); the ray of light leaving is the reflected ray (R in the

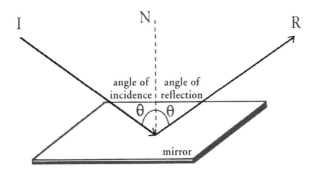

Figure 10. Angle of incidence, angle of reflection. (Courtesy of José F. Candelaria)

diagram). At the point of incidence where the ray strikes the mirror, a line can be drawn perpendicular to the surface of the mirror (the normal line, labeled N in the diagram). This line divides the angle between the incident ray and the reflected ray into two equal angles. The angle between the incident ray and the normal is known as the angle of incidence; the angle between the reflected ray and the normal is known as the angle of reflection. The law, then, states that when light bounces off a surface, the angle of incidence is equal to the angle of reflection.

In Mackey's *Broken Bottle* series, the operant rule is not equivalence but rather a principle Jarred Bottle in *Bedouin Hornbook* calls "*[t]he fallacy of adequation.... The lack of any absolute fit*" (171), reiterated by N. in *Djbot Baghostus's Run* as "a principle of non-equivalence, an upfront absence of adequation" (49). The figure N. invokes to demonstrate the lack of absolute fit is the asymptote. An asymptote is defined by the *American Heritage Dictionary* as a "line considered a limit to a curve in the sense that the perpendicular distance from a moving point on the curve to the line approaches zero as the point moves an infinite distance from the origin." The limit of the curve, visible in figure 11, is measured by the ever-narrowing gap between the line of the curve and the reference lines *x* and *y*. The term *asymptote* comes from the Greek, meaning nonintersecting, not converging, for the curve, by definition, approaches the axes or reference lines but never actually touches them.

In a text studded with geometrical curves—ellipses, hyperbolas, circles, and

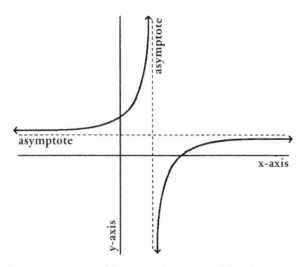

Figure 11. Asymptote. (Courtesy of José F. Candelaria)

spirals, many set into motion and/or set to music[14]—the asymptote is *Bedouin Hornbook*'s most characteristic dynamic, the arc of its emotional, intellectual, physical, and musical operations. Members of the band suffer "asymptotic shivers" (*Bedouin* 46), Jarred Bottle moves along an "asymptotic slope" (169), a musician plays "an elliptic, asymptotic wisp of a theme" (202), and all take care to respect the "arced, asymptotic 'inch'" (216) that generates their creativity. This "ontic, unbridgeable distance, a cosmogonic, uncrossable gap" (170) in *Bedouin Hornbook* becomes in the next volume the "run" of *Djbot Baghostus's Run:* its pace, act, slope, distance, momentum, and freedom, "asymptotic sprint," "asymptotic pursuit," and "arch asymptotic aria" (*Djbot* 191).

Mackey's asymptotic semiotics are anticipated in a second foundational document of radical modernism, Gertrude Stein's "A Carafe, That Is a Blind Glass," the overture to *Tender Buttons.* Bouncing off a title that has the syntax of an equation—an *x,* that is a *y*—Stein's word portrait enacts the fallacy of adequation, the lack of any absolute fit. Her carafe is a variant of other modernist vessels, among them Williams's "bottle: unbottled" (*Paterson* 142), H.D.'s "tale of a jar or jars" ("Tribute to the Angels" 105), Stevens's jar ajar in Tennessee ("Anecdote" 76), and all the gleaming light catchers in the paintings of Picasso and Braque. "A Carafe, That Is a Blind Glass," Stein writes: "A kind in glass and a cousin, a spectacle and nothing strange a single hurt color and an arrangement in a system to pointing. All this and not ordinary, not unordered in not resembling. The difference is spreading" (9). Like the rest of *Tender Buttons,* this paragraph is a "run" that swerves away from any gesture of equalization or adequation. It emphasizes "not resembling" in the same instant it insists, like an asymptotic diagram, on the fact it is also "not unordered." Its waver of "the same—different—the same" is, punceptually, a waiver or deferral of fit.[15] The litotes "not unordered," the oxomoronic "blind glass," the paradoxical phrase "a system to pointing" all gesture toward a gap that language cannot quite cross. In case we miss this idea on a conceptual level, the paragraph performs it again for the ear in "the same—different—the same" of rhyme: a blind glass/a kind in glass, in/cousin, strange/arrange, not ordinary/not unordered. The meaning of "A Carafe, That Is a Blind Glass" is not—cannot be—equivalence. In its operatic tilt, this lack of adequation is not a failure but a release: a "difference [that] is spreading,"[16] a generative ongoingness and the diaspora of punceptual thinking.[17]

*   *   *

The theories of language that underlie "Tribute to the Angels" and *Djbot Baghostus's Run* suggest yet another difference in the ways in which the poetics of these two writers differ in response to the politics and ethics of their times.

For H.D., the working model is once again a match or adequation, here between word and thing or, less loosely, signifier and signified. "The Walls Do Not Fall," *Trilogy*'s first section, charts a straightforward and untroubled transit from concept to thing through the mediation of the word:

> Without thought, invention,
> you would not have been, O Sword,
>
> without idea and the Word's mediation,
> you would have remained
>
> unmanifest in the dim dimension
> where thought dwells,
>
> and beyond thought and idea,
> their begetter,
>
> Dream,
> Vision. (18)

In the fourfold passage from dream or vision to thought to word and at last to thing, the Word is a go-between: a messenger, mediator, and reconciler of differences. H.D.'s object of address in this passage—"O Sword"—is symptomatic, for the difference between *Word's* and *Sword* is not essence but position: *Sword* is *Word's* anagram. As in the biblical story of the Creation, the word makes manifest, brings forth, generates, or realizes—makes real—that which has been "unmanifest in the dim dimension / where thought dwells." This genealogy lays the foundation for the linguistic alchemy of the next section, "Tribute to the Angels," in which *marah, mar,* and *mater* are transformed to *Mary* and *mother* by recombining the consonants *m, t, h,* and *r*. Although the letters are rearranged, as in an anagram, they exist in equivalence: they are made to balance, more or less, equally.

Mackey's principle of nonequivalence moves his thought in an opposite direction. Where H.D. tends to mute or suppress the discrepant, Mackey amplifies and foregrounds it. For him, the relation of words to things is oblique and angular—less an engagement of discrepancies than a "discrepant engagement." *Discrepant Engagement* is, of course, the title Mackey gave his collection of essays on Amiri Baraka, Robert Duncan, Robert Creeley, Charles Olson, Kamau Brathwaite, Wilson Harris, and other twentieth-century innovative and improvisatory writers. The title is asymptotic, "coined," Mackey explains, "in reference to practices that, in the interest of opening presumably closed orders of identity and signification, accent fissure, fracture, incongruity, the rickety, imperfect fit between word and world" (19).

Unlike H.D.'s vision of the Word, which glances back at Genesis, Mackey's looks back to the creation myth of the Dogon of West Africa. In Dogon cosmology, as the sage Ogotemmêli explains it to the anthropologist Marcel Griaule, the making of cloth represents the cycle of life. The various components of the process—the warp, the woof, the footrest, the shuttle, the heddle, the block on which the loom rests—stand for aspects of generativity: the opening and shutting of the womb, the phallic in-and-out of the serpent-shuttle, the stretched threads that represent procreation, the woven cloth that wraps the dead. "The craft of weaving," Ogotemmêli concludes, "is the tomb of resurrection, the marriage bed and the fruitful womb" (73).

The loom rests on a solid piece of hard wood to which the Dogon give the name "the creaking of the word." This creaking is, Mackey explains, "the noise upon which the word is based, the discrepant foundation of all coherence and articulation, of the purchase upon the world fabrication affords. Discrepant engagement, rather than suppressing or seeking to silence that noise, acknowledges it. In its anti-foundational acknowledgment of founding noise, discrepant engagement . . . voic[es] reminders of the axiomatic exclusions upon which positings of identity and meaning depend" (*Discrepant* 19). The buzz, the resonance, the semiotic spread in Mackey's texts performs his version of the creaking of the word in a refusal of adequation that is as sustained and resolute as Stein's. Like the eponymous perfume whose traces emanate from the shards of a broken bottle, like notes that fan out into chords or compositions reprised in multiple keys, words in Mackey's texts again and again split out into bracketed pairs or triplets, multiplying "ascent" into "accent" and "assent" (*Bedouin* 25), for example, or breaking "compost" down to "compose" (92).

Although H.D.'s story of the word's mediation moves in the direction of adequation rather than discrepancy, *Trilogy* also buzzes with not quite coincident aural doublets and triplets. In two often cited examples, "Venice" slides into "Venus," a word previously split out into "venereous," on the one hand, and "venerate," on the other hand (74–75, 78), as "Osiris" builds into "O, Sire, is" (57) and breaks down into *zrr-hiss, / lightning in a not-known, // unregistered dimension*" (58). This thick and flickering ascent and breakdown in the work of H.D. and Mackey, this over-the-top extravagance, is the work of operatic extremity, operatic tilt.

*   *   *

To an unsympathetic reader, operatic extremity, operatic tilt may seem merely operatic: histrionic, that is, or, worse, hysterical. As if to blunt such a reading, both H.D. and Mackey embed it preemptively in their texts. The detractor in the first section of *Trilogy* sneers at the poet's

perilous ascent,
ridiculous descent; rhyme, jingle,

overworked assonance, nonsense,
juxtaposition of words for words' sake,

without meaning, undefined. (44)

The detractor in *Bedouin Hornbook*—the first speaker at a press conference in a record store—is more succinct. His target is not convergence—"overworked assonance"—but dispersal: the Mystic Horn Society, he says, has a "tendency to . . . 'go off on tangents.'" "[A] piece of music should *gather*," he adds, to the applause of a knot of people in the classical section, "rather than *disperse* its component parts" (16). Set like a trap at the beginning of each serial work, these critiques acknowledge that operatic extremity is perilous, perhaps even, in minimalist times, "ridiculous," but neither H.D. nor Mackey concedes that it is "without meaning, undefined," decorative, decadent, or irrelevant.

In the work of H.D. and Mackey, operatic tilt is an act, a habit, a praxis that moves outward and away from the "I," eroding the basis for any criticism that tries, as Robin Blaser puts it in his essay on Jack Spicer, "to wrap itself around a personality" (272). Operatic extremity cannot be recuperated to a pathology, for it does not point inward toward the psyche or soul. Blaser's name for this poetics is "the practice of outside" (269). Constitutive rather than descriptive, the truth of this practice lies in what it makes rather than what it describes. What it seeks, Blaser says, is a *"reopened language,"* one that "lets the unknown, the Other, the outside in again as a voice in the language" (276).

The parallel to reopened language is reopened form: the run, the slip, or the serial composition, which occurs, N. tells the Angel of Dust, in "submission to a processional muse" (*Bedouin* 26).[18] H.D.'s definition—led by the triplet *have no, haven, heaven*—moves toward a similar conclusion. *"[W]e are voyagers,"* H.D. writes,

> *discoverers*
> *of the not-known,*
>
> *the unrecorded;*
> *we have no map;*
>
> *possibly we will reach haven,*
> *heaven.* (59)

Exploring the dynamics of serial composition in a letter to Blaser, Spicer emphasized the necessity "not to search for the perfect poem but to let your way of writing of the moment go along its own paths, explore and retreat but never be fully realized (confined) within the boundaries of one poem" (*Collected Books* 61). This process, which Spicer attributes to Robert Duncan, Duncan absorbed at least partially from H.D. and passed on, in turn, to Mackey.[19] There is, however, an additional twist to the serial progressions of H.D. and Mackey: if with no set outcome—no heaven, no haven—the choice lies between the random and the experimental, H.D. and Mackey pick the latter over the former. Unlike aleatory postmodernists, their procedure is to move not only from event to event but also from event toward law.

The mystical mathematics or mathematical mysticism of "Tribute to the Angels" and *From a Broken Bottle* record a passage through destruction into generativity. What falls, H.D.'s law of angles implies, rises again, be it moisture, fire, a city, or a civilization, be it "angles of light" (150) or, in a deft slippage— a metathesis intensified by a transegmental drift—"angels of flight." "Tribute to the Angels" ends with the assurance that the war's "*zrr-hiss, / lightning in a not-known, // . . . dimension*" (58), the incendiary "whirr and roar in the high air" (19), is equal to the *this is* of another here and now: "*This is*," "Tribute" concludes, "*the flowering of the rod, / this is the flowering of the burnt-out wood*" (110).

The mathematics of angles in H.D. meets the mathematics of the asymptote in Mackey at just this point: the point of genesis or generativity. Here, N. tells the Angel of Dust, "the muse of inclusiveness awakens one to a giddy sense of spin, a pregnant, rotund integrity eternally and teasingly and whirlingly out of reach . . . a sense of asymptotic wobble" (*Djbot* 71). At the end of *Djbot Baghostus's Run,* Jarred Bottle returns to amplify N.'s point by invoking "the tiny primeval seed the Dogon call *po*" (190)—the place of all-flowering—in two incidents, one musical and the other cosmogonical.

The incidents occur in two quotations in Djbot Baghostus's mind in the final scene of *Djbot Baghostus's Run.* After the drummer Dannie Richmond had been in Mingus's band for nine months, the first story goes, Mingus asked him, "'[S]uppose you had to play a composition alone. How could you play it on the drums?'" and then supplied an answer: "'Okay, if you had a dot in the middle of your hand and you were going in a circle, it would have to expand and go round and round, and get larger and larger and larger. And at some point it would have to stop, and then this same circle would have to come back around, around, around to the little dot in the middle of your hand'" (190). This spiral movement in two directions coincides with Ogotemmêli's figure for creation in the second quotation: "'The internal movement of germination was prefigured by this spiral movement in two directions, which is the movement of the *po*. It is said: "The seed grows by turning." Inside, while germinating, it first spins in one direction, then, after bursting, that is, after the emergence of the germ, it spins in the other direction, in order to produce its root and stalk'" (qtd. in Mackey, *Djbot* 190). This radical wobble—improvisational, alchemical—is the creative force in action.

"It's exactly here," N. tells the Angel of Dust, "that revelation and recuperation lock horns, the latter almost inevitably the victor" (*Djbot* 71). The binaries that stop the spin or abort the wobble are to interpreters of the last three decades of the twentieth century what scholasticism was to Pound and Fenollosa in the first two: a mark of the limits of Western logic that poetry bids to bypass. In the moment of recuperation, N. explains, "the potential breakthru, the asymmetrical fissure which begins to be glimpsed, is almost immediately closed off, almost immediately traded away for the consolations of a binary opposition" (71).

The operatic poetics of radical modernists like Pound, Stein, H.D., and Mackey is a struggle—not always, or even often, successful—to dodge these consolations. Although both "Tribute to the Angels" and *Djbot Baghostus's Run* respond to gendered and racialized readings, neither text follows a binary logic of realism. This is a strength, not, as has sometimes been implied, an embarrassment or deficit. In their excess, their operatic tilt, H.D. and Mackey swerve away from the accessible and familiar politics of opposition. "My view," Mackey writes in the introduction to *Discrepant Engagement,* "is that there has been far too much emphasis on accessibility when it comes to writers from socially marginalized groups. This has resulted in shallow, simplistic readings that belabor the most obvious aspects of the writer's work and situation, readings that go something like this: 'So-and-so is a black writer. Black people are victims of racism. So-and-so's writing speaks out against racism'" (17–18).

The inaugural readings of H.D.—the readings that made her accessible to my generation—speak out eloquently against oppression based on gender and on race, but it is time to complicate the oppositions of these readings by following her into more intricate, metaphysical, and chaotic territories. This is one benefit of reading H.D. next to Mackey or, to turn the spiral in Hollenberg's collection of essays, reading H.D. and Mackey next to Mackey reading H.D. "We find the traditions that feed us," Mackey tells Peter O'Leary. "[W]e make them up in part, we invent the traditions and the senses of the past, the genealogies, that allow us to follow certain dispositions that we have, to be certain things we want to be, to do certain things we want to do" (O'Leary 37).

The benefits of reading Mackey in accord/in a chord with H.D. are not only an intensification of important complexities in his thought but also an appreciation of his radical modernist genealogy, a lineage he traces back through

Duncan to H.D., Pound, and Williams as well as forward from Clarence Major and Amiri Baraka to Kamau Brathwaite and Wilson Harris. As Aldon Lynn Nielsen argues in *Black Chant,* his important study of the languages of African-American postmodernism, "[I]f an intertextual history of African-American poetics is to succeed, it must also take as part of its assignment a study of the multitudinous ways in which black writings relate themselves to those writings by whites that seem to afford openings for transracial signifying practices. If American postmodernity is to be comprehended in its transracial plenitude, critical readings will have to follow black poets as they read and transform the texts of whites" (36). The resonance of transracial and transgender signifying practices in the work of H.D. and Mackey not only gives access to elements we cannot see if we concentrate only on the binaries of their antitotalitarian politics but also lets us hear the peril in the chime of "not see" and "Nazi" and perhaps also the promise of an off-tonic operatic tilt that is "not C" but, perhaps, in a couple of variants, the writing signet H.D. and the indefinite number N.

Notes

1. As we have seen, H.D.'s fixed stare in the movie *Borderline* and her taping of portions of *Helen in Egypt* both use twentieth-century broadcast media to facilitate the transmission of thought from one mind to another. The two chapters of part 3 position this drift between sender and receiver as an interchange in ink. As Mackey emphasizes, however, this print transmission, like film and tape, also draws on the eye and ear—"glimpse" and "resonance"—in the interplay of graphotext and phonotext.

2. In addition to the ten poets who write essays for her volume, Hollenberg lists Robin Blaser, George Bowering, Hayden Carruth, Jane Cooper, Robert Creeley, Beverly Dahlen, Diane DiPrima, Robert Duncan, Sandra Gilbert, Judy Grahn, Barbara Guest, Thom Gunn, Donald Hall, Lindy Hough, Susan Howe, Dale Kushner, Denise Levertov, Dorothy Livesay, Charlotte Mandel, Hilda Morley, Robert Pinsky, Joan Retallack, Adrienne Rich, May Swenson, Edith Walden, and Anne Waldman (xi). The list could be extended to include Meredith Stricker, Liz Waldner, and several younger poets just now publishing their first full-length collections.

3. "So first off," Rachel Blau DuPlessis writes in "Haibun: 'Draw your / Draft,'" her essay for Hollenberg's volume, "it's not so much the influence of H.D. on me but (don't get me wrong) my influence on H.D." (117). DuPlessis's account of writing a poem called "Eurydice" then stumbling across H.D.'s "Eurydice" is an excellent example of this process, for DuPlessis's initial refusal of scripted myths allowed her to discern the early feminist critique in H.D.'s poem and to use that poem to develop her own theory of "revisionary mythopoesis" (*Writing* 105). For DuPlessis's theory of mythopoesis, see *Writing beyond the Ending,* chap. 7.

4. Like H.D.'s permutations on the initials that form her name, the name of Mackey's narrator, N., has many possible extensions, among them Nathaniel (his own first name), Narrator (his function), and N. (the mathematical symbol for an indefinite number).

5. Mackey's name for his protagonist—Jarred Bottle—recalls the "bottle: unbottled" by the fire in book 3 of William Carlos Williams's *Paterson:* "An old bottle, mauled by the fire / gets a new glaze, the glass warped / to a new distinction, reclaiming the / undefined" (142–43).

6. In a letter in *Djbot Baghostus's Run,* N. cautions the Angel of Dust "against confusing solemnity with truth" (144). Like Jonathan Culler and the other essayists who contribute to Culler's collection of essays *On Puns,* H.D. and Mackey find echoic wordplay "not a marginal form of wit but an exemplary product of language or mind" (Culler, "Call" 4).

7. For the full anecdote, see Bede, *Ecclesiastical History,* book 2, chap. 1 (99–100).

8. For an extended discussion of puncepts in classical writing, see Ahl. For the Dogon myth of the "creaking of the word," see Mackey, *Discrepant Engagement* 19–21, 183–90.

9. In *Bedouin Hornbook,* N. makes this point in reference to the improvisations of the saxophonist John Coltrane: "It's like those people who used to say that Coltrane sounded like he was searching for some 'right' note on those long runs of his that at the time were called 'sheets of sound.' What he was up to was no such cover at all. He wanted each and every one of those notes to be heard, not to be erased by the eventual arrival at some presumably 'correct' (or at least sought-after) note" (28–29).

10. "Radical modernism" is a term Charles Bernstein uses in his essay "In the Middle of Modernism in the Middle of Capitalism on the Outskirts of New York," presented at the Socialist Scholars Conference in 1987. Although, like Bernstein, I use this term to emphasize the political and institutional ramifications of this writing, Bernstein's emphasis is on the term's socialist valence, mine on its linguistic valence.

11. For an excellent discussion of the dynamics of improvisation—and a convincing argument that "the composition/improvisation dichotomy doesn't exist" (140)—see Bailey. For a discussion of Stein's improvisatory methods, see Hejinian, "Common Sense" 374–75.

12. This redoubling resembles Mackey's own after-the-fact recognition of H.D.'s initials in his phrase "hieratic drift" ("Palimpsestic Stagger" 225). It also tempts the reader to see Mystic Horn Society's initials as yet another layer in the time-lapse equation of the title "Three M's and an H."

13. "I am invisible," Ellison's narrator emphasizes, "simply because people refuse to see me" (7).

14. See, for example, N.'s *"Deaf Diagrammatic Perspective on the Toupouri Wind Ensemble's Harvest Song"* in *Bedouin Hornbook* (134) or in *Djbot Baghostus's Run* the diagram N. labels "SUSPECT-SYMMETRICAL STRUCTURE OF MISCONCEPTUAL SEED'S PARALLACTIC DISPATCH" (109).

15. For Stewart's play with the term "waiver," see "Modernism's Sonic Waiver."

16. The erotic resonance of Stein's "spreading" resonates with Mackey's many allusions to the unquenchable desire that drives his writing, "a sexual 'cut'" that signifies "'an exegetic refusal to be done with desire'" (*Bedouin* 38, 52).

17. Another mathematical term Mackey uses for the leftover or remainder is the "aliquant factor": "[r]emainder and thus reminder of what's left over, what's left out." The aliquant factor is the difference that "[blows] the lid off totalizing assumptions" (*Djbot* 151).

18. N. goes on in this passage to invoke the geometry of the asymptotic curve. Noting that submission to a processual muse is a kind of rowdiness that "openly takes to the streets," he adds, "I hope I can say this and still keep clear of a strictly euclidian sense of 'the streets.' . . . I should stress the word 'openly' perhaps" (*Bedouin* 26).

19. Mackey's Ph.D. dissertation, "Call Me Tantra: Open Field Poetics as Muse," took up the work of Robert Duncan. "It was . . . Duncan who ushered me into H.D.'s work," Mackey writes, "albeit indirectly. It wasn't that I hadn't read H.D. before meeting him or that I hadn't read her prior to reading his readings of her in *The H.D. Book*. . . . Reading more and more of Duncan's work led me to read H.D. more deeply" ("Palimpsestic" 226). For Mackey's essays on Duncan, see *Discrepant Engagement*.

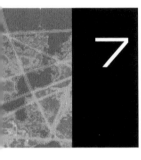

7

Transformations:
H.D., Spicer, and Scalapino

[Tradition] means generations of different poets in different
countries patiently telling the same story, writing the same poem,
gaining and losing something with each transformation—but,
of course, never really losing anything.
—Jack Spicer, *After Lorca*

Activity is the only community. The conservative gesture, always a
constant (any ordering, institutional and societal) is to view both
activity and time *per se* as a condition of tradition. As such, both
time and activity are a "lost mass" at any time.
—Leslie Scalapino, "The Radical Nature of Experience"

It's not lost. This will go on somewhere.
—H.D., epigraph to "The Sword Went Out to Sea (Synthesis of
a Dream)"

This book begins with a series of microlinguistic fissions and
fusions of the sort Geoffrey Hartman describes as aural events
with conceptual consequences. "Split the atom of sound,"
Hartman writes, "and you detonate an astonishing charge of
meaning" (341). Although Hartman is not thinking of H.D.,
his description captures the event that occurs in her poetry
when a phrase like "Sea Rose" dissolves into "zeroes" or a word
like "Osiris" splits into "O, Sire, is" then fuses in the "*zrr-hiss*"
of Nazi rockets falling over London (*Trilogy* 57, 58). These
transformations are part of the ongoingness of language that
led H.D.'s thought as she struggled to make the dissolutions
of her century socially, ethically, and philosophically intelligi-

ble. In the chapter that ends this book, I want to turn from Hartman's figure of speech toward an event it at once evokes and occludes: the detonation of the atom bomb over Hiroshima and Nagasaki in August 1945.

In the light cast by nuclear weapons exploded, stockpiled, rattled, "improved," and proliferated across the last half of the twentieth century, this chapter's epigraphs can be read as a series of attempts to test the charge the words "loss," "tradition," and "go on" retain in face of technologies of global annihilation. In the first blast over Hiroshima, 13,983 people disappeared without a trace: these are not the dead—who numbered in the hundreds of thousands—but the vaporized (Maclear 31).[1] In face of such loss—bodies unbodied, shadows seared into walls—what does it mean to "go on"? What elements transmitted from generation to generation, what modes of thought or behavior, custom or usage, retain significance? Where is the "somewhere" of persistence? What, if anything, does survival have to do with fissions and fusions of meaning in poetry?

The words "Hiroshima" and "Nagasaki"—like the word "Auschwitz" in Adorno's declaration of the barbarism of poetry "after Auschwitz"[2]—mark a limit at which customary structures of feeling and thought cease to be adequate to experience. The three poets at the heart of this chapter—H.D., Jack Spicer, and Leslie Scalapino—come from three generations that surround the first catastrophic explosions of nuclear weapons: H.D., born in 1886, was fifty-nine years old in the year the bomb was tested in New Mexico and dropped on Hiroshima and Nagasaki; Jack Spicer, born in 1925, was twenty years old, a year away, by his own reckoning, from the moment of his real birth when he met Robin Blaser and Robert Duncan at the University of California at Berkeley (Gizzi xix); Leslie Scalapino, born in 1947, is a member of the first generation to enter a world always already altered by the nuclear firestorms of August 1945.

The mushroom cloud over ground zero is a still-frame of singularity: a snapshot of catastrophe, a violent inversion, a moment that is, for all three poets, at once *ruin* and *rune*.[3] Taken variously to signify scientific breakthrough and apocalyptic collapse, an end to World War II and a beginning of global annihilation, this icon has been endlessly reproduced in paintings, drawings, silk screens, and collages, on postage stamps and billboards, in advertisements for new and improved commodities, even in the contours of an angel-food cake served at a Washington, D.C., party celebrating the completion of the 1946 atomic tests at Bikini.[4] Like the stricken replay of the footage of the September 11, 2001, collapse of New York's World Trade Center towers, this reiteration testifies to the force of an event that the language and traditions of contemporary imagination cannot explain, contain, or master, an event that wrecks our minds.

*   *   *

In his essay "The Noble Rider and the Sound of Words," written in the midst of World War II, before Hiroshima and Nagasaki and before the full disclosure of the atrocities at Auschwitz, Wallace Stevens declared the imagination sufficient to its trials. "The mind," he writes, "is a violence from within that protects us from a violence without. It is the imagination pressing back against the pressure of reality. It seems, in the last analysis, to have something to do with our self-preservation; and that, no doubt, is why the expression of it, the sound of its words, helps us to live our lives" (36). In his claim that the imagination holds its ground against the onslaught of contemporaneity, Stevens invokes a familiar drama of force and counterforce. The dynamics of pressing and pressing back are part of the story of objects and forces in collision, rebound, advance, retreat, and stalemate described by Newtonian physics. This explanation of the world, illustrated by falling apples and colliding billiard balls and played out in the push, shove, and stalemate of trench warfare, hit its limit in the spectacle of fission and fusion, lost mass, and vaporization at Hiroshima and Nagasaki.

In 1919, in his essay "Tradition and the Individual Talent," T. S. Eliot constructed his brief for the adequacy and equanimity of the poet's imagination. More elaborate than Stevens's model, Eliot's comes not from physics but from chemistry. The interaction between the poet and "the whole of the literature of Europe from Homer and within it the whole of the literature of his own country" (4), Eliot argues, resembles "the action which takes place when a bit of finely filiated platinum is introduced into a chamber containing oxygen and sulphur dioxide" (7). Like the platinum shred in whose presence these two gases form sulphurous acid, he is saying, the poet's mind is a catalyst: it precipitates a process that happens not *to* it but because of it. Eliot's emphasis is the poet's depersonalization: the poet's mind is, he continues, "a receptacle for seizing and storing up numberless feelings, phrases, images, which remain there until all the particles which can unite to form a new compound are present together" (8). What is surprising in this argument for the separation of "the man who suffers and the mind which creates" (8) is not so much its tenor—this is a point Pound and T. E. Hulme had pressed for almost a decade—but its vehicle: to Eliot's contemporaries, the chemistry of gases interacting in a canister would call to mind not a laboratory reaction but a weapon of terror introduced four years earlier on the battlefields of World War I.

The first use of "asphyxiating bombs" is credited to the German army, which dispersed chlorine gas over Allied lines near Ypres on 22 April 1915. "The attack of last Thursday evening," Will Irwin reported in his 27 April dispatch to the *New York Tribune,* "was preceded by the rising of a cloud of vapor, greenish gray and iridescent. That vapor settled to the ground like a swamp mist and drifted toward the French trenches on a brisk wind. Its effect on the French was a violent nausea and faintness, followed by an utter collapse. It is believed that the Germans, who charged in behind the vapor, met no resistance at all, the French at their front being virtually paralyzed."[5] Rapidly deployed by all sides, chemical weapons played a significant part in the carnage of 1916–17. By 1918, it is estimated, one of every four artillery shells carried noxious, paralyzing, or corrosive gas.[6]

Like Stevens, Eliot imagines a mind that remains not only intact but fundamentally unaltered by the volatility it confronts. Eliot's comparison between the poet's mind and the platinum shred admits no trauma, contextual or psychological. His point, in fact, is the *lack* of exchange between the poet and the violence without: the combination of sulphur dioxide and oxygen into sulphurous acid, which occurs only in the presence of the platinum shred, "contains no trace of platinum, and the platinum itself is apparently unaffected; has remained inert, neutral, and unchanged" (7). As detached, objective, and depersonalized as Carl Gart formulating the "Gart theorum of mathematical biological intention" (*HERmione* 4), Eliot's poet stands apart from the processes he observes. There is, in Spicer's terms, no "gaining and losing something with each transformation"; in Scalapino's, no "lost mass" between the mind of the poet, the traditions in which the poet works, and the language that carries and sustains those traditions.

For the three poets who are the subject of this chapter, by contrast, the mind exists in a continuous mutually constitutive exchange with the phenomena around it. In "The Radical Nature of Experience," an essay that undoes nearly every premise of Eliot's argument, Scalapino uses a trope from atomic physics—the physics of World War II—to undermine the notion of tradition as an entity apart from the poet's mind. "The conservative gesture, always a constant," Scalapino argues, "is to view both activity and time *per se* as a condition of tradition. As such, both time and activity are a 'lost mass' at any time" (3). In contrast to a chemical process in which the catalyst remains inert, neutral, and unchanged, the reference here is to a fusion reaction that transforms mass into energy. For Scalapino, time and activity—including the activity of the poet's mind—participate in a continuous demassification of institutions, categorizations, customs, and canons. Energy is, then, as Einstein's equations demonstrated, not lost mass but mass transformed. This transformation is Scalapino's "thought/form as discovery" (3), a process in which nothing is "lost," as H.D. would have it, that does not "go on somewhere," "gaining and losing something," as Spicer puts it, "with each transformation."

Because "[w]riting," in Scalapino's formulation, "is . . . an experiment of reality" (8), it prompts the future by radically transforming the categories of the past. The bombing of Hiroshima and Nagasaki is an event that does not leave the mind intact and apart from the violence without. The strange turns in H.D.'s writing, the incursions of an outside into Spicer's writing, and the syntactic and conceptual impermanence of Scalapino's writing are transformations that happen if and only if the mind allows itself to be opened, altered, or, in a term Scalapino borrows from Philip Whalen, "wrecked."[7] Like Hartman's vision of the microlinguistic turmoil released by splitting phonemes, the conceptual fissions and fusions in the poetry of H.D., Spicer, and Scalapino "detonate an astonishing charge of meaning."[8] These poems need to be read, therefore, as links in a chain reaction, segments of an ongoing series of interior and exterior events, each one of which creates the conditions within which the next can occur.

*   *   *

Although Spicer and Scalapino both admire H.D.'s work—Spicer tells Blaser he has mailed "Hildy Doolittle" a complimentary copy of *After Lorca* (Ellingham and Killian 122) and Scalapino writes eloquently on H.D.'s *Trilogy* and *Helen in Egypt*[9]—in this chapter I am interested not in tracing lines of influence but in witnessing the strategies through which these poets come to terms, separately and together, with the physics of destruction and creation that preoccupied them in the wake of Hiroshima and Nagasaki.

In "Interior Scrutiny," her most sustained essay on H.D., Scalapino begins by locating the gist of H.D.'s writing in "the syntax or language-shape that is [its] action" (205). Scalapino does not mean that H.D. writes well about action but rather that her writing *is* itself action: an unfolding of "mind-phenomena" in which "relativity itself is the sole ground of observation" (204). The form of such a meditation cannot be a lyric burst or epic narration, for its focus is neither interior psychological nuance nor exterior progression of events but an inside/outside that joins the mind's operations and the phenomena those operations apprehend.

Instead of lyric or narrative, H.D., Spicer, and Scalapino work in a form Scalapino, in an essay on Robert Creeley's sequences *For Love, Words,* and *Pieces,* calls "*thinking serially*" (*Public World* 44). The customary designation for this form is Spicer's term "the serial poem," created, he told Robin Blaser, "jokingly" (273), with a glance at radio serials and comic strips. For Creeley,

Spicer, Scalapino, and H.D., the virtue of this form is its capacity to monitor continuous transformations. Stopping and starting, crossing divisions that are at one and the same time fissions and fusions, the poet continues to rearrange events well after they have occurred, using the ongoing now of composition to pull the past into the future. As Scalapino acutely observes in her comments on H.D.'s *Trilogy,* this is a form that tends to arise out of the "greatest crisis"—a crisis like the bombing of London or the annihilation of Hiroshima and Nagasaki—because in it the "'present' *ha[s]* to transcend history" ("Interior Scrutiny" 204).

Just as syntax or language-shape is a continuous patterning or formation of grammatical elements, poems like H.D.'s *Helen in Egypt,* Spicer's *The Holy Grail,* and Scalapino's *As: All Occurrence in Structure, Unseen—(Deer Night)* are spectacles of combination and recombination, reiteration and transformation. In these poems, there is no past that cannot be rethought in the now of composition in order to make way for an oncoming—or a going-on—future. In these works, therefore, relationships between characters like Helen, Paris, and Achilles, Gawain, Lancelot, and Guinivere, or Ariel, Caliban, and Prospero, and events like the Trojan War, the imprisonment of Merlin, or Caliban's enslavement remain undetermined even after they have "occurred." "It's almost," Scalapino says of *Helen in Egypt,* "a molecular structure: history transcending as 'one' (as if all the events and motions are in the mind of one)" ("Interior Scrutiny" 204).[10] Insofar as the serial poetry of H.D., Spicer, and Scalapino enacts the churn of loss, tradition, and "going on," it joins the project Hal Foster identifies with all "historical and neo-avant-gardes": "a continual . . . protension and retension, a complex relay of reconstructed past and anticipated future—in short . . . a deferred action that throws over any simple scheme of before and after, cause and effect, origin and repetition" (30).

A desire to overthrow "simple scheme[s] of before and after, cause and effect," helps to explain the return in H.D., Spicer, and Scalapino's serial poems to core texts of Western culture. Although their rewriting of foundational texts recalls similar returns in Ezra Pound's *Cantos* or T. S. Eliot's *The Waste Land,* on the one hand, and Jean Rhys's *Wide Sargasso Sea* or Margaret Atwood's *Circe/Mud Poems,* on the other hand, these poems are not primarily demonstrations of how we have fallen from or how we might improve on past configurations. Although they contain both ironical and hopeful gestures, that is, they are more exploratory than exhortatory. H.D. describes her relationship with prior texts as a rewriting that is also, more precisely, an overwriting: the creation of a "palimpsest"—or, in Michael Davidson's variant of this term, a "palimtext"—in which one writing is inscribed on top of a series of others.[11]

H.D.'s *Trilogy* and *Helen in Egypt* explore foundational Judeo-Christian and classical mythologies, transforming some elements, deforming or obscuring others; Spicer's *The Holy Grail* reinvents Sir Thomas Malory's many-times-retold tales from *Le Morte d'Arthur;* Scalapino's *As: All Occurrence in Structure, Unseen—(Deer Night)* recasts Shakespeare's *The Tempest,* itself, of course, like the Bible, Homer, and Malory, composed of retellings of previously reinscribed narratives.

In a palimpsest, each scribbling over or partial occlusion of the text(s) below brings a loss of legibility but also, as knowledge recoalesces across contexts, a gain in information and perspective. The most interesting aspect of H.D., Spicer, and Scalapino's deployment of the palimpsest, however, is not cognitive but political. To the extent that they reconfigure concepts foundational to Western culture, palimpsestic overwritings undo existing cultural agreements.[12] In this sense, as Spicer observes in *After Lorca,* "A poet is a time mechanic not an embalmer" (25). Like the Terminator in James Cameron's *Terminator 2: Judgment Day,* H.D. in *Trilogy* and *Helen in Egypt,* Spicer in *After Lorca* and *The Holy Grail,* and Scalapino in *As* travel back to the tales of the past to make an adjustment to avert a catastrophe in the future that is now.[13]

To comprehend this twist it is necessary to recognize a third and related characteristic of these palimpsestic serial poems: their switch from a Newtonian to an Einsteinian conception of time. Rather than a linear progression, that is, H.D., Spicer, and Scalapino imagine time as a fold or overlap "in which all times exist at once. And occur as activity without excluding each other" (Scalapino, "Radical Nature" 3). The palimpsestic narratives in the poetry of H.D., Spicer, and Scalapino reveal tradition to be a set of structures and events that exist in the mass-energy Scalapino's subtitle to *The Public World* identifies as "syntactically impermanence." Like the entity Werner Heisenberg describes in his formulations—the impossible-but-nonetheless-actual mass-energy, now wave, now particle—the linguistic formation Scalapino names "syntactically impermanence" exists in an always incomplete conversion between states. This is, as the subtitle of *As* puts it, "all occurrence in structure, unseen": an event, a paradigm, a flickering, newly perceptible in the aftermath of the firestorms of August 1945 and intermittently caught in the formulations of H.D.'s *Trilogy* as glimpsed through Scalapino's *The Return of Painting, The Pearl, and Orion: A Trilogy,* Spicer's *The Holy Grail,* and Scalapino's *As.*

*   *   *

Published a half-century after H.D.'s *Trilogy,* Scalapino's *Trilogy* is a 230-page volume containing three sequences: "The Return of Painting," "The Pearl," and "Orion." Scalapino describes these pieces as "one thing, although they're discrete" (Interview 116). Each poem is composed of sections, each section of paragraphs, each paragraph of units that range from single words to complex collocations of phrases and sentences. On all three levels—sections, paragraphs, and words, phrases, or sentences—the constituent parts jostle without resolution. Although sections sometimes show up under rubrics such as "A Novel" or "A Novel II (a separate novel)," the action is less a plot that joins the actions, speech, and thoughts of the characters than an unceasing spin of transformations. Looming into and out of focus through the three poems are a detective who is hired to do a number of jobs—she's variously a dishwasher, a check-out girl, a security escort, and a private eye in search of a hillbilly's daughter—and a cast of characters who would be right at home in a Dick Tracy comic strip: a fat, cigar-smoking lolling man, a man out walking a cat on a leash, a building contractor who may or may not be running drugs, a truck driver, a woman with thin appendages and a large rear, and a series of dubious public officials, including cops, a mayor, a senior government source, CIA operatives, and state oil monopoly henchmen. The background against which these figures appear and disappear is a bright and distorted litter of corpses and bums, tough guys, true hearts, and hangers-on.

Each of the titles of Scalapino's three poems points outward: "The Return of Painting" refers to an observation by the artist Julian Schnabel; "The Pearl" refers to a late fourteenth-century poet's vision of the death of a child who may or may not be his daughter;[14] and "Orion" refers to the mythological hunter, son of Poseidon and Euryale, who appears to lie on his side in the southern hemisphere because from the point of view of earth a series of stars that are in reality light years apart can be connected into a picture. The most consistent model for Scalapino's *Trilogy,* however, is not art, religion, or the parade of constellations but their noncanonized or low-art double: the comic strip. Read horizontally or vertically, one frame at a time—"pow on the side of the head and she reels from it" (126)—the comic strip is the pulp equivalent of "the serial novel" (158), the pictorial equivalent of the serial poem.

Although they begin as narrative blocks, over the course of *Trilogy,* Scalapino's paragraphs take on the shape and syncopation of elements in a serial poem. A few are fragments—"Of them" (93), for example, "That there isn't" (122), or "—necessarily—" (95)—but most have the stand-alone sequentiality of pages in a flipbook, snapshots in an album, panels in a comic strip, or frames in film noir. "The (other) woman goes downstairs and out of the bar—and down the street at night," one paragraph reads. "Her heels ring on the pavement of the empty block" (63). In another paragraph, the same woman or maybe another—it's hard to tell—"drives—at night, a truck is behind her. The (other) pulls wildly into a gas station. Standing wildly, asking directions. The man black in the lamp answers calmly looking up from crouching" (91). In yet another, "Others arriving with the ashes of an other. Outside it's quiet" (103).

These enigmas give Scalapino's *Trilogy* the suspense of a detective novel: Who did it, we want to know, to whom and when and how and why? And what, exactly, was it that they did, if in fact they did it? Like Sergeant Friday and Officer Gannon, readers are positioned to seek the facts but, unlike Friday and Gannon, they are at the same time forced to acknowledge that they inhabit a universe in which there's no longer any such thing as "just a fact."[15] The scene is strewn with corpses—a boy in a ditch, a man in a plane, a filling-station attendant who may or may not have killed himself, a building contractor doused with alcohol and thrown in the river, a Mohawk skinhead boy, a flower child—but it's never clear who killed these people, much less why or when. Because the rare bits of dialogue consist of clichés—"Then he calls her up. You're all I've got. Whining. Obviously manipulating" (95)—any semblance of psychological inwardness evaporates like a puddle on a roadway as the reader zooms on by. Lines like this tell us so little about who or even why, the reader turns with relief to the question how. In this emphasis on thought/form as process, Scalapino's *Trilogy* detaches from Chester Gould's comic strip and aligns itself with H.D.'s *Trilogy* to suggest another way to read the postatomic serial poem.

*   *   *

One of very few footnoted lines in "The Pearl" gives us a place to start: "Flatness," the text reads, "was construed as (was made to be) a barrier put up against the viewer's normal wish to enter a picture and dream, to have it be a space apart from life in which the mind would be free to make its own connections" (133). This observation—attributed in the footnote to T. J. Clark's *The Painting of Modern Life: Paris in the Art of Manet and His Followers*—is a standard description of modernism's refusal of the realist's dream of transparency, belief in "accurate" or "authentic" representation, and complacency about the normalcy of his or her views of life in the world. "The return of painting"—to cite the phrase from Schnabel that titles the first poem in Scalapino's *Trilogy*—marks the countermoment when postimpressionists, cubists, expressionists, and others used the application of paint to reopen epistemological and ontological questions that realism seemed to have foreclosed.

As Marjorie Perloff suggests in *Radical Artifice: Writing Poetry in the Age of Media,* realism's comforting illusions, dreams, and reassurances are now the stuff of Hollywood films, talk shows, soap operas, and advertising campaigns.[16]

"We know we're being shitted when we're four years old," Scalapino comments, "and yet we could be going on eighty and still be living in this shitting" (137). In both trilogies, persistence in illusion is not an inevitability but a willed accession to norms imposed by a ubiquitous, unspecified, slightly sinister, slightly comic consensus-formation known as "they."[17] "They" are the "smug and fat," the ones, H.D. continues, who "were angry when we were so hungry" (*Trilogy* 5). "They"—the makers of fantasies, romances, and advertisements—create a warp, then, Scalapino adds, "They think that we are in that warp. . . . They created this saying this is reality when there is not such. It isn't that. That isn't the center. It isn't" (*Return* 138). The stumble in syntax, the spin of fragments, the repetition of "they," the insistent "isn't . . . isn't . . . isn't" mark Scalapino's effort to hack out a space of contemplation that escapes realist illusion in order to permit philosophical and ethical inquiry.

Both H.D.'s *Trilogy* and Scalapino's *Trilogy* situate themselves in a landscape of death, destruction, and despair without endorsing nihilism; both mobilize the resources of dream vision, mystical tradition, and religious writing without embracing institutionalized faith. The achievement of these poems is neither a modernism understood as a search for transcendent mythic systems nor a postmodernism conceived as endless aleatory play, but a third position that emerges in the wake of disaster. Too mobile to be schematic, too abstract to be pragmatic, these poems propose a habit of contemplation as a form of action.

The mode of apprehension in these trilogies is painterly in intensity, concentration, and self-reflexivity. Like Cézanne looking at an apple or Stevens studying a pear, H.D. and Scalapino gaze at occurrences and structures until their edges dissolve into an outside or elsewhere that exceeds the categories of language. In *Notes on Thought and Vision*, H.D. stages this gaze as the meditation of the Ming dynasty poet Lo-fu. "He sat in his orchard and looked about in a vague, casual way," H.D. tells us. At first, he is preoccupied by practicalities—"that shoot should have been pruned, it hangs too low"—but slowly, in the force of his gaze, form dissolves into flow, and he sees "the globes of the apples red, yellow, red with flecks of brown and red, yellow where the two colours merged, and flecks of brown again on the yellow, and green as the round surface curved in toward the stem" (43).[18] The curvilinear plane produced in this gaze is a shimmer of form and color, mass and energy, space and time. In this mutually interactive field, mind merges with and co-creates the phenomena it observes.

To apprehend the world, for a moment, in this fashion loosens categories of before, during, and after, paradigms of cause and effect, hierarchies of first and last. The dissolution the poem generates is, for H.D.'s Lo-fu, a "means of approach to something else" (*Notes* 45). Both H.D. and Scalapino refuse to name this "something else," but it is clear that for both it functions as a transition: a gate, or, in H.D.'s swift elision, agate. "I can not invent it," H.D. says in "Tribute to the Angels," but

> I said it was agate,
>
> I said, it lived, it gave—
> fragrance—was near enough
>
> to explain that quality
> for which there is no name. (77)

In "Orion," the concluding poem of Scalapino's *Trilogy,* in the midst of cafés, consumers, flags, taxis, and bums, there is—wavering in and out of sight, emerging abruptly and usually lodged on its own line—an entity, a state, a condition Scalapino calls, in her turn, "the jewel."[19] Unspecified and uncategorized, the jewel is, or seems to be, a glimpse of an outside: a mass-energy that is "not being in one's own civilization" (163) or, in the poem's "syntactically impermanence" precision, "not being in the other civilization / but rather not in her own" (167).

For both H.D. and Scalapino, the jewel marks a liminal terrain attained, if at all, briefly, through meditation or quest, no sooner envisioned than dispelled. In the light of this liminality, language—any language—appears contingent, constructed, frail, temporary, dangerous, even, in its tendency toward fixities, deadly. H.D.'s glimpse of an elsewhere emerges from and returns to the ground zero of London, where the bombing does not cease; Scalapino's glimpse of an elsewhere emerges from and returns to a contemporary toxic postatomic waste, where, nonetheless, life goes on.

Both Scalapino and H.D. recognize—but do not completely dodge—the risk in the formation of a concept like "the jewel": when language names it, the process solidifies and stops. H.D. combats this massification by imagining not so much the jewel as the jewel-in-formation, introducing it, that is, through a description of an alchemical process of continuous change. Scalapino, in the crucible of her poem, introduces the concept of the jewel in a linguistic flicker, allowing it to appear and disappear in "syntactically impermanence." For both poets, the jewel as an entity is not an answer: not a place to go, a place to stay, a place to hide. It is not equilibrated with the question of how to live, what to do. To get closer to the "lost mass" the jewel suggests, we need to turn to another quest, another set of questions, generated in Jack Spicer's transformations of the stories of the Grail tradition.

*   *   *

"'You ask the wrong questions,'" says the Fool-killer to the Fool in Jack Spicer's serial poem *The Holy Grail* (193). "Who was the fool-killer?" asks someone sitting in Warren Tallman's Vancouver living room during Spicer's lecture on seriality and *The Holy Grail*. "The fool-killer ain't in the Grail legend," Spicer replies (*House* 60). "It's coming out in a movie with Tony Perkins," someone else—or maybe the same person—comments. Spicer asks, "What's coming out?" The answer is *The Fool Killer* (1965), billed by reel.com as an "[u]nusual horror-tinged Western about [an] orphan in [the] post–Civil War South encountering [a] disturbed ex-soldier."[20] A publicity still from the movie features Anthony Perkins standing on a chimney on top of what appears to be a home in the American heartland. He has a bland, impassive face and a Beatles haircut, and he holds an ax in the air as if it were an American flag (see fig. 12). This quest is going nowhere. Let's start again.

"'You ask the wrong questions,'" says the Fool-killer to the Fool in Jack Spicer's serial poem *The Holy Grail*, a poem written—or at least received—in 1962.[21] What was happening in 1962? On Valentine's Day, President Kennedy announced that U.S. military advisers in Vietnam would fire if fired upon. On

Figure 12. Publicity still for *The Fool Killer* (1965), with Anthony Perkins.

20 February, Lieutenant Colonel John Glenn circled the earth three times in the Mercury capsule *Friendship 7.* In July, the first U.S. communications satellite was launched. On 1 October, after three thousand troops moved in to put down riots, James Meredith matriculated as the first black student at the University of Mississippi. On 22 October, Kennedy appeared on television to announce a Soviet missile build-up in Cuba. As he spoke to the nation, the Pentagon put two dozen Strategic Air Command bombers into the air, each carrying four H-bombs, thus tripling the number of bomb-laden planes always already aloft as a matter of cold war policy. On 24 October, the United States entered Defense Condition 2—DefCon2—one stage away from all-out nuclear war, where it stayed until Kennedy announced a stand-down on 2 November 1962. In 1962, Ed Sanders founded *Fuck You: A Magazine of the Arts,* Robert Creeley published *For Love,* and Rachel Carson serialized *Silent Spring* in the pages of *The New Yorker.*

The question Carson asks concerns birds, mice, rabbits, and foxes found in violent contortions after a mosquito-control campaign near Duxbury, Massachusetts, a gypsy moth battle in eastern Long Island, and an all-out war against fire ants in the southern states. The June 1962 *New Yorker* included this tableau from her book: "There was once a town in the heart of America where all life seemed to live in harmony with its surroundings. Then a strange blight crept over the area and everything began to change. There was a strange stillness. The few birds seen anywhere . . . trembled violently and could not fly. It was a spring without voices. . . . [O]nly silence lay over the fields and woods and marsh" (35). Carson's research showed that insecticides, weed killers, and massive crop spraying—America's weapons of choice in the war against pests—had inserted poisons more devastating than radiation directly into the food chain. Monsanto, Velsicol, American Cyanamid, and other global chemical corporations responded with threats of lawsuits and characterizations of Carson as a hysterical woman whose questions were of little more consequence than those of the neurasthenic in *The Waste Land* who intones "What are you thinking of? What thinking? What?" "What is that noise?" "What is that noise now? What is the wind doing?" (57).

In the Grail legend, as we know if we pursue *The Waste Land*'s annotations, the quester must enter a land in which no birds sing, find the castle of the impotent king, journey to the Chapel Perilous, and ask the right question. Given the colonialism, imperialism, racism, global capitalism, nuclear brinkmanship, and widespread destruction of cycles of generativity at work in 1962, Carson's question seems to be a good one: it grew out of and engaged her training in zoology, aquatic biology, and environmental science, launched productive research in her discipline, reconfigured our understanding of the public world, and inspired effective and long-lasting environmental activism. It is, however, a scientist's question. What were the inquiries that activated and engaged the response of poets to the waste land of the early sixties?

"What had you been thinking about?" John Ashbery asks in "The Tennis Court Oath" (*Norton Anthology* 1261).[22] "[W]hat were you thinking in [your] secret heart then?" Allen Ginsberg inquires in "To Aunt Rose" (1219). "And what of the dead?" Anne Sexton wonders in "The Truth the Dead Know" (1305). "Pure?" Sylvia Plath sneers. "What does it mean?" (1425). "Nothing very bad happen to me lately," John Berryman's Henry confesses. "How you explain that?" (914). "My old flame, my wife!" Robert Lowell exclaims. "Remember our lists of birds?" (968). These questions—raw, disaffected, nostalgic—turn inward, away from the world of politics, race riots, chemical corporations, and nuclear threats, to generate answers we already know: the dead "lie without shoes / in their stone boats" (1305), purity is a scam, in just a minute something bad will happen to Henry, and, as for Lowell's old flame, who knows what she remembers.

Spicer's *Holy Grail* follows *The Waste Land* protocol: the king is sick, the landscape is deserted—"There were no leaves dropping or sounds anybody could hear" (191)—and the questions the Grail Knights know how to ask are few and futile. The first two—"Heal it how?" (187) and "Who won?" (188)—are set-ups: no one knows how to heal it, nobody wins. The best question is Merlin's—"Carefully now will there be a Grail or a Bomb which tears the heart out of things?"—but this too goes nowhere. "I say," Merlin continues in a tapering fall, "there will be no fruit in Britain for seven years unless something happens" (205). Given the "[u]nusual horror-tinged Western" that has been normal life since Hiroshima and Nagasaki, what can poets do to make something happen? What counts as an effective question in the practice of poetry after 1945?

*   *   *

One reason we ask the wrong questions—feeble questions, useless questions—is that, like the audience at Spicer's lecture, we only know how to ask questions that lead to answers we already know. Spicer calls these closed loops "answer-question[s,] always the same" (*Holy Grail* 210). Answer-questions preset the options. "Will there be a Grail or a Bomb?" Merlin asks. "Go to jail," Spicer comments. "Go directly to jail. Do not pass Go. Do not collect $200.00" (202). Like Merlin, the major players in *The Holy Grail* draw from a limited pack of chance cards:

> . . . They are saying mass in the Grail Castle
> The dumb old king
> Awaits
> The scourge, the vinegar, the lance, for the umptiumpth time
> Not Christ, but a substitute for Christ as Christ was a substitute. (199)

Gawain "[d]id / More or less what they asked" (190); "The hermit said dance and [Percival] danced" (193); "The cup said 'Drink me' so [Galahad] drank" (207). Spicer's Grail Knights did not think about how they think.

The tales that fascinate Spicer and Scalapino are tales of ratiocination: radio serials, novels of detection,[23] movies about Martians, body snatchers, pod people, and the dead, always the dead. In these genres, the trick is to think nimbly enough to break free of preset options. In the discipline of poetry, as H.D., Spicer, and Scalapino practice it, the way past the answer-question runs through structures that support a multitude of combinations—puns, syntactic indeterminacies, serial speculations—all of which force readers to dwell for a time within unclosable complexities and contradictions. As curvilinear, disjunctive, metonymic, polyvalent, and recombinative practices, these methods of thought offer a scatter, a stumble, a stagger of lines, acts, episodes, installments, panels, and frames, each with its own array of choice points at which the reader, not knowing what to think, must think about *how* he or she thinks. At these choice points, something happens: for a moment, but again and again, as Scalapino puts it, "cognition [is] changed by its articulation" (*Public World* 18), perspective readjusts perception, and, in Susan Howe's phrase, "Standpoint melts into open" (*Articulation* n.p.).

Spicer's parable of the Fool-killer and the Fool is a lesson in this kind of thinking:

> Fool-killer and I were fishing in the same ocean
> "And at the end of whose line?" I asked him once when I met him in my
>   shadow.
> "You ask the wrong questions" and at that my shadow jumped up and
>   beat itself against a rock, "or rather the wrong questions to the wrong
>   person"
> At the end of whose line
> I now lie
> Hanging. (*Holy Grail* 193)

The question from Spicer's Vancouver audience—"Who was the Fool-killer?"—is a feasible question given the phrase "Fool-killer and I," but the syntax dissolves at its forward edge: the speaker, playing the fool, meets the Fool-killer in his shadow. The Fool-killer, then, is the negative space of the Fool, both parts played by Spicer with the panache of Orson Welles, in Spicer's favorite radio serial, playing Lamont Cranston playing the Shadow who knows the Evil That Lurks in the Hearts of Men. In the next line, however, the Shadow jumps up and beats itself against a rock at the moment it is addressed by the speaker who is, it seems . . . : Where are we? These two, these three, these three-in-one are—is?—"fishing in the same ocean." What is caught flips the hook in the intervals between syntactical units. The parable ends with three diminishing recombinative lines:

> At the end of whose line
> [silence]
> I now lie
> [silence]
> Hanging.
> [silence].

Lie down? Lie in wait? Tell a lie? "lie / Hanging." In a state of "syntactically impermanence," it depends.

Instead of Anthony Perkins posed stiffly on a chimney holding his axe and looking, for all the world, like a Nice Boy caught in an odd moment, the Fool-killer/Fool in Spicer's poem is a composite as volatile as Bruce Conner's BOMB-HEAD (see fig. 13). The bottom half of Conner's lithograph-and-photocopy collage from 1989 is a broad-shouldered torso in a generic military jacket, a crisp white shirt, and a black tie asserted by a simple pin bearing the logo of the International Atomic Energy Commission. The torso is rigid and massive: except for a tuft of vegetation cresting each shoulder like an epaulet, its bulk blots out the entire landscape. The top half of the collage is a mushroom cloud that boils upward against the sky from the torso's dissolving neck.

Bruce Conner's desire to escape the cold war mentality he was convinced would result in a global nuclear holocaust led him into a series of projects he understood as "'a process of testing and acting as if I did not exist as an ego'" (qtd. in Rothfuss 169). Like Spicer, Robin Blaser, Robert Duncan, Philip Whalen, Gary Snyder, Michael McClure, Jay De Feo, Joan Brown, Wallace Berman, and other artists at work in San Francisco during the early sixties, Conner responded to the Cuban Missile Crisis, the colonialism in Vietnam, and the racism in the American South by rejecting labels, taxonomies, and ultimately language itself. In a past-and-future, cause-and-effect, linear reading of Conner's BOMBHEAD, the inflexibility of the collage's lower half could be said to generate the explosion that is its top, but the point of interest and

Figure 13. BOMBHEAD by Bruce Conner. (Reprinted from *2000 BC: The Bruce Conner Story Part II* [Minneapolis: Walker Art Center, 1999], by permission of the artist)

energy in this collage is the turbulence at the neck. Between the rigidity of the uniform and the dissipation of the cloud is a shape-shift in which hierarchy, order, and ego come apart. This is the moment of "syntactically imperma-nence": its poetic equivalent is the crypt words, torqued plots, line endings, and section breaks of the serial poem.

The cultural work done by H.D.'s *Trilogy,* Scalapino's *Trilogy,* Spicer's *Holy*

Grail, and Scalapino's *As* is to interrupt the join between rigidified cultural thinking and the holocaust that such thinking makes inevitable. Elaborated on the basis of classical mythology, Judeo-Christian mythology, the Grail legend, and *The Tempest,* these poems function as "'*thoughtpath[s]*'" (Susan Howe qtd. in Scalapino, *Public World* 9), "tracking[s]" (*Public World* 45), or guided meditations. They are not, then, an answer-question but a protest, an ethics, a spiritual discipline, an effort to make something happen. What they want is simple: before we wreck the world, these poems, in Philip Whalen's words, "'just want to wreck your mind'" (qtd. in *Public World* 5).

*   *   *

"'You ask the wrong questions,'" says the Fool-killer (one last time) to the Fool in Jack Spicer's serial poem *The Holy Grail* (193). What, then, are the right questions? In his Vancouver lecture on seriality, Spicer tells his audience that the young poet "ought to do just exactly what somebody would do in one of those mystical Asian sects that Ginsberg likes so well—trying to get his personality out of himself and letting something else come in, whatever the hell it is" (*House* 85). In Buddhism—which isn't exactly a "mystical Asian sect," but never mind—the right question is the opposite of the "answer-question." To search for the question that undoes the categories we know is a discipline. In Spicer's parable, it involves fishing in the ocean. In Zen practice, it involves fishing in the troubled waters of the koan. A compound of two syllables that mean, respectively, "public" and "matter," a koan is a problem that is insoluble without profound change in the consciousness of the thinker, a change that, presumably, has repercussions for the way we inhabit the public world. To do what you're told, like Gawain, or to drink what you're given, like Galahad, gets you nowhere. The mass-energy that titles Scalapino's essays, *The Public World/ Syntactically Impermanence,* suggests a different route.

The epigraph to Scalapino's volume is a piece of impermanent syntax attributed to the Buddhist philosopher Nāgārjuna. It reads, in full: "As: Nāgārjuna's 'destruction of all philosophical views'—obviously this would include all modes of articulation, and any definitions or procedures of 'discourse.'" When Spicer says his poems are dictated by Martians, he means the same thing Robin Blaser means in describing Spicer's poems as "the practice of outside" and something close to what Scalapino means in the locution "not being in the other civilization / but rather not in her own" (*Trilogy* 167): poems like *The Holy Grail* work toward Nāgārjuna's "destruction of all philosophical views." Both the Fool and the Fool-killer fish in this ocean. What they snag, whatever it is that flips at the end of their line, is not—it must be noted—the end of the world but the end of the philosophical views that have brought us one step away from total nuclear destruction.

*   *   *

Although no less elusive than Spicer's, Scalapino's descriptions of her practice are more sustained and nuanced. While her affinities with poets like Whalen, Blaser, Lyn Hejinian, and Michael Palmer situate her firmly in a tradition of thinkers who use formal and linguistic innovations to interrogate philosophical views, her study of non-Western philosophies gives her access to an array of techniques and terms that she uses to think otherwise. *As,* the most sustained and ambitious segment of *The Public World/Syntactically Impermanence,* is enriched by the ideas broached in the essays that introduce it, but its most remarkable aspect is its transformation of serial thinking into a thought/form that could be described as a "serial play."[24]

The full title of the middle section of part 2 of *The Public World* is *As: All Occurrence in Structure, Unseen—(Deer Night).* The *As* from which the subtitle depends is both demonstration and commentary: it packs into a word that could be an adverb, conjunction, pronoun, or preposition meanings that gesture toward the perpetual unfolding of mind-phenomena, the simultaneity of past, present, and future, and the co-arising of occurrence and the intangible structures through which it is perceived. This piece—a "poem/play" (88) to be imagined, not performed—is "'such stuff as dreams are made on'" (*The Tempest* qtd. in *As* 88). Arising in the reader/spectator's mind as a perception that is at the same time a conception, it both configures and is configured by a public world that has been falsely divided from the private. The events of the play make no distinction between subjective and objective, inner and outer, psychic and civic: nightmares, flecks of physical pain, and flickers of desire exist in the same phantasmagoria as people shipped in cattle cars or shot, gangs of men burning tar in gorges, forced collectivization in wheat fields, child slavery in the brothels of Thailand, "The McDonalds and Sony companies by the brothels" (94), and Exxon, Standard Oil, and the Bechtel Corporation everywhere else.

Like Spicer's Vancouver lectures, the essays that precede this serial play undertake the task of folding the conceptual structures that have brought the public world to its impasse back upon themselves in order to reopen a future. In this play, as in *Trilogy,* Scalapino compresses past, present, and future into a multidimensional now, but *As* adds two additional strategies: the generation of a dimension we might call "phrase space"—a space in which contraries exist separately, at once, and without mutual destruction—and the use of this space of coexisting contraries to help the mind get outside of the continual imposition of its own forms and allow it, encourage it, or force it "to outrace its own closure" (*Public World* 50). To borrow a phrase from the third volume of Scalapino's detective trilogy, serial thinking is the discipline of "continual conceptual rebellion" ("Dahlia's Iris" n.p.): the art of wrecking the mental constructs that have brought us to the verge of wrecking the earth.

Like the transegmental drifts in H.D.'s "Sea Rose" and "Storm," the "phrase space" of *As* captures the simultaneous coming apart/coming together—the dynamic interplay of destruction and creation—that Conner depicts in the turmoil at the neck of the figure in BOMBHEAD. The term "phrase space" is apt not only in its evocation of the materiality of the words and phrases that are the play's action, scenery, and cast but also in its echo of the term "phase space," which describes the charts early chaos scientists employed to capture phenomena they had no language to describe. As James Gleick explains in describing the work of the scientist Stephen Smale, phase space—the space in which a strange attractor materializes—is "a way of turning numbers into pictures, abstracting every bit of essential information from a system of moving parts . . . and making a flexible road map to all its possibilities" (134). In Smale's graphics, Gleick explains, "Any state of the system at a moment frozen in time was represented as a point in phase space; all the information about its position or velocity was contained in the coordinates of that point. As the system changed in some way, the point would move to a new position in phase space. As the system changed continuously, the point would trace a trajectory" (49–50).

Just as phase space is a model of the history of "system time" (134), the "phrase space" of a serial play is a model of mass-energy in motion. In Scalapino's challenging summary of this effect, such a play is "activity being separated from the language and going on at the same time" ("Radical Nature" 12). The intent of this display is to make the audience see language as a concoction at the same time as it also sees the flow of activity language occludes. It is, again in Scalapino's terms, "Writing not having any relation to event / being it—by being exactly its activity" (12).

In rewriting *The Tempest* without using Shakespeare's characters, plot, or language, Scalapino makes a more radical revision than H.D. or Spicer did in their respective rewritings of the Trojan War and the Grail legend. Abandoning the "occurrence" of this fable in order to witness its "structure (unseen)," the poem recreates the *how* rather than the *what* of Shakespeare's text. The emphasis in the play is "conception-making at present *as* the line of text" (93, my emphasis). "The intention," as Scalapino describes it in the notes to *As,* "was for the work to be a state of freedom (eventually), subverting capitalism's 'imperialism' from the inside" (133).

Part of the trick of the serial play is that there is no such thing as an outside. In this, the form replicates a point made by the following anecdote from *Trilogy:* a couple, Scalapino tells us, tries to escape the institutions of school and war by fleeing to a desert, where they first name and raise then slaughter "reddish white-faced calves." Thinking to escape language and war, they find instead that they helplessly replicate their unseen structures. There is an alternative to killing—"seeing the steers look at him," the man "doesn't kill any more of the cattle"—but there is no alternative to "[l]iving out there in a trailer in that heat—with them . . . on the waste range" (89).

Scalapino's refusal to separate outside from inside, institution from escape from institutions, language from action—her refusal, in short, to provide an answer—is not to be confused with defeatism, escapism, or submission to a postnuclear waste land. As an intensive investigation into the co-arising of perception and conception, *As* enacts a decision to live as an activist inside the question. If the syntax of imperialism is the answer-question that forces a speaker to submit to hierarchical distinctions, to separate event from commentary, and to imagine that he or she speaks from a pure or uncontaminated objectivity, the formations of "syntactically impermanence" perform a choice to live not as an outsider or an insider but in the contradictions and complicities in between:

> One as the outsider sees oneself as observing actively and at the same time being inactive in the past event and the insider as active yet unobservant there. The event itself occurs "between" these.
>   (My) intention—in poetry—is to get complete observing at the same instant (space) as it being the action. (Public World 16)

Like Rachel Carson's *Silent Spring,* Scalapino's project is an attempt to ask a useful question. Her obsession, like Carson's, is a spread of unseen but deadly toxins through the ecosphere, which is inevitable if we understand ourselves—our minds, our bodies, our species—to be separate from all that surrounds us. In the light of the threat of nuclear holocaust and global poisoning, we need to think differently. This is the project—the cultural work—performed by difficult poets like H.D., Spicer, and Scalapino, whose continual conceptual activism attempts, with intermittent success, to wreck our minds by outracing our answers.

Eliot's trajectory in "Tradition and the Individual Talent" is unidirectional: "what happens when a new work of art is created is something that happens . . . to all the works of art which preceded it" (5). It is also true, however, that older works of art, reread, open toward newer formulations. In the light of *The Holy Grail* and *As,* H.D.'s *Trilogy* does not close as neatly as it seemed to close when read side by side with high modernist documents like *The Waste Land* or *The Cantos.* In the light of H.D.'s *Trilogy,* similarly, Scalapino's *Trilogy,* Spicer's *Holy Grail,* and Scalapino's *As* regain—or perhaps retain—some of the openness that drew these writers to read H.D. in their quest to learn how to live, what to do.

Notes

The third epigraph on page 204 follows the dedication of "The Sword Went Out to Sea" to Bryher, or "Gareth," as she is called in this text. It repeats Gareth's reassurance to Delia Alton, H.D.'s name for herself in the novel, after Hugh Dowding's rejection of messages she believed she had received from airmen lost in the Battle of Britain. The rejection "left me cold," Delia writes, "as the impact of the high explosives and the bombs had done." " 'It's not lost,' " Gareth says. " 'This will go on somewhere.' [Gareth] had a way of saying simply things of the most profound significance" (8–9).

   1. This statistic comes from Kyo Maclear's meditation on the meaning of the word "witness" in face of the events at Hiroshima and Nagasaki.
   2. Adorno's comment appears at the conclusion of his essay "Cultural Criticism and Society." "Cultural criticism," Adorno writes, "finds itself faced with the final stage of the dialectic of culture and barbarism. To write poetry after Auschwitz is barbaric. . . . Critical intelligence cannot be equal to this challenge as long as it confines itself to self-satisfied contemplation" (34).
   3. The terms "catastrophe" and "singularity," defined by the mathematician René Thom and reiterated by Susan Howe in her collection *Singularities,* specify "the point where there is a sudden change to something completely else. It's a chaotic point. It's the point chaos enters cosmos, the instant articulation" (Howe, "*Talisman* Interview" 173). This is the point straddled by H.D.'s pun on the words *ruin* and *rune* in *Trilogy.*
   4. For the many meanings of this cultural icon, see Maclear 6–7. For a reproduction of the mushroom cloud in an advertisement for Soviet jeans, see Maclear 92. For a photograph of Vice Admiral W. H. P. Blandy, the commander of the 1946 atomic tests, cutting into a mushroom-cloud cake, see Boyer 87.
   5. See "Armory: Gas Warfare," part of the "World War I: Trenches on the Web" at <http://www.worldwar1.com/armory.htm#gas>, for more information on the use of gas in World War I. In addition to historical information, this site contains images and artwork that provide a vivid sense of the terror generated by the new weapons. "The first reported use of gas," the site indicates, "was by the Germans on the eastern front on 3-Jan-1915. It was a tearing agent dispersed by artillery shell. The first use on the

western front came several months later on 22-Apr-1915 at the village of Langemarck near Ypres. At 1700 hours the Germans released a 5 mile wide cloud of chlorine gas from some 520 cylinders (168 tons of the chemical). The greenish-yellow cloud drifted over and into the French and Algerian trenches where it caused wide spread panic and death. The age of chemical warfare had begun." Two articles by Will Irwin from the *New York Tribune* reporting the panic the new weapon caused are archived at <http://www.lib.byu.edu/~rdh/wwi/1915/chlorgas.html>.

6. The sulphurous acid to which Eliot refers is used, like chlorine, to manufacture bleach. Although it is not one of the gases dispersed in World War I, it is a close chemical relative of sulfuric acid, used in the manufacture of fertilizer, gunpowder, nitroglycerin, and a variety of other explosives.

7. Philip Whalen comes to his formulation—"'I just,'" he writes, "'want to wreck your mind'" (qtd. in Scalapino, "Radical Nature" 5)—through the rigors of Zen practice.

8. In "The Heads of the Town," Spicer, like Hartman, identifies astonishment as the residue of poetry: "'Esstoneish me,' the words say that hide behind my alarm clock or my dresser drawer or my pillow. 'Etonnez moi,' even the Word says" (*Collected Books* 178).

9. For Scalapino's commentary on H.D., see especially "Interior Scrutiny" and "An H.D. Book." In an important clarification of the tie between their writings, Scalapino writes, "I'm comparing gestures of mine as possibly being akin to H.D., rather than saying these come from her" ("Interior Scrutiny" 206).

10. For important discussions of the characteristics of serial poems, see Blaser and Conte, chaps. 2 and 3.

11. On palimpsests in H.D., see, for example, DuPlessis, *H.D.* 55–56. For Davidson's "palimtext," see Davidson 64–93.

12. For extended examples of this process, see Friedman on H.D.'s rewriting of the image of Helen in *Psyche Reborn* 232–36, DuPlessis on the technique she calls "Revisionary Mythopoesis" in *Writing beyond the Ending,* and Nixon on postcolonial rewritings of Shakespeare's plot in his essay "Caribbean and African Appropriations of *The Tempest.*"

13. The comparison between this technique and time travel in *Terminator 2* is suggested by Leslie Scalapino in "Dahlia's Iris."

14. Like the poems of H.D.'s *Trilogy* and Scalapino's *Trilogy,* the fourteenth-century poem "The Pearl" is bound with other long poems that can themselves be read together or separately. The poems bound with "The Pearl" are "Sir Gawain and the Green Knight," "Purity," and "Patience."

15. In this text, it's the ones who think they have the answers who are most contemptible: the newspaper man, the bigot, the "person who'd always raise their hand in class. Waving I have the answer, I have the answer" (111).

16. This is, significantly, the same complaint H.D. and her cohort made in their vituperations against Hollywood in the pages of *Close Up.*

17. For an example from H.D.'s *Trilogy*, see section 2 of "The Walls Do Not Fall," especially the sequence beginning "they were angry when we were so hungry" (*Trilogy* 5).

18. The precondition of this state is an abnegation of "doing": "You sit—," Scalapino writes, describing a similar dissolve in "The Pearl," "and it's just that—just sitting. Not—doing—something. There are not actions" (97).

19. For references to this jewel, see 163, 167, 168, 173, 175, 177, 180, and 199.

20. The publicity blurb for *The Fool Killer* is online at <http://www.reel.com/movie.asp?MID=4267>.

21. The subject of Spicer's lecture the preceding night, "Dictation and 'A Textbook of Poetry,'" had been the process of composition, which for Spicer comes "from the outside rather than from the inside" (*House* 5). In this sense, for Spicer, writing is received rather than produced.

22. This series of questions is drawn from the canonized poetry of the early 1960s codified by the *Norton Anthology of Modern Poetry*.

23. Avid readers of detective fiction, both Spicer and Scalapino also write detective novels. Spicer's unfinished *The Tower of Babel* was published in 1994 by Talisman House; Scalapino's trilogy of detective novels includes *R-hu,* published by Atelos in 2000, *Orchid Jetsam,* published under the pseudonym Dee Goda, by Tuumba Press, in 2001, and "Dahlia's Iris: Secret Autobiography and Fiction," forthcoming from Fiction Collective 2 in 2003.

24. In an analogous shift, Scalapino calls her volume *The Front Matter, Dead Souls* (1996) "a serial novel for publication in the newspaper," also suitable for "billboards or outdoors as murals" (1).

Works Cited

Adorno, Theodor W. "Cultural Criticism and Society." In *Prisms.* Trans. Samuel Weber and Shierry Weber. Cambridge: Massachusetts Institute of Technology Press,
1981. 17–34.

———. "Lyric Poetry and Society." *Telos* 20 (1974): 56–71.

Adorno, T. W., and M. Horkheimer. "The Culture Industry: Enlightenment as Mass
Deception." In *Mass Communication and Society.* Ed. James Curran, Michael Gure-
vitch, and Janet Woollacott. London: Edward Arnold, 1977. 349–83.

Ahl, Frederick M. *Metaformations: Soundplay and Wordplay in Ovid and Other Classical Poets.* Ithaca, N.Y.: Cornell University Press, 1985.

Albright, Daniel. *Quantum Poetics: Yeats, Pound, Eliot, and the Science of Modernism.*
Cambridge: Cambridge University Press, 1997.

Allen, Donald, ed. *The New American Poetry, 1945–60.* New York: Grove Press, 1960.

Antin, David. "whos listening out there." In *tuning.* New York: New Directions, 1984.
269–96.

"Armory: Gas Warfare." In *World War I Trenches on the Web: An Internet History of the
Great War.* 15 Jan. 2000; 15 June 2000. <http://www.worldwar1.com/arm006.htm>.

Arnheim, Rudolf. *Radio.* Trans. Margaret Ludwig and Herbert Read. London: Faber,
1936.

Attridge, Derek. "Unpacking the Portmanteau; or, Who's Afraid of *Finnegans Wake?*"
In *On Puns,* ed. Culler. 140–55.

Atwood, Margaret. "Circe/Mud Poems." In *Selected Poems.* New York: Simon and
Schuster, 1976. 201–23.

Auden, W. H. "In Memory of W. B. Yeats." In *The Collected Poetry of W. H. Auden.* New
York: Random House, 1945. 48–51.

Augustine, Jane. "A Note on the Text and Its Arrangement." In *The Gift: The Complete
Text,* by H.D. Ed. Jane Augustine. Gainesville: University Press of Florida, 1998. ix–xi.

Bailey, Derek. *Improvisation: Its Nature and Practice in Music.* New York: Da Capo, 1993.

Baker, William E. *Syntax in English Poetry, 1870–1930.* Berkeley: University of California Press, 1967.

Bakhtin, Mikhail Mikhailovich. "The *Bildungsroman* and Its Significance in the History of Realism." In *Speech Genres and Other Late Essays.* Ed. Caryl Emerson and Michael Holquist. Trans. Vern W. McGee. Austin: University of Texas Press, 1986. 10–59.

———. "Forms of Time and Chronotope in the Novel." In *The Dialogic Imagination: Four Essays.* Ed. Michael Holquist. Trans. Caryl Emerson and Michael Holquist. Austin: University of Texas Press, 1981. 84–258.

Ballet mécanique. dir. Fernand Léger and Dudley Murphy. Video Yesteryear, 1924.

Baraka, Amiri. "The Changing Same (R&B and New Black Music)." In *The Leroi Jones/ Amiri Baraka Reader.* Ed. William J. Harris. New York: Thunder's Mouth, 1989. 186–209.

Barthes, Roland. "Listening." In *The Responsibility of Forms: Critical Essays on Music, Art, and Representation.* Trans. Richard Howard. New York: Hill, 1985. 245–60.

———. *The Pleasure of the Text.* Trans. Richard Miller. New York: Hill, 1975.

———. *Roland Barthes.* Trans. Richard Howard. New York: Hill, 1977.

———. *S/Z.* Trans. Richard Howard. New York: Hill, 1974.

Beach, Christopher. *Poetic Culture: Contemporary American Poetry between Community and Institution.* Evanston, Ill.: Northwestern University Press, 1999.

Bede, the Venerable, Saint. *Ecclesiastical History.* Book 2: *A History of the English Church and People.* Rev. ed. Trans. Leo Sherley-Price. Harmondsworth, U.K.: Penguin, 1968.

Bedient, Calvin. "Kristeva and Poetry as Shattered Signification." *Critical Inquiry* 16 (1990): 807–29.

Bell, Ian F. A. *Critic as Scientist: The Modernist Poetics of Ezra Pound.* London: Methuen, 1981.

Benét, William Rose. "Round about Parnassus" (review of *Red Roses for Bronze,* by H.D.). *Saturday Review of Literature,* 16 Jan. 1932, 461.

Benjamin, Walter. "The Work of Art in the Age of Mechanical Reproduction." In *Illuminations.* London: Fontana, 1973. 219–53.

Bernstein, Charles. *Content's Dream: Essays, 1975–1984.* Los Angeles: Sun and Moon, 1986.

———. "In the Middle of Modernism in the Middle of Capitalism on the Outskirts of New York." In *A Poetics* 90–105.

———. Introduction to *Close Listening: Poetry and the Performed Word.* Ed. Charles Bernstein. New York: Oxford University Press, 1998. 3–26.

———. *Live at the Ear.* Oracular Laboratory Recordings, 1994.

———. *A Poetics.* Cambridge, Mass.: Harvard University Press, 1992.

———. "Pounding Fascism (Appropriating Ideologies—Mystification, Aestheticization, and Authority in Pound's Poetic Practice)." In *A Poetics* 121–27.

———. "Thought's Measure." In *Content's Dream* 61–86.

Bernstein, Jeremy. *Einstein.* New York: Penguin, 1976.

Bernstein, Michael André. *The Tale of the Tribe: Ezra Pound and the Modern Verse Epic.* Princeton, N.J.: Princeton University Press, 1980.

Bethlehem Book Committee. *Bethlehem of Pennsylvania: The Golden Years, 1841–1920.* Bethlehem, Pa.: Lehigh Litho, 1976.

Biocca, Frank A. "The Pursuit of Sound: Radio, Perception and Utopia in the Early Twentieth Century." *Media, Culture, and Society* 10 (1988): 61–79.

Blackmur, R. P. "The Lesser Satisfactions" (review of *Red Roses for Bronze,* by H.D.). *Poetry* 41 (1932): 94–100.

Blaser, Robin. "The Practice of Outside." In Spicer, *Collected Books* 269–329.

Bolter, Jay David, and Richard Grusin. *Remediation: Understanding New Media.* Cambridge: Massachusetts Institute of Technology Press, 1999.

Boone, Elizabeth Hill, and Walter D. Mignolo, eds. *Writing without Words: Alternative Literacies in Mesoamerica and the Andes.* Durham, N.C.: Duke University Press, 1994.

Borderline. Dir. Kenneth Macpherson. Perf. Helga Doorn [H.D.] and Paul Robeson. POOL, 1930.

Boughn, Michael. "The Bibliographic Record of H.D.'s Contributions to Periodicals." *Sagetrieb* 6.2 (1987): 171–94.

———. "Elements of the Sounding: H.D. and the Origins of Modernist Prosodies." *Sagetrieb* 6.2 (1987): 101–22.

Boyer, Paul. *By the Bomb's Early Light: American Thought and Culture at the Dawn of the Atomic Age.* Chapel Hill: University of North Carolina Press, 1994.

Briggs, John. *Fractals: The Patterns of Chaos.* New York: Simon and Schuster, 1992.

Bryher [Winifred Ellerman]. *The Days of Mars: A Memoir, 1940–1946.* London: Calder, 1972.

———. "Hollywood Code II." *Close Up* 3.4 (1931): 280–82.

Buck, Claire. *H.D. and Freud: Bisexuality and a Feminine Discourse.* New York: St. Martin's Press, 1991.

Budge, E. A. Wallis. *Easy Lessons in Egyptian Hieroglyphics.* Vol. 3 of *Books on Egypt and Chaldaea.* London: Kegan Paul, 1902.

———. *A Hieroglyphic Vocabulary to the Theban Recension of the Book of the Dead.* Vol. 31 of *Books on Egypt and Chaldaea.* London: Kegan Paul, 1911.

Burke, Kenneth. "On Musicality in Verse." In *The Philosophy of Literary Form: Studies in Symbolic Action.* 3d ed. Berkeley: University of California Press, 1973. 369–78.

Burnett, Gary. *H.D. between Image and Epic: The Mysteries of Her Poetics.* Ann Arbor: University of Michigan Research Press, 1990.

Byrd, Donald. *The Poetics of the Common Knowledge.* Albany: State University of New York Press, 1994.

Carpenter, Humphrey. *A Serious Character: The Life of Ezra Pound.* London: Faber and Faber, 1988.

Carson, Rachel. "Silent Spring." *The New Yorker,* 16 June 1962, 31+; 30 June 1962, 35+.

"Charles Doolittle" (obituary). *The Observatory* 42 (1919): 219–20.

"Charles Doolittle" (obituary). *Publications of the Astronomical Society of the Pacific* 31 (1919): 103–4.

Chisholm, Dianne. *H.D.'s Freudian Poetics: Psychoanalysis in Translation.* Ithaca, N.Y.: Cornell University Press, 1992.

Clark, Ronald W. *Freud: The Man and the Cause.* New York: Random House, 1980.

Clark, T. J. *The Painting of Modern Life: Paris in the Art of Manet and His Followers.* Rev. ed. Princeton, N.J.: Princeton University Press, 1999.

Clayton, Jay. "The Voice in the Machine: Hazlitt, Hardy, James." In *Language Machines: Technologies of Literary and Cultural Production.* Ed. Jeffrey Masten, Peter Stallybrass, and Nancy J. Vickers. New York: Routledge, 1997. 209–32.

Collecott, Diana. *H.D. and Sapphic Modernism.* Cambridge: Cambridge University Press, 2000.

———. "Images at the Crossroads: The 'H.D. Scrapbook.'" In *H.D.,* ed. King. 319–67.

Conceiving Ada. Dir. Lynn Hershman-Leeson. Perf. Tilda Swinton and Timothy Leary. Fox Lorber, 1999.

Conner, Bruce. "BOMBHEAD." In *2000 BC: The Bruce Conner Story Part II.* Minneapolis: Walker Art Center, 1999.

Connor, James A. "RADIO free JOYCE: Wake Language and the Experience of Radio." In *Sound States: Innovative Poetics and Acoustical Technologies.* Ed. Adalaide Morris. Chapel Hill: University of North Carolina Press, 1997. 17–31.

Conte, Joseph M. *Unending Design: The Forms of Postmodern Poetry.* Ithaca, N.Y.: Cornell University Press, 1991.

Cory, Mark E. "Soundplay: The Polyphonous Tradition of German Radio Art." In *Wireless Imagination,* ed. Kahn and Whitehead. 331–71.

Coudert, Allison. *Alchemy: The Philosopher's Stone.* Boulder, Colo.: Shambhala, 1980.

Crane, Hart. *Complete Poems of Hart Crane.* Ed. Marc Simon. New York: Liveright, 2000.

Creeley, Robert. *Collected Poems of Robert Creeley, 1945–1975.* Berkeley: University of California Press, 1982.

———. *For Love.* In *Collected Poems* 103–258.

———. Introduction to *Collected Prose,* by Charles Olson. Ed. Donald Allen and Benjamin Friedlander. Berkeley: University of California Press, 1997. xi–xvi.

———. "The Measure." In *Collected Poems* 290.

———. "'Poems are a complex.'" In *Collected Essays of Robert Creeley.* Berkeley: University of California Press, 1989. 489–90.

Crisell, Andrew J. *Understanding Radio.* 2d ed. New York: Routledge, 1994.

Crook, Tim. *International Radio Journalism: History, Theory, and Practice.* New York: Routledge, 1998.

Crown, Kathleen. "'Let Us Endure': Atomic-Age Anxiety in H.D.'s *Sagesse.*" *Sagetrieb* 15.1–2 (1996): 247–72.

Cullen, Countee. *Color.* 1925. Reprint, New York: Arno Press and the New York Times, 1969.

Culler, Jonathan. "The Call of the Phoneme: Introduction." In *On Puns,* ed. Culler. 1–16.

———. "Changes in the Study of the Lyric." In *Lyric Poetry: Beyond New Criticism.* Ed. Chaviva Hošek and Patricia Parker. Ithaca, N.Y.: Cornell University Press, 1985. 38–54.

———, ed. *On Puns: The Foundation of Letters.* New York: Blackwell, 1988.

Czitrom, Daniel J. *Media and the American Mind: From Morse to McLuhan.* Chapel Hill: University of North Carolina Press, 1982.

Davidson, Michael. *Ghostlier Demarcations: Modern Poetry and the Material Word.* Berkeley: University of California Press, 1997.

Davies, Hugh. "A History of Recorded Sound." In *Poésie Sonore Internationale.* Ed. Henri Chopin. Paris: Jean-Michel Place, 1979. 13–40.

DeKoven, Marianne. *A Different Language: Gertrude Stein's Experimental Writing.* Madison: University of Wisconsin Press, 1983.

Deutsch, Babette. "The Glory That Is Greece" (review of *Red Roses for Bronze,* by H.D.). *New York Herald Tribune Books,* 14 Feb. 1932, 12.

Donald, James, Anne Friedberg, and Laura Marcus, eds. *Close Up, 1927–1933: Cinema and Modernism.* Princeton, N.J.: Princeton University Press, 1998.

Doolittle, Charles L. *A Treatise on Practical Astronomy as Applied to Geodesy and Navigation.* New York: Wiley, 1885.

Doubiago, Sharon. "From 'Perdita's Father.'" In *H.D. and Poets After,* ed. Hollenberg. 53–74.

Drouet, Francis. "Francis Wolle's Filamentous Myxophyceae." *Field Museum of Natural History* Botanical Series 20.2 (1939): 17–64.

Duncan, Robert. "Beginnings: Chapter 1 of the H.D. Book Part 1." *Coyote's Journal* 5–6 (1966): 8–31.

———. "From the Day Book, Part II, First Series." *Origin,* 2d ser. 10 (July 1963): 1–47.

———. "From the *H.D. Book,* Part II, Chapter 5." *Sagetrieb* 4.2–3 (1985): 39–86.

———. "Nights and Days, Chapter 2." *Sumac* 1.1 (1968): 101–46.

———. *The Truth and Life of Myth: An Essay in Essential Autobiography.* Fremont, Mich.: Sumac Press, 1968. Reprinted in *Fictive Certainties.* New York: New Directions, 1985. 1–59.

DuPlessis, Rachel Blau. "Haibun: 'Draw your/Draft.'" In *H.D. and Poets After,* ed. Hollenberg. 112–29.

———. *Genders, Races, and Religious Cultures in Modern American Poetry, 1908–1934.* Cambridge: Cambridge University Press, 2001.

———. *H.D.: The Career of That Struggle.* Brighton, U.K.: Harvester Press, 1986.

———. "A Note on the State of H.D.'s *The Gift.*" *Sulfur* 9 (1984): 178–82.

———. "'Perceiving the other-side of everything': Tactics of Revisionary Mythopoesis." In *Writing beyond the Ending* 105–22.

———. "Romantic Thralldom in H.D." In *Writing beyond the Ending* 66–83.

———. *Writing beyond the Ending: Narrative Strategies of Twentieth-Century Women Writers.* Bloomington: Indiana University Press, 1985.

DuPlessis, Rachel Blau, and Susan Stanford Friedman. "'Woman Is Perfect': H.D.'s Debate with Freud." *Feminist Studies* 7.3 (1981): 417–30.

Eagleton, Terry. *Literary Theory: An Introduction.* Minneapolis: University of Minnesota Press, 1983.

Easthope, Antony, and John O. Thompson, eds. *Contemporary Poetry Meets Modern Theory*. Toronto: University of Toronto Press, 1991.

Edmunds, Susan. *Out of Line: History, Psychoanalysis, and Montage in H.D.'s Long Poems*. Stanford, Calif.: Stanford University Press, 1994.

Einstein, Alfred. *Ideas and Opinions*. New York: Dell, 1973.

Eisenstein, Sergei M. "The Cinematographic Principle and the Ideogram." In *Film Form: Essays in Film Theory*. Trans. and ed. Jay Leyda. New York: Harcourt, 1949. 28–44.

———. "The Fourth Dimension in the Kino." *Close Up* 6.3 (Mar. 1930): 185–94; 6.4 (Apr. 1930): 253–68.

Eksteins, Modris. *Rites of Spring: The Great War and the Birth of the Modern Age*. New York: Houghton, 1989.

Eliot, T. S. *Selected Essays*. New York: Harcourt, 1964.

———. "Tradition and the Individual Talent." 1919. In *Selected Essays* 3–11.

———. *The Waste Land*. In *Collected Poems, 1909–1962*. New York: Harcourt, 1963. 51–76.

Ellingham, Lewis, and Kevin Killian. *Poet Be Like God: Jack Spicer and the San Francisco Renaissance*. Hanover, N.H.: University Press of New England, 1998.

Ellis, Havelock. *The Dance of Life*. Boston: Houghton, 1923.

———. "The Play-Function of Sex." In *Little Essays of Love and Virtue*. New York: Doran, 1922. 116–33.

Ellison, Ralph. *Invisible Man*. New York: Random House, 1952.

Evans-Pritchard, E. E. Introduction to *The Gift: Forms and Functions of Exchange in Archaic Societies,* by Marcel Mauss. Trans. Ian Cunnison. New York: Norton, 1967. v–x.

Fenollosa, Ernest. *The Chinese Written Character as a Medium for Poetry*. Ed. Ezra Pound. San Francisco: City Lights, 1963.

Ferris, Timothy. *The Red Limit: The Search for the Edge of the Universe*. Rev. ed. New York: Quill, 1983.

The Fool Killer. Dir. Servando Gonzalez. Perf. Anthony Perkins and Edward Albert. American International Pictures, 1965.

Forché, Carolyn, ed. *Against Forgetting: Twentieth-Century Poetry of Witness*. New York: Norton, 1993.

Foster, Edward. "Leslie Scalapino." In *Postmodern Poetry: The Talisman Interviews*. Ed. Edward Foster. Hoboken, N.J.: Talisman, 1994. 115–23.

———. "Nathaniel Mackey." In *Postmodern Poetry: The Talisman Interviews*. Ed. Edward Foster. Hoboken, N.J.: Talisman, 1994. 69–83.

Foster, Hal. "What's Neo about the Neo-Avant-Garde?" *October* 70 (1994): 5–32.

Frank, Joseph. *The Widening Gyre: Crisis and Mastery in Modern Literature*. New Brunswick, N.J.: Rutgers University Press, 1963.

Fraser, Kathleen. "The Blank Page: H.D.'s Invitation to Trust and Mistrust Language." In *H.D. and Poets After,* ed. Hollenberg. 163–71.

———. "The tradition of marginality . . . and the emergence of *HOW(ever)* (1985)." In *Translating the Unspeakable: Poetry and the Innovative Necessity.* Tuscaloosa: University of Alabama Press, 2000. 25–38.

Freud, Sigmund. *Beyond the Pleasure Principle.* Trans. and ed. James Strachey. New York: Liveright, 1970.

———. "On Beginning the Treatment (Further Recommendations on the Technique of Psycho-analysis I)." In *The Standard Edition of the Complete Psychological Works of Sigmund Freud.* Vol 12. Trans. and ed. James Strachey. London: Hogarth, 1958. 121–44.

———. "Recommendations to Physicians Practising Psycho-analysis." In *The Standard Edition of the Complete Psychological Works of Sigmund Freud.* Vol. 12. Trans. and ed. James Strachey. London: Hogarth, 1958. 109–20.

Fried, Debra. "Rhyme Puns." In *On Puns,* ed. Culler. 83–99.

Friedberg, Anne. "'And I Myself Have Learned to Use the Small Projector': On H.D., Woman, History, Recognition." *Wide Angle: A Film Quarterly of Theory, Criticism, and Practice* 5.2 (1982): 26–31.

———. "Approaching *Borderline.*" In *H.D.,* ed. King. 369–90.

———. Introduction to part 5. "*Borderline* and the POOL Films." In *Close Up, 1927–1933,* ed. Donald, Friedberg, and Marcus. 212–20.

Friedman, Susan Stanford. *Analyzing Freud: Letters of H.D., Bryher, and Their Circle.* New York: New Directions, 2002.

———. "Chronology: Dating H.D.'s Writing." In *Penelope's Web* 360–66.

———. *Penelope's Web: Gender, Modernity, H.D.'s Fiction.* Cambridge: Cambridge University Press, 1990.

———. *Psyche Reborn: The Emergence of H.D.* Bloomington: Indiana University Press, 1981.

Friedman, Susan Stanford, and Rachel Blau DuPlessis. "'I Had Two Loves Separate': The Sexualities of H.D.'s *Her.*" *Montemora* 8 (1981): 7–30.

———, eds. *Signets: Reading H.D.* Madison: University of Wisconsin Press, 1990.

Fries, Adelaide L. *The Moravian Church: Yesterday and Today.* Raleigh: Edwards, 1926.

———. *The Road to Salem.* Chapel Hill: University of North Carolina Press, 1944.

Frye, Northrop. *Anatomy of Criticism: Four Essays.* Princeton, N.J.: Princeton University Press, 1957.

Gage, John T. *In the Arresting Eye: The Rhetoric of Imagism.* Baton Rouge: Louisiana State University Press, 1981.

Gallop, Jane. *Thinking through the Body.* New York: Columbia University Press, 1988.

Gardiner, Sir Alan. *Egyptian Grammar, Being an Introduction to the Study of Hieroglyphs.* 3d ed. Oxford: Oxford University Press, 1957.

General Electric Radio. "Don't Cry Mother" (advertisement). *Life,* Jan.–Feb. 1940, inside front cover.

Gilbert, Sandra M., and Susan Gubar. *The Madwoman in the Attic: The Woman Writer and the Nineteenth-Century Literary Imagination.* New Haven, Conn.: Yale University Press, 1979.

Gilligan, Carol. *In a Different Voice: Psychological Theory and Women's Development.* Cambridge, Mass.: Harvard University Press, 1982.

Gizzi, Peter. Introduction to *The House That Jack Built: The Collected Lectures of Jack Spicer.* Ed. Peter Gizzi. Hanover, N.H.: University Press of New England, 1998. xix–xxiv.

Gleick, James. *Chaos: Making a New Science.* New York: Viking, 1987.

Godelier, Maurice. *The Enigma of the Gift.* Trans. Nora Scott. Chicago: University of Chicago Press, 1999.

Golding, Alan. *From Outlaw to Classic: Canons in American Poetry.* Madison: University of Wisconsin Press, 1995.

Gollin, Gillian Lindt. *Moravians in Two Worlds: A Study of Changing Communities.* New York: Columbia University Press, 1967.

Goody, Jack, and Ian Watt. "The Consequences of Literacy." In *Literacy in Traditional Societies.* Ed. Jack Goody. Cambridge: Cambridge University Press, 1968. 27–68.

Graff, Gerald. *Professing Literature: An Institutional History.* Chicago: University of Chicago Press, 1987.

Graham, Jorie. Introduction to *The Best American Poetry, 1990.* Ed. Jorie Graham with David Lehman. New York: Macmillan, 1990. xv–xxxi.

Gregory, Eileen. *H.D. and Hellenism: Classic Lines.* Cambridge: Cambridge University Press, 1997.

———. [Introductory paragraphs to] "Speech of Acceptance to the American Academy of Arts and Letters," by H.D. *H.D. Newsletter* 3.1 (1990): 4–5.

———. "Rose Cut in Rock: Sappho and H.D.'s *Sea Garden.*" In *Signets,* ed. Friedman and DuPlessis. 129–54.

Gregory, Horace. Introduction to *Helen in Egypt,* by H.D. New York: New Directions, 1961. vii–xi.

Griaule, Marcel. *Conversations with Ogotemmêli: An Introduction to Dogon Religious Ideas.* London: Oxford University Press, 1965.

Gubar, Susan. "The Echoing Spell of H.D.'s *Trilogy.*" *Contemporary Literature* 19.2 (1978): 196–218.

———. "Sapphistries." *Signs* 10.1 (1984): 43–62.

Guest, Barbara. *Herself Defined: The Poet H.D. and Her World.* Garden City, N.Y.: Doubleday, 1984.

———. "The Intimacy of Biography." *Iowa Review* 16.3 (Fall 1986): 58–71.

Guillory, John. *Cultural Capital: The Problem of Literary Canon Formation.* Chicago: University of Chicago Press, 1993.

Harding, Sandra. *The Science Question in Feminism.* Ithaca, N.Y.: Cornell University Press, 1986.

Hartman, Geoffrey. "The Voice of the Shuttle: Language from the Point of View of Literature." In *Beyond Formalism: Literary Essays, 1958–1970.* New Haven, Conn.: Yale University Press, 1970. 337–55.

Hatlen, Burton. "Renewing the Open Engagement: H.D. and Rachel Blau DuPlessis." In *H.D. and Poets After,* ed. Hollenberg. 130–62.

Havelock, Eric A. *The Muse Learns to Write: Reflections on Orality and Literacy from Antiquity to the Present.* New Haven, Conn.: Yale University Press, 1986.

———. *Preface to Plato.* Cambridge, Mass.: Harvard University Press, 1963.

Hayles, N. Katherine. *Chaos Bound: Orderly Disorder in Contemporary Literature and Science.* Ithaca, N.Y.: Cornell University Press, 1990.

———. "The Condition of Virtuality." In *Language Machines: Technologies of Literary and Cultural Production.* Ed. Jeffrey Masten, Peter Stallybrass, and Nancy J. Vickers. New York: Routledge, 1997. 183–206.

———. *The Cosmic Web: Scientific Field Models and Literary Strategies in the Twentieth Century.* Ithaca, N.Y.: Cornell University Press, 1984.

———. *How We Became Posthuman: Virtual Bodies in Cybernetics, Literature, and Informatics.* Chicago: University of Chicago Press, 1999.

———. "Turbulence in Literature and Science: Questions of Influence." In *American Literature and Science.* Ed. Robert J. Scholnick. Lexington: University Press of Kentucky, 1992. 229–50.

H.D. "Advent." In *Tribute to Freud* 115–87.

———. *Asphodel.* Ed. Robert Spoo. Durham, N.C.: Duke University Press, 1992.

———. "Autobiographical Notes." Ts. H.D. Papers. Beinecke Library, Yale University, New Haven, Conn.

———. *Between History and Poetry: The Letters of H.D. and Norman Holmes Pearson.* Ed. Donna Krolik Hollenberg. Iowa City: University of Iowa Press, 1997.

———. *Bid Me to Live (A Madrigal).* 1960. Reprint, Redding Ridge, Conn.: Black Swan Books, 1983.

———. "The Borderline Pamphlet." 1930. In *Close Up, 1927–1933,* ed. Donald, Friedberg, and Marcus. 221–36.

———. "The Cinema and the Classics I: Beauty." 1927. In *Close Up, 1927–1933,* ed. Donald, Friedberg, and Marcus. 105–9.

———. "The Cinema and the Classics II: Restraint." 1927. In *Close Up, 1927–1933,* ed. Donald, Friedberg, and Marcus. 110–14.

———. "The Cinema and the Classics III: The Mask and the Movietone." 1927. In *Close Up, 1927–1933,* ed. Donald, Friedberg, and Marcus. 114–20.

———. *Collected Poems, 1912–1944.* Ed. Louis L. Martz. New York: New Directions, 1983.

———. "Compassionate Friendship." Ts. H.D. Papers. Beinecke Library, Yale University, New Haven, Conn.

———. "The Death of Martin Presser." *Quarterly Review of Literature* 13.3–4 (1965): 241–61.

———. *End to Torment: A Memoir of Ezra Pound.* Ed. Norman Holmes Pearson and Michael King. New York: New Directions, 1979.

———. "A Friendship Traced: H.D.'s Letters to Silvia Dobson." Ed. Carol T. Tinker. *Conjunctions* 2 (1982): 115–57.

———. "The Gift." Ts. H.D. Papers. Beinecke Library, Yale University, New Haven, Conn.

———. *The Gift* (abridged). New York: New Directions, 1982.

———. *The Gift: The Complete Text*. Ed. Jane Augustine. Gainesville: University Press of Florida, 1998.

———. "H.D." ("Response to Questionnaire"). *The Little Review* 12.2 (1929): 38–40.

———. "H.D. by Delia Alton" ("Notes on Recent Writing"). *Iowa Review* 16.3 (1986): 180–221.

———. *H.D.: Selected Poems*. Ed. Norman Holmes Pearson. New York: Grove, 1957.

———. *The Hedgehog*. London: Brendin, 1936.

———. *Hedylus*. 1928. Reprint, Redding Ridge, Conn.: Black Swan, 1980.

———. *Helen in Egypt*. 1961. Reprint, New York: New Directions, 1974.

———. *Helen in Egypt*. Audiocassette. 1981. Watershed Tapes, C-158.

———. "Hermetic Definition." In *Hermetic Definition* 1–55.

———. *Hermetic Definition*. New York: New Directions, 1972.

———. *HERmione*. New York: New Directions, 1981.

———. "Hirslanden Notebooks." Ms. H.D. Papers. Beinecke Library, Yale University, New Haven, Conn.

———. *Ion: A Play after Euripides*. 1937. Reprint, Redding Ridge, Conn.: Black Swan, 1986.

———. Letters to Elizabeth Ashby, Bryher, Silvia Dobson, Robert Herring, Clifford Howard, Viola Jordan, Brigit Patmore, Norman Holmes Pearson, George Plank, and May Sarton. H.D. Papers. Beinecke Library, Yale University, New Haven, Conn.

———. "Majic Ring." Ts. H.D. Papers. Beinecke Library, Yale University, New Haven, Conn.

———. "Marianne Moore." *The Egoist* 3 (1916): 118–19.

———. "Narthex." In *The Second American Caravan: A Yearbook of American Literature*. Ed. Alfred Kreymborg, Lewis Mumford, and Paul Rosenfeld. New York: Macaulay, 1928. 225–84.

———. [John Helforth]. *Nights*. 1935. Reprint, New York: New Directions, 1986.

———. "Notes." In *The Gift: The Complete Text*. Ed. Jane Augustine. Gainesville: University Press of Florida, 1998. 225–78.

———. *Notes on Thought and Vision & The Wise Sappho*. San Francisco: City Lights, 1982.

———. *Paint It Today*. Ed. Cassandra Laity. New York: New York University Press, 1992.

———. *Palimpsest* ("Hipparchia: War Rome," "Murex," "Secret Name: Excavator's Egypt"). 1926. Reprint, Carbondale: Southern Illinois University Press, 1968.

———. *Pilate's Wife*. Ed. Joan A. Burke. New York: New Directions, 2000.

———. [Rhoda Peter]. "Pontikonisi (Mouse Island)." *Pagany* 3.3 (1932): 1–9.

———. *Red Roses for Bronze*. Boston: Houghton, 1931.

———. Review of *Goblins and Pagodas*, by John Gould Fletcher. *The Egoist* 3.12 (1916): 183–84.

———. "Sagesse." In *Hermetic Definition* 57–84.

———. *Sea Garden*. 1916. Reprint, London: St. James, 1975.

———. "Speech of Acceptance to the American Academy of Arts and Letters." *H.D. Newsletter* 3.1 (1990): 4–6.

———. "The Sword Went Out to Sea (Synthesis of a Dream)." Ts. H.D. Papers. Beinecke Library, Yale University, New Haven, Conn.

———. *Tribute to Freud.* New York: New Directions, 1974.

———. *Trilogy* ("The Walls Do Not Fall," "Tribute to the Angels," "The Flowering of the Rod"). New York: New Directions, 1973.

———. *The Usual Star.* Dijon: Darantière, 1934.

———. "Winter Love." In *Hermetic Definition* 85–117.

———. *Within the Walls.* Iowa City: Windhover, 1993.

Hejinian, Lyn. "Barbarism." In *Language of Inquiry* 318–36.

———. "A Common Sense." In *Language of Inquiry* 355–82.

———. *The Language of Inquiry.* Berkeley: University of California Press, 2001.

———. "The Rejection of Closure." In *Language of Inquiry* 40–58.

Herring, Robert. "A New Cinema, Magic and the Avant Garde." In *Close Up, 1927–1933,* ed. Donald, Friedberg, and Marcus. 50–57.

———. Letters to H.D. Beinecke Library, Yale University, New Haven, Conn.

Hill, Jonathan. *The Cat's Whisker: 50 Years of Wireless Design.* London: Oresko, 1978.

Hillman, James. *Re-Visioning Psychology.* New York: Harper, 1975.

Hollander, John. *Vision and Resonance: Two Senses of Poetic Form.* 2d ed. New Haven, Conn.: Yale University Press, 1985.

Hollenberg, Donna Krolik. *H.D.: The Poetics of Childbirth and Creativity.* Iowa City: University of Iowa Press, 1991.

———, ed. *H.D. and Poets After.* Iowa City: University of Iowa Press, 2000.

Hošek, Chaviva, and Patricia Parker, eds. *Lyric Poetry: Beyond New Criticism.* Ithaca, N.Y.: Cornell University Press, 1985.

Howe, Susan. *Articulation of Sound Forms in Time.* Windsor, Vt.: Awede, 1987.

———. "Thorow." In *Singularities.* Hanover, N.H.: Wesleyan University Press, 1990. 39–59.

———. "*Talisman* Interview, with Edward Foster." In *The Birth-Mark: Unsettling the Wilderness in American Literary History.* Hanover, N.H.: Wesleyan University Press, 1993. 155–81.

Hulme, T. E. *Further Speculations.* Ed. Sam Hynes. Lincoln: University of Nebraska Press, 1962.

———. *Speculations: Essays on Humanism and the Philosophy of Art.* Ed. Herbert Read. London: Routledge, 1924.

Hyde, Lewis. *The Gift: Imagination and the Erotic Life of Property.* New York: Random House, 1983.

———. *Trickster Makes This World: Mischief, Myth, and Art.* New York: Farrar, 1998.

Ingalls, Jeremy. "The Epic Tradition: A Commentary." *East-West Review* 1.1 (1964): 42–69.

———. "The Epic Tradition: A Commentary II." *East-West Review* 1.2 (1964): 173–211.

Irigaray, Luce. "Women on the Market." In *This Sex Which Is Not One.* Trans. Catherine Porter, with Carolyn Burke. Ithaca, N.Y.: Cornell University Press, 1985. 170–91.

Irwin, Will. "22 April 1915: The Use of Poison Gas." *New York Tribune,* 25–27 Apr. 1915. World War I Document Archive. 10 June 2000. <http://www.lib.byu.edu/~rdh/wwi/ 1915/chlorgas.html>.

Jacobson, Roman, with Krystyna Pomorska. "The Time Factor in Language." In *On Language.* Ed. Linda R. Waugh and Monique Monville-Burston. Cambridge: Harvard University Press, 1990. 164–75.

Jaffer, Frances. "A Gift of Song: My Encounter with H.D." In *H.D. and Poets After,* ed. Hollenberg. 95–103.

"The 'Jacky' Projector" (advertisement). 1930. In *Close Up, 1927–1933,* ed. Donald, Friedberg, and Marcus. 288.

Jay, Martin. *Downcast Eyes: The Denigration of Vision in Twentieth-Century French Thought.* Berkeley: University of California Press, 1993.

Jeans, Sir James Hopwood. *The Mysterious Universe.* Rev. ed. Cambridge: Cambridge University Press, 1932.

———. *The Stars in Their Courses.* Cambridge: Cambridge University Press, 1931.

Kahn, Douglas. *Noise, Water, Meat: A History of Sound in the Arts.* Cambridge: Massachusetts Institute of Technology Press, 1999.

Kahn, Douglas, and Gregory Whitehead, eds. *Wireless Imagination: Sound, Radio, and the Avant-Garde.* Cambridge: Massachusetts Institute of Technology Press, 1992.

Kaplan, Alice Yaeger. *Reproductions of Banality: Fascism, Literature, and French Intellectual Life.* Minneapolis: University of Minnesota Press, 1986.

Kawin, Bruce F. *Telling It Again and Again: Repetition in Literature and Film.* Ithaca, N.Y.: Cornell University Press, 1972.

Keller, Evelyn Fox. *Reflections on Gender and Science.* New Haven, Conn.: Yale University Press, 1985.

Kelly, Robert. "H.D.: A Joining." In *H.D. and Poets After,* ed. Hollenberg. 32–44.

Kenner, Hugh. *The Mechanic Muse.* New York: Oxford University Press, 1987.

———. *The Pound Era.* Berkeley: University of California Press, 1971.

Kerblat, Jeanne. "*Helen in Egypt:* Variations sur un thème sonore." *GRES* 2 (Apr. 1978): 23–46.

King, Michael, ed. *H.D.: Woman and Poet.* Orono, Maine: National Poetry Foundation, 1986.

Kittler, Friedrich A. *Discourse Networks, 1800/1900.* Trans. Michael Metteer, with Chris Cullens. Stanford, Calif.: Stanford University Press, 1990.

———. *Gramophone, Film, Typewriter.* Trans. Geoffrey Winthrop-Young and Michael Wutz. Stanford, Calif.: Stanford University Press, 1999.

Kloepfer, Deborah Kelly. "Flesh Made Word: Maternal Inscription in H.D." *Sagetrieb* 3.1 (1984): 27–48.

————. *The Unspeakable Mother: Forbidden Discourse in Jean Rhys and H.D.* Ithaca, N.Y.: Cornell University Press, 1989.

Kristeva, Julia. *Desire in Language: A Semiotic Approach to Literature and Art.* Ed. Leon S. Roudiez. Trans. Thomas Gora, Alice Jardine, and Leon S. Roudiez. New York: Columbia University Press, 1980.

————. *Revolution in Poetic Language.* Trans. Margaret Waller. New York: Columbia University Press, 1984.

Lawrence, Amy. *Echo and Narcissus: Women's Voices in Classical Hollywood Cinema.* Berkeley: University of California Press, 1991.

Levertov, Denise. "An Approach to Public Poetry Listenings." In *Light Up the Cave.* New York: New Directions, 1981. 46–56.

Lévi-Strauss, Claude. *La Pensée Sauvage.* Paris: Plon, 1983.

"Listenin'!" (postcard). 1923. In Hill, *Cat's Whisker* 67.

Lord, Albert P. *The Singer of Tales.* Cambridge, Mass.: Harvard University Press, 1960.

"The Lorenz Attractor." In Gleick, *Chaos* 114 (inset).

Lury, Celia. *Prosthetic Culture: Photography, Memory, and Identity.* New York: Routledge, 1998.

Mackey, Nathaniel. 1986. *Bedouin Hornbook.* Los Angeles: Sun and Moon, 1997.

————. "Call Me Tantra: Open Field Poetics as Muse." Ph.D. dissertation, Stanford University, 1974.

————. "The Changing Same: Black Music in the Poetry of Amiri Baraka." In *Discrepant Engagement* 22–48.

————. *Discrepant Engagement: Dissonance, Cross-Culturality, and Experimental Writing.* Cambridge: Cambridge University Press, 1993.

————. *Djbot Baghostus's Run.* Los Angeles: Sun and Moon, 1993.

————. "Palimpsestic Stagger." In *H.D. and Poets After,* ed. Hollenberg. 225–34.

Maclear, Kyo. *Beclouded Visions: Hiroshima-Nagasaki and the Art of Witness.* Albany: State University of New York Press, 1999.

Macpherson, Kenneth. "As Is." 1927. In *Close Up, 1927–1933,* ed. Donald, Friedberg, and Marcus. 36–40.

————. "As Is." 1930. In *Close Up, 1927–1933,* ed. Donald, Friedberg, and Marcus. 236–38.

————. *Poolreflection.* Territet, Switz.: POOL, 1927.

Mandel, Charlotte. "Magical Lenses: Poet's Vision beyond the Naked Eye." In *H.D.,* ed. King. 301–17.

————. "The Redirected Image: Cinematic Dynamics in the Style of H.D." *Literature/ Film Quarterly* 11.1 (1983): 36–45.

Man with a Movie Camera. Dir. Dziga Vertov. Film Arts Guild, 1929.

March, Robert H. *Physics for Poets.* 2d ed. New York: McGraw, 1970.

Marcus, Laura. Introduction to part 6. "Cinema and Psychoanalysis." In *Close Up, 1927–1933,* ed. Donald, Friedberg, and Marcus. 240–46.

Marinetti, F. T. "Destruction of Syntax—Wireless Imagination—Words in Freedom."
1913. In *Stung by Salt and War: Creative Texts of the Italian Avant-Gardist F. T. Marinetti.* Trans. Richard J. Pioli. New York: Lang, 1987. 45–53.

Martz, Louis L. Introduction to H.D., *Collected Poems,* xi–xxxvi.

Marvin, Carolyn. *When Old Technologies Were New: Thinking about Electric Communication in the Late Nineteenth Century.* New York: Oxford University Press, 1988.

Materer, Timothy. *Modernist Alchemy: Poetry and the Occult.* Ithaca, N.Y.: Cornell University Press, 1995.

Mauss, Marcel. *The Gift: Forms and Functions of Exchange in Archaic Societies.* Trans. Ian Cunnison. New York: Norton, 1967.

———. "Gift, Gift." In *The Logic of the Gift: Toward an Ethic of Generosity.* Ed. Alan D. Schrift. New York: Routledge, 1997. 28–32.

Mayr, Ernst. *Animal Species and Evolution.* Cambridge, Mass.: Harvard University Press, 1963.

McCauley, Lawrence H. "The Wail Cannot Di-Jest Me: Puns, Poetry, and Language in H.D.'s *Trilogy.*" *Sagetrieb* 14.1–2 (1995): 141–60.

McGann, Jerome. *Black Riders: The Visible Language of Modernism.* Princeton, N.J.: Princeton University Press, 1993.

———. *The Textual Condition.* Princeton, N.J.: Princeton University Press, 1991.

McHale, Brian. *Postmodernist Fiction.* New York: Methuen, 1987.

McLuhan, Marshall. *The Gutenberg Galaxy: The Making of Typographic Man.* Toronto: University of Toronto Press, 1962.

———. *Understanding Media: The Extensions of Man.* New York: McGraw, 1964.

Mermoz, Gérard. "On the Synchronism between Artistic and Scientific Ideas and Practices: An Exploration of Hypotheses, 1900–1930s." *Common Denominators in Art and Science.* Proceedings of a discussion conference held under the auspices of the School of Epistemics, University of Edinburgh, Nov. 1981. Ed. Martin Pollock. Aberdeen: Aberdeen University Press, 1983. 134–44.

Miller, Toby, ed. "Radio-Sound." *Continuum: The Australian Journal of Media and Culture* 6.1 (1992): 5–11.

Mingus, Charles. "Free Cell Block F, 'tis Nazi USA." *Changes Two.* Recorded 27, 28, and 30 Dec. 1974. LP. Atlantic, 1975.

Moretti, Franco. *Modern Epic: The World-System from Goethe to García Márquez.* Trans. Quintin Hoare. New York: Verso, 1996.

Murtagh, William J. *Moravian Architecture and Town Planning: Bethlehem, Pennsylvania, and Other Eighteenth-Century American Settlements.* Chapel Hill: University of North Carolina Press, 1967.

"Music, 1903." Microsoft Bookshelf. CD-ROM. Redmond, Wash.: Microsoft, 1998.

Nänny, Max. *Ezra Pound: Poetics for an Electric Age.* Bern: Francke Verlag, 1973.

Nelson, Cary. *Repression and Recovery: Modern American Poetry and the Politics of Cultural Memory, 1910–1945.* Madison: University of Wisconsin Press, 1989.

————, ed. *Anthology of Modern American Poetry*. New York: Oxford University Press, 2000.

Nicholls, Peter. "Of Being Ethical: Reflections on George Oppen." *Journal of American Studies* 31 (1997): 153–70.

Nielsen, Aldon Lynn. *Black Chant: Languages of African-American Postmodernism*. Cambridge: Cambridge University Press, 1997.

Nixon, Rob. "Caribbean and African Appropriations of *The Tempest*." *Critical Inquiry* 13.3 (1987): 557–78.

Noland, Carrie. *Poetry at Stake: Lyric Aesthetics and the Challenge of Technology*. Princeton, N.J.: Princeton University Press, 1999.

The Norton Anthology of Modern Poetry. Ed. Richard Ellmann and Robert O'Clair. 2d ed. New York: Norton, 1988.

O'Leary, Peter. "An Interview with Nathaniel Mackey." *Chicago Review* 43.1 (1997): 30–46.

Olson, Charles. "Projective Verse." In *Collected Prose*. Ed. Donald Allen and Benjamin Friedlander. Berkeley: University of California Press, 1997. 239–49.

Ong, Walter J. *Orality and Literacy: The Technologizing of the Word*. London: Methuen, 1982.

————. *Presence of the Word: Some Prolegomena for Cultural and Religious History*. Minneapolis: University of Minnesota Press, 1981.

"On the Way WING BEAT!" (advertisement for *Wing Beat*). 1927. In *Close Up, 1927–1933*, ed. Donald, Friedberg, and Marcus. 18.

Ostriker, Alicia. "No Rule of Procedure: The Open Poetics of H.D." *Agenda* 25.3–4 (1987–88): 145–54.

————. "'A Wish to Make Real to Myself What Is Most Real': My H.D." In *H.D. and Poets After*, ed. Hollenberg. 1–13.

Parry, Milman. *The Making of Homeric Verse: The Collected Papers of Milman Parry*. Ed. Adam Parry. Oxford: Clarendon Press, 1971.

Pearson, Norman Holmes. "The American Poet in Relation to Science." *American Quarterly* 1.2 (1949): 116–26.

————. Foreword to H.D., *Hermetic Definition* v–vii.

————. "Norman Holmes Pearson on H.D.: An Interview." *Contemporary Literature* 10.4 (1969): 435–46.

————. Notes for H.D. Biography. Ms. H.D. Papers. Beinecke Library, Yale University, New Haven, Conn.

————. "*Trilogy* (annotated)." Ms. H.D. Papers. Beinecke Library, Yale University, New Haven, Conn.

Perelman, Bob. *The Marginalization of Poetry: Language Writing and Literary History*. Princeton, N.J.: Princeton University Press, 1996.

Perloff, Marjorie. "Can(n)on to the Right of Us, Can(n)on to the Left of Us: A Plea for Difference." In *Poetic License: Essays on Modernist and Postmodernist Lyric*. Evanston, Ill.: Northwestern University Press, 1990. 7–29.

———. *The Dance of the Intellect: Studies in the Poetry of the Pound Tradition.* Cambridge: Cambridge University Press, 1985.

———. *The Poetics of Indeterminacy: Rimbaud to Cage.* Princeton, N.J.: Princeton University Press, 1981.

———. *Radical Artifice: Writing Poetry in the Age of Media.* Chicago: University of Chicago Press, 1991.

———. *Wittgenstein's Ladder: Poetic Language and the Strangeness of the Ordinary.* Chicago: University of Chicago Press, 1996.

Piombino, Nick. "The Aural Ellipsis and the Nature of Listening in Contemporary Poetry." In Bernstein, *Close Listening* 53–72.

"Poets in Public." *Evening Standard,* 15 Apr. 1943.

Pondrom, Cyrena N. "H.D. and the Origins of Imagism." *Sagetrieb* 4.1 (1985): 73–97.

Pound, Ezra. *ABC of Reading.* New York: New Directions, 1960.

———. *Cantos.* New York: New Directions, 1970.

———. *Gaudier-Brzeska: A Memoir.* New York: New Directions, 1970.

———. "How to Read." In *Literary Essays of Ezra Pound.* Ed. T. S. Eliot. New York: New Directions, 1968. 15–40.

———. "I Gather the Limbs of Osiris [IV]: A Beginning." *New Age,* 21 Dec. 1911, 178–80.

———. "I Gather the Limbs of Osiris [II]: A Rather Dull Introduction." *New Age,* 7 Dec. 1911, 130–31.

———. "In a Station of the Metro." In *Selected Poems of Ezra Pound.* New York: New Directions, 1957. 35.

———. *The Letters of Ezra Pound, 1907–1941.* Ed. D. D. Paige. New York: Harcourt, 1950.

———. *Literary Essays of Ezra Pound.* Ed. T. S. Eliot. New York: New Directions, 1968.

———. "A Retrospect." In *Literary Essays of Ezra Pound.* Ed. T. S. Eliot. New York: New Directions, 1968. 3–14.

———. *The Spirit of Romance.* New York: New Directions, 1968.

———. "Three Cantos." In *Poetry: A Magazine of Verse* 10.3 (1917): 113–21.

Quartermain, Peter. *Disjunctive Poetics: From Gertrude Stein and Louis Zukofsky to Susan Howe.* Cambridge: Cambridge University Press, 1992.

Quinn, Vincent. *Hilda Doolittle (H.D.).* New Haven, Conn.: College and University Press, 1967.

Rainey, Lawrence S. "Canon, Gender, and Text: The Case of H.D." In *Representing Modernist Texts: Editing as Interpretation.* Ed. George Bornstein. Ann Arbor: University of Michigan Press, 1991. 99–123.

———. *Institutions of Modernism: Literary Elites and Public Culture.* New Haven, Conn.: Yale University Press, 1998.

Rasula, Jed. *The American Poetry Wax Museum: Reality Effects, 1940–1990.* Urbana, Ill.: National Council of Teachers of English, 1996.

Rhys, Jean. *Wide Sargasso Sea.* New York: Norton, 1966.

Rich, Adrienne. *Of Woman Born: Motherhood as Experience and Institution.* New York: Norton, 1976.

Riddel, Joseph N. "H.D. and the Poetics of 'Spiritual Realism.'" *Contemporary Literature* 10.4 (1969): 447–73.

Robinson, Janice S. *H.D.: The Life and Work of an American Poet.* Boston: Houghton, 1982.

Roche, John. *Moravian Heresy, wherein the Principal Errors of That Doctrine . . . Are Fully Set Forth, Proved, and Refuted.* Dublin: The author, 1751.

Rorty, Richard. *Philosophy and the Mirror of Nature.* Princeton, N.J.: Princeton University Press, 1979.

Rossiter, Margaret W. *Women Scientists in America: Struggles and Strategies to 1940.* Baltimore: Johns Hopkins University Press, 1982.

Rothfuss, Joan. "Escape Artist." In *2000 BC: The Bruce Conner Story Part II.* Minneapolis: Walker Art Center, 1999. 159–83.

Rubin, Gayle. "The Traffic in Women: Notes on the 'Political Economy' of Sex." In *Toward an Anthropology of Women.* Ed. Rayna R. Reiter. New York: Monthly Review, 1975. 157–210.

Sagan, Carl. *Cosmos.* New York: Random House, 1980.

Sahlins, Marshall. *Stone Age Economics.* New York: Aldine de Gruyter, 1972.

Scalapino, Leslie. *As: All Occurrence in Structure, Unseen—(Deer Night).* In *The Public World* 88–133.

———. "Dahlia's Iris: Secret Autobiography and Fiction." Forthcoming.

———. *The Front Matter, Dead Souls.* Hanover, N.H.: University Press of New England, 1996.

———. "An H.D. Book." In *Objects in the Terrifying Tense/Longing from Taking Place.* New York: Roof, 1993. 3–7.

———. "Interior Scrutiny: Example of H.D." In *H.D. and Poets After,* ed. Hollenberg. 203–10.

———. [Dee Goda]. *Orchid Jetsam.* Berkeley, Calif.: Tuumba, 2001.

———. *The Public World/Syntactically Impermanence.* Hanover, N.H.: University Press of New England, 1999.

———. *R-hu.* Berkeley, Calif.: Atelos, 2000.

———. "The Radical Nature of Experience." In *The Public World* 3–14.

———. *The Return of Painting, The Pearl, and Orion: A Trilogy.* San Francisco: North Point, 1991.

———. "'Thinking Serially' in *For Love, Words* and *Pieces.*" In *The Public World* 44–52.

Schaffner, Perdita. "Sketch of H.D.: The Egyptian Cat." In H.D., *Hedylus* 142–46.

———. "A Profound Animal." In H.D., *Bid Me To Live (A Madrigal)* 185–94.

Schrift, Alan D. "Introduction: Why Gift?" In *The Logic of the Gift: Toward an Ethic of Generosity.* Ed. Alan D. Schrift. New York: Routledge, 1997. 1–22.

Sessler, Jacob John. *Communal Pietism among Early American Moravians.* New York: Holt, 1933.

Shakespeare, William. *Macbeth.* Cambridge: Cambridge University Press, 1997.

———. *The Winter's Tale.* Cambridge: Cambridge University Press, 1950.

Shaw, Lytle. "Seven Types of Materiality: Michael Davidson's *Ghostlier Demarcations.*" *Qui Parle* 11.1 (1997): 173–80.

Shaw, Robert. "Strange Attractors, Chaotic Behavior, and Information Flow." *Zeitschrift für Naturforschung* 36a (1981): 79–112.

Sherry, Vincent. *Ezra Pound, Wyndham Lewis, and Radical Modernism.* Oxford: Oxford University Press, 1993.

Shoaf, R. A. "The Play of Puns in Late Middle English Poetry: Concerning Juxtology." In *On Puns,* ed. Culler. 44–61.

Showalter, Elaine. "Feminist Criticism in the Wilderness." In *The New Feminist Criticism: Essays on Women, Literature, and Theory.* Ed. Elaine Showalter. New York: Pantheon, 1985. 243–70.

Silliman, Ron. *The New Sentence.* New York: Roof, 1987.

Silverman, Kaja. *The Acoustic Mirror: The Female Voice in Psychoanalysis and Cinema.* Bloomington: Indiana University Press, 1988.

Some Imagist Poets: An Anthology. Boston: Houghton, 1915.

Spicer, Jack. *After Lorca.* In *Collected Books* 9–52.

———. *The Collected Books of Jack Spicer.* Ed. Robin Blaser. Los Angeles: Black Sparrow, 1975.

———. *The Holy Grail.* In *Collected Books* 185–213.

———. *The House That Jack Built: The Collected Lectures of Jack Spicer.* Ed. Peter Gizzi. Hanover, N.H.: University Press of New England, 1998.

———. "Vancouver Lecture I: Dictation and 'A Textbook of Poetry.'" In *The House That Jack Built* 1–48.

———. "Vancouver Lecture 2: The Serial Poem and *The Holy Grail.*" In *The House That Jack Built* 49–96.

———. *Jack Spicer's Detective Novel: The Tower of Babel.* Hoboken, N.J.: Talisman, 1994.

Stack, Carol B. *All Our Kin: Strategies for Survival in a Black Community.* New York: Harper, 1974.

Stein, Gertrude. "A Carafe, That Is a Blind Glass." In *Tender Buttons.* Los Angeles: Sun and Moon, 1990. 9.

———. "Forensics." In *How to Write.* New York: Dover, 1975. 383–95.

———. "Patriarchal Poetry." In *Gertrude Stein: Writings, 1903–1932.* Ed. Catherine R. Stimpson and Harriet Chessman. New York: Library of America, 1998. 567–607.

———. "Portraits and Repetition." In *Lectures in America.* New York: Random House, 1935. 163–206.

Stevens, Wallace. "Anecdote of the Jar." In *Collected Poems* 76.

———. *The Collected Poems of Wallace Stevens.* New York: Knopf, 1961.

———. "How to Live. What to Do." In *Collected Poems* 125–26.

———. "The Noble Rider and the Sound of Words." In *The Necessary Angel: Essays on Reality and the Imagination.* New York: Knopf, 1951. 1–36.

Stewart, Garrett. "Modernism's Sonic Waiver: Literary Writing and the Filmic Difference." In *Sound States: Innovative Poetics and Acoustical Technology.* Ed. Adalaide Morris. Chapel Hill: University of North Carolina Press, 1997. 237–73.

———. *Reading Voices: Literature and the Phonotext.* Berkeley: University of California Press, 1990.

Stock, Noel. *The Life of Ezra Pound.* Expanded ed. San Francisco: North Point, 1982.

Strauss, Neil, ed. *Radiotext(e).* Special issue of *Semiotext(e)* 6.1 (1993).

Stricker, Meredith. "new species." *HOW(ever)* 5.4 (Oct. 1989): 1, 19–20.

Sword, Helen. "H.D.'s *Majic Ring.*" *Tulsa Studies in Women's Literature.* 14.2 (1995): 347–62.

———. "Necrobibliography: Books in the Spirit World, Ghosts in the Library." In *Ghostwriting Modernism.* Ithaca, N.Y.: Cornell University Press, 2002. 10–31.

Tedlock, Dennis. "Learning to Listen: Oral History as Poetry." *Boundary2* 3 (1975): 707–26.

———. "Toward an Oral Poetics." *New Literary History* 8 (1977): 507–19.

Ten Days That Shook the World [*October; Oktyabr*]. Dir. Sergei Eisenstein. Amkino Corporation, 1927.

Terminator 2: Judgment Day. Dir. James Cameron. Perf. Arnold Schwarzenegger and Linda Hamilton. TriStar Pictures, 1991.

Terrell, Carroll F. *A Companion to the Cantos of Ezra Pound.* Vol. 1: *Cantos 1–71.* Berkeley: University of California Press, 1980.

Thom, René. *Mathematical Models of Morphogenesis.* Chichester: Horwood, 1983.

———. *Structural Stability and Morphogenesis: An Outline of a General Theory of Models.* Reading, Mass.: Benjamin, 1975.

Tiffany, Daniel. *Toy Medium: Materialism and Modern Lyric.* Berkeley: University of California Press, 2000.

Toulmin, Stephen. *The Return to Cosmology: Postmodern Science and the Theology of Nature.* Berkeley: University of California Press, 1982.

Ulmer, Gregory. "The Puncept in Grammatology." In *On Puns,* ed. Culler. 164–89.

Vargish, Thomas, and Delo E. Mook. *Inside Modernism: Relativity Theory, Cubism, Narrative.* New Haven, Conn.: Yale University Press, 1999.

Wallace, Emily Mitchell. "Athene's Owl." *Poesis: A Journal of Criticism* 6.3-4 (1985): 98–123.

Walton, Eda Lou. "The Poetic Method of H.D." (review of *Red Roses for Bronze,* by H.D). *The Nation,* 2 Mar. 1932, 264.

Watten, Barrett. "The Constructivist Moment: From El Lissitzky to Detroit Techno." *Qui Parle* 11.1 (1997): 57–100.

———. "Missing 'X': Formal Meaning in Crane and Eigner." In *Total Syntax* 168–90.

———. "The Politics of Poetry: Surrealism & L=A=N=G=U=A=G=E." In *Total Syntax* 31–64.

———. "Social Formalism: Zukofsky, Andrews, and Habitus in Contemporary Poetry." *North Dakota Quarterly* 55.4 (Fall 1987): 365–82.

———. *Total Syntax.* Carbondale: Southern Illinois University Press, 1985.

Welsh, Andrew. *Roots of Lyric: Primitive Poetry and Modern Poetics.* Princeton, N.J.: Princeton University Press, 1978.

White, Eric Walter. *Images of H.D. from* The Mystery, [by] H.D. London: Enitharmon Press, 1976.

Whitehead, Gregory. "Out of the Dark: Notes on the Nobodies of Radio Art." In *Wireless Imagination,* ed. Kahn and Whitehead. 253–63.

Wilby, Pete, and Andy Conroy. *The Radio Handbook.* New York: Routledge, 1994.

Williams, William Carlos. "A Letter from William Carlos Williams to Norman Holmes Pearson Concerning Hilda Doolittle and Her Mother and Father (July 11, 1955)." *William Carlos Williams Newsletter* 2.2 (1976): 2–3.

———. *Paterson.* New York: New Directions, 1963.

Winnicott, D. W. *Playing and Reality.* New York: Tavistock, 1989.

Wolle, Rev. Francis. *Desmids of the United States.* 2d ed. Bethlehem, Pa.: Moravian Publication Office, 1892.

———. *Diatomaceae of North America.* Bethlehem, Pa.: Comenius, 1890.

———. *Fresh-Water Algae of the United States.* 2 vols. Bethlehem, Pa.: Comenius, 1887.

Wolle, Francis. *A Moravian Heritage.* Boulder, Colo.: Empire, 1972.

Woolf, Virginia. "On Being Ill." In *Collected Essays.* Vol. 4. London: Hogarth, 1967. 193–203.

Yeats, William Butler. "Byzantium." In *Poems.* New York: Macmillan, 1960. 243–44.

Zumthor, Paul. *Oral Poetry: An Introduction.* Trans. Kathryn Murphy-Judy. Minneapolis: University of Minnesota Press, 1990.

Index

Index

ADALAIDE MORRIS is the John C. Gerber Professor of English at the University of Iowa. She is the author of *Wallace Stevens: Imagination and Faith* (1974), a coeditor of *Extended Outlooks: The Iowa Review Collection of Contemporary Women Writers* (1982), and the editor of *Sound States: Innovative Poetics and Acoustical Technologies* (1997).

The University of Illinois Press
is a founding member of the
Association of American University Presses.

University of Illinois Press
1325 South Oak Street
Champaign, IL 61820-6903
www.press.uillinois.edu